*Scientific knowledge and
sociological theory*

D0777582

Monographs in Social Theory

Editor: Arthur Brittan, *University of York*

Titles in the Series

Barry Barnes   *Scientific knowledge and sociological theory*

Zygmunt Bauman   *Culture as praxis*

Keith Dixon   *Sociological theory*

Anthony D. Smith   *The concept of social change*

A catalogue of books in other series of Social Science
books published by Routledge & Kegan Paul will be found
at the end of this volume.

Barry Barnes

Science Studies Unit
University of Edinburgh

Scientific knowledge and sociological theory

Routledge & Kegan Paul
London and Boston

First published in 1974
by Routledge & Kegan Paul Ltd
Broadway House, 68–74 Carter Lane,
London EC4V 5EL and
9 Park Street,
Boston, Mass. 02108, USA
Printed in Great Britain by
Clarke, Doble & Brendon Ltd, Plymouth
© Barry Barnes 1974

ISBN 0 7100 7961 3 (c)
     0 7100 7962 1 (p)
Library of Congress Catalog Card No. 74-81994

F11

Contents

Preface   vii

1   The diversity of beliefs about nature and the problem of explaining it   1

2   The sociologist and the concept of rationality   22

3   The culture of the natural sciences   45

4   Belief, action and determinism: the causal explanation of scientific change   69

5   'Internal' and 'external' factors in the history of science   99

6   Science and ideology   125

Epilogue   153

Notes   159

Bibliography   181

Author Index   189

Subject Index   191

This is an essay in the sociology of scientific knowledge written with the sociology of knowledge and culture, generally, very much in mind. As a sociological study it is unusual in that the form and content of scientific knowledge is the main concern and not its organization or distribution. There are, however, good reasons why this neglected subject should be of particular interest at the present time.

After a long period of neglect we have seen a marked revival of interest in the sociology of knowledge. Moreover, in this revival, cautious, positivistic approaches to the study of belief systems have given way to more speculative and comparative work, which has assumed that the study of knowledge is of central importance in the development of sociological theory. This welcome change has been stimulated by anthropologists such as Mary Douglas and R. Horton, and by the growing influence of phenomenology and ethnomethodology. It has generated a fascinating and important literature, which promises to lead to a fully general sociological understanding of knowledge as a whole.

This literature does, however, tend to skirt around the question of what the world has to do with what is believed, and this is a question which must be answered, at least schematically, by a fully developed sociological theory of knowledge. Occasionally, existing work leaves the feeling that reality has *nothing* to do with what is socially constructed or negotiated to count as natural knowledge, but we may safely assume that this impression is an accidental by-product of over-enthusiastic sociological analysis, and that sociologists as a whole would acknowledge that the world in some way constrains what it is believed to be. The question however remains: what is the nature of this constraint and how strong is it?

It is impossible to avoid this question when scientific knowledge is the subject of sociological study. Here, one is forced to examine very seriously how far beliefs can be represented as rational responses to reality, and how far this restricts the scope of the sociology of knowledge. Scientific knowledge is, of course, frequently cited by those who see the sociology of knowledge as, at best, a limited enterprise, and would have it called the sociology of belief. These critics remain largely unanswered: some sociologists tacitly accept their claims and avoid the consideration of science, assuming it must be different from other belief systems; others assume that science must fit sociological theories, but they are unable to see how, and consequently avoid consideration of science also.

Here is where the present study may have something of general significance to offer. Through actual consideration of scientific beliefs, and through an examination of how reality may constrain them, it will be shown that there is no need to restrict the scope of the sociology of knowledge. The important tenets of recent work in this area apply to the knowledge of natural science as well as elsewhere; those tenets which do not apply to science are generally inapplicable and deserve no place in the field in any case. Thus, the argument protects the flank of the sociology of knowledge against rationalistic criticism, and emphasizes its status as a fully general approach. Hopefully, however, it will do more than this, for it suggests that, instead of being avoided, scientific knowledge should be actively studied and reflected upon in the quest for a general sociological understanding of the nature of knowledge as a whole. A body of knowledge with so many unique features cannot be safely ignored in such an undertaking; after all, science is the most elaborated and systematized of all forms of knowledge, and the least anthropomorphic. Moreover, in many ways it is the easiest of all forms of knowledge to study. It is accessible and, for the most part, unconstrained by norms of secrecy and restricted access; it is remarkably well defined and bounded by those who transmit it; and its history is well documented and can be studied more reliably than that of an oral tradition. Scientific knowledge should be one of the most valuable resources in the sociologist's attempt to understand natural knowledge and its variation, not one of the greatest obstacles.

It should be emphasized that the discussion is centred upon the sociologist's concern to understand and explain beliefs about nature and their variation. It does not seek to advocate or to criticize the beliefs discussed, nor is it concerned with their justification. (The reader is asked to overlook those harmless and readily identified slips from this ideal which I have not troubled to eliminate.) This point is stressed since, in the current intellectual milieu, simply to talk of science in other than reverential terms may be seen as criticism. Existing discussions of scientific beliefs tend either to assume their validity or to be demonstrations of it. The investigation of science as a phenomenon has been incompletely differentiated from its justification. As a result, it is now being realized by everyone concerned with the study of science that our present understanding of the nature of its knowledge is hopelessly conflated with ideas of what it ought to be, or 'must' be. Perhaps those outside sociology concerned to change this situation will find this essay of some interest, since, in a sense, it attempts to take science as it finds it.

If this proved to be the case it would merely slightly offset an enormous debt. The material used here has been drawn from a number of different academic fields; so many indeed that, given the present organization of academic knowledge, the work stands in danger of being condemned as specialized. I have, however, striven to minimize the resulting problems, and to make the main text readily intelligible to sociologists and reasonably accessible to others. As a result, there will be those who find particular examples or illustrations intolerably oversimplified, but the dilemma involved here will be clear enough. With regard to terminology, only sociological concepts are left unelaborated, and these are not used so extensively as to present insuperable difficulties to readers from outside the discipline. It should be noted, however, that the term 'knowledge' is used throughout with the sense of 'accepted belief', not with the sense of 'correct belief'.

Turning to more particular debts, it is a pleasure to thank all the colleagues and friends, in Edinburgh and elsewhere, who have commented upon and criticized various aspects of the argument. Particular acknowledgment is due to Donald MacKenzie of the Science Studies Unit here, who read the manuscript and made a number of particular criticisms and suggestions which were incorporated into the text. Indubitably, however, it is my colleague David Bloor to whom my greatest thanks are due. I have been grateful for his criticisms of the manuscript, but his influence upon it has been much more profound, since my thinking upon this subject has taken shape during innumerable informal discussions with him. Responsibility for what is said must, of course, fall entirely upon myself, as must that for any errors in the text. These would without doubt have been more numerous but for the help of Mrs Corinne Robertson who generously undertook most of the typing involved, and my wife, who read the manuscript. I am grateful to both for detecting and eliminating many of my slips and oversights.

BARRY BARNES

Edinburgh
September 1973

chapter 1

The diversity of beliefs about nature and the problem of explaining it

I

For most people, whatever their way of life, the beliefs they accept and utilize are held unselfconsciously, and are rarely reflected upon. Moreover, when reflection does occur, it tends merely to depict these beliefs as natural representations of 'how things are'. Critical, analytical examination of beliefs, their origins, functions, and claims to validity, is the province of specialized academic roles in modern societies, and is a phenomenon of little general significance. The 'Western layman' lives in a taken for granted world; solid, objective and intelligible; on the whole he thinks with his beliefs, but not about them.

In highly differentiated, modern societies there is always a sharp distinction between the social and the natural. People invariably distinguish two spheres of belief, one relating to a world of objects, facts or concrete events, one to a system of values, obligations, conventions and institutional categories. Both spheres are taken for granted as permanent and valid; both, in this sense, are real. But, today, it is our construction of the natural or physical world which is the most secure and unquestioned. We appeal to nature for our basic metaphors of order and permanence. Our ontological tastes lean to the material and substantial rather than to the abstract or spiritual, so that we find a satisfying congruence between the use of the term 'concrete' as an adjective and its use as a noun. Peter Berger, writing of the taken for granted nature of everyday beliefs and practices, assumes this ontological preference in his audience and writes: 'For most of us, as we grow up, and learn to live in society, its forms take on an appearance of structures as self-evident and as solid as those of the natural cosmos' (1961, pp. 10-11).

With an undifferentiated society, it might have proved more apposite to show how perceptions of nature became as solid and self-evident as those of social life (Horton, 1967). But modern industrial society does not provide its members with such a clear-cut pattern of order and ready intelligibility. For us, natural order is a model for understanding social order. Sociologists and politicians, in their different ways, articulate the metaphor of society as an organism to attempt to gain, or to convey, an understanding of its regularities. Crusading ladies use metaphors from epidemiology to characterize the spread of drug-taking or pornography.

Whereas alternatives to our presently constructed social order are usually found threatening and dangerous, such is the confidence engendered by our conceptions of natural order that alternatives to them are merely treated as odd, or perhaps amusing. And no powerful social group or society exists with an alternative natural world view that may serve to shake our faith in our own. Quaint cosmologies in our midst, or the anthropomorphic physics of primitive societies, disturb us no more than the existence of those who believe in them. Whereas we like to think our values are the best, we know our view of nature is the right one.

Indeed, there is an *obvious* rightness about our own world view. It seems, in some way, to mirror reality so straightforwardly that it must be the consequence of direct apprehension rather than effort and imagination. Conversely, alternative beliefs possess an obvious wrongness. The more natural our own perspective becomes, the more puzzling become the strange propositions of ancestors, aliens and eccentrics. How did such mistaken ideas come to be held? However have they remained uncorrected for so long? A whole series of categories exists which can be readily deployed by anyone in modern societies needing to answer such questions: inferior or impaired mentality, stupidity, prejudice, bigotry, hypocrisy, ideology, conditioning and brain-washing are but a few. All imply a distortion of what is really perceived, a disturbance of a person's normal direct apprehension of the world. Common sense theories of the incidence of beliefs involve the actor treating his own as in need of no explanation and the varying beliefs of others as intelligible in terms of pathologies and biasing factors.

Many academic theories about beliefs, whether philosophical, psychological or sociological, are closely related to this common sense approach. Typically, they divide beliefs about nature into 'true' and 'false' categories, treating the former as unproblematic in the sense that they derive directly from awareness of reality, whereas the latter must be accounted for by biasing and distorting factors. It is sometimes thought that philosophers should develop criteria which establish the truth or falsity of beliefs, and psychologists and sociologists should account for the falsehoods they expose by unearthing causes of bias.[1] Such theories are more explicit, and a degree less parochial, than common sense approaches but their structure remains the same.

None the less, this particular perspective, treating truth as unproblematic and falsehood as needing causal explanation, can be made the basis of thoroughly sceptical approaches to the incidence of beliefs. We need only cite Bacon, warning against the pervasiveness of the idols which beset the human mind, and Marx asserting the systematic distortion of perception in all class societies, to illustrate how fruitful and iconoclastic the approach has been within two widely varying philosophical traditions. Neither of these two writers found much within their own cultures in the way of valid or true beliefs. Both had views on the distortion of perception and belief which remain influential today. Indeed, most sociological attempts to give causal explanations for beliefs about the world fall more or less into one of these traditions.

Talcott Parsons's analysis of ideology (1959) provides a suitable example. He regards the empirical claims of ideologies as in need of explanation in so far as they deviate from what is valid. In practice, this may only be determined to the extent that science has generated relevant standards of correctness; suspect beliefs must be compared and judged in terms of the available 'value-science integrate', which provides a reliable but never complete basis for judgment (1959, p. 295):

> Secondary selection and distortion can only be demonstrated by reference to their deviation from the cultural standards of the value-science integrate . . . once an ideology has been clearly identified by reference to deviation from these cultural standards, . . . [other] considerations can be brought into play . . . One is the problem of explaining the *sources* of ideological selection and distortion.

Other writers have sought to employ the term 'ideology' rather differently from Parsons, and have criticized his definition of it. Geertz, for example, opposes Parsons's 'evaluative' usage, which permits only incorrect beliefs to be termed ideological, yet it is clear that he too seeks causes when beliefs cease to accord with 'reality' (1964, p. 69):

> The social function of science vis-à-vis ideologies is first to understand them—what they are, how they work, what gives rise to them—and second to criticize them, to force them to come to terms with [but not necessarily to surrender to] reality.

There is, of course, a very wide range of particular approaches to the explanation of beliefs within the social sciences. Some of them are much more subtle and complex than the preceding. Yet that simple scheme does capture one important element which most theories share. The causal explanation of beliefs correlates with distortion or inadequacy, and hence operates as an implicit condemnation. Beliefs which are valued, for whatever reason, are spared a deterministic account. There are glimmerings of other possibilities, notably in Durkheim, Lukacs and Mannheim, but these remain inadequately explored. The frequently made claim that the sociology of knowledge applies to true and false beliefs alike is not reflected in its concrete achievements. Mannheim, it will be remembered, accepted that mathematics and the natural sciences lay beyond the scope of his theories.

It should be noted at this point that it is only causal elucidation by reference to bias, or interference with normal faculties of reason and cognition, which is held to be inapplicable to true beliefs. Other kinds of causal account remain possible. The origin of some class of true beliefs may be due to the growth of interest in some previously neglected field of experience, or to a set of phenomena being encountered and recorded for the first time. Another kind of acceptable causal account is that which describes the removal of a biasing factor. One might, for example, relate the rise of true beliefs to a weakening of religious or political control within a society. Both these kinds of causal account invoke no disturbances of human cognitive processes.

An interesting variant on the second kind of explanatory scheme can be discerned in the work of Robert Merton, which has been seminal to the sociology of science. Here, it is assumed that truth, or at least an increase in the truth content of beliefs, does follow from the unhampered operation of reason, from proceeding rationally. But it is not obvious that people naturally do proceed rationally, rather than, for example, on the basis of emotion or tradition. For people to operate almost entirely rationally they need to have internalized some non-rational commitment to rationality. Science as an institution maintains and transmits this commitment to truth as revealed by reason. Scientists espousing error not only deviate from the natural indications of their own reason, but from institutional norms as well. Hence the peculiarly high level of rationality in science and the peculiar reliability of its beliefs. (For an excellent discussion of this 'happy coincidence' see King, 1971.)

Merton's attribution of special status to scientific beliefs has been accepted without question by most sociologists. Although it would be generally agreed that biasing factors occur, in different degrees, in most institutional contexts, and hence that most belief systems embody some degree of error and distortion, the natural sciences are generally accepted as true and undistorted bodies of knowledge; their methods as impartial, unbiased models of investigation. Thus, science can function as a model of how we would be able to orient ourselves to the world in the absence of our psychological biases and social prejudices. Such has been the enthusiasm for science in Western cultures that statements of its truth have taken on almost the nature of tautologies; science has been allowed to define what we hold to be true about the world. Although it is still possible meaningfully to ask whether parts of science might not be false, in practice, any epistemology which implied that the generality of scientific beliefs were biased or mistaken would be stillborn. Similarly, the scheme for explaining beliefs discussed in the preceding paragraphs would be unable to maintain its credibility without science as an exemplar of true belief.

The idea of truth as a normal, straightforward product of human experience, and that of natural science as a paradigm of a true system of beliefs, have been of considerable importance in academic work. One of their most important consequences has been the conception of scientific knowledge as a growing stockpile of facts. As science is a collection of unchanging truths it can only grow by producing yet more truths to add to the collection. Each truth resembles a brick being incorporated permanently in the structure of a rising building. Science grows by gathering more detail in areas already investigated, and by stumbling across new sets of facts in areas of experience never previously investigated. This conception has been very influential in older approaches to the history of science (Agassi, 1963), and has been implicitly influential in a sociology of science tradition which has given much attention to priority of discovery in science, but little to theoretical controversy.

Another consequence of these ideas is that the existence and distribution of scientific beliefs is readily explained; essentially, they are believed because they are true; people will tend to accept them wherever human cognition and reason are unconstrained (this, of course, fits well with the traditional stress on autonomy within science as an institution). Thus, the sociology of knowledge approach, which seeks to account for the content of beliefs by social causation, will be, *a priori*, irrelevant to an understanding of scientific belief systems. It is interesting to note how influential this analysis has been within the sociology of knowledge tradition itself, where the study of scientific beliefs has been almost entirely neglected.

Conversely, false beliefs must be identified and accounted for, and the pronouncements of the sciences are ready at hand for use as definitive discriminating criteria. Other belief systems can be compared with science to expose the false elements within them; these can then be given sociological explanations. Such procedures are particularly evident in social anthropology, where they are important in the identification of *magical* beliefs and practices, *mystical* beliefs, and *ritual* and *symbolic* activities. (Although anthropologists generally talk about the non-efficacy rather than the falsehood of magic they rely on the truth of science to identify non-efficacy. They have no other justification for claiming that ceremonies do not cause the rain which follows, or that chanting does not aid the growth of corn. For interesting discussions of these questions in the context of anthropology see Goody (1961), Beattie (1966, 1970), Jarvie and Agassi (1967).)

It is, of course, the fully accepted beliefs of our current science that are used as touchstones of truth. The history of science presents something of a problem, for it is inescapably apparent that illustrious scientists of the past held views widely at variance with present ones. The situation can be saved by replacing the notion of truth with that of 'what rationally follows from the available evidence'. This defines unproblematic beliefs uniquely, and all others need explanation as before. Alternatively, the term 'truth' may be used implicitly with the above meaning. What matters is that Newton's beliefs, or those of some other hero, are 'right' and not in need of causal explanations, whereas other beliefs linked with the same evidence are 'wrong', even though Newton's beliefs are not accepted as final today. Science is conceived as a uniquely rational process leading to present truth; that which can be set on a teleologically conceived sequence leading to the present is assumed to be naturally reasonable and not in need of causal explanation. That which lies off the path is aberrant, and interesting to the historian of science only indirectly.

II

Here, then, is what has been a very common way of understanding beliefs. We have one world, with a wide range of conflicting beliefs about it; this is intelligible in terms of one set of true, or uniquely reasonable, beliefs, and a wide range of causes of error and distortion. Today, there is a good deal of dissatisfaction with this point of view, but it remains implicitly influential among many who no longer explicitly argue its merits. Theories such as this one cannot be merely abandoned, they have to be exorcized. Hence it will be useful to examine the grounds which have been provided for accepting the theory, and the difficulties which it has encountered.

Eventually, this will involve some discussion of the work of philosophers, particularly epistemologists and philosophers of science. This will often involve using their ideas in a way which they did not themselves intend. We shall be seeking an account of how beliefs actually can arise. They will generally be intending to justify beliefs as knowledge. An example will serve to make the point.

Suppose a philosopher gives an account of how true or reasonable beliefs arise by citing (say) sensory inputs, memory, induction and deduction. Now imagine a critic who accepts the account, as account, but claims that it is a story about how human beings are deluded by appearances. Truth, he suggests, is only to be approached by shutting out deceptive sensory inputs and meditating on the nature of reality. This might produce further arguments from the philosopher, but the sociologist could safely leave the discussion at this point.[2]

The sociologist, if he accepts the model suggested earlier, is really only interested in the philosopher's view as a *naturalistic* account. He wants to know what beliefs arise in the absence of bias, and can be content to leave the issue there. He can *call* such beliefs true beliefs about the world, but it is their naturalness which really matters to him. Simply to give an account of how cognition and reason generate beliefs naturally, is to justify the sociologist's use of the theory in question. Thus, it will be with an entirely naturalistic interest that philosophers' accounts will be considered, and the following comments will be, accordingly, neither philosophy nor criticisms of philosophy.

Ideally, then, the sociologist needs an account which shows how beliefs arise naturally from cognitive and rational processes, given a particular field of experience. He also needs to know that essentially only one set of beliefs may so arise, or at least that incompatible sets of beliefs may not so arise.[3] Thus, he will look to philosophers who argue for the truth of particular sets of beliefs about the world, and account all alternatives as false. Many philosophical approaches have been of this form. Perhaps the best way of classifying them is according to whether they stress the role of the mind in the generation of knowledge, or minimize it and emphasize instead the external constraint of the world itself, or the sensuous given, or the data of experience.

For present purposes, it will suffice to limit discussion to the second kind of approach, as typified by the old fashioned varieties of inductivism. This is the approach which is usually implicit in the social sciences when true or reasonable beliefs are separated from falsehoods. Briefly, we can say that it characterizes naturally reasonable beliefs as those which are held on the basis of induction from experience.[4]

Clearly, if this characterization were adequate, the theories described earlier would be vindicated. And it does seem to have much to recommend it. Our senses provide us with direct awareness of the world in a form beyond our conscious control. They provide it in the form of 'facts', 'observations', 'events', 'perceptions' or some other primitive units (possibly 'measurements'). And our own direct awareness seems to be the same as everyone else's, indicating the reliability with which our senses monitor the world.[5] As to induction, the process of moving from the particular to the general, this can well be regarded as a naturally reasonable procedure. After all, it is impossible to imagine any institutionalized pattern of human belief and action which does not involve inductively generated expectation.

None the less, there are difficulties in this account which are sufficiently compelling to make the sociologist turn from the notion of true or uniquely reasonable beliefs as baselines for explanation. These are not, however, the difficulties which the philosophers have found with inductivism as a theory of knowledge. Philosophers dislike the uncertainty of inductive inference (exceptions may always turn up). They are worried by its scope (what can be induced from repeated failures to cure cancer, and what from repeated success in curing disease?). But, most important of all, they are disturbed because, as Hume showed long ago, induction cannot be justified by deductive arguments.

Many philosophers feel very strongly that induction ought to be deductively justifiable. Indeed the strength of this feeling can be such that it overcomes normal professional habits. We sometimes find the conflict of feeling referred to as the 'paradox of induction' (a paradox being normally a situation where logical procedures produce contradictions). This is one context where the sociologist with his naturalistic interests need not follow the philosophers; to him the universal occurrence of induction is of far more importance than its lack of a deductive justification. It really does seem plausible as a natural process in the development of beliefs. All humans induce; all societies believe that the sun will rise tomorrow, and the next day. (None seem to have induced simply 'Suns are prone to pass overhead'!) Induction is constitutive to human thought at every level.[6]

For the sociologist, the difficulty with inductivism is its incapacity to provide what might be called a complete rational reconstruction of the origin of reasonable beliefs. Let us accept for the moment its account of experience and of factual beliefs, in order to concentrate on the origin of more general beliefs. (The institutionalized beliefs of all societies are almost invariably in some way general in form; only the particular events of myth or accepted history could be argued to constitute exceptions to this.)

The process of inductive inference itself is all that is available to account for such general beliefs. Even if they were all of the nature of inductive generalizations from 'the facts' the task would be extraordinarily difficult.[7] As it is, the greater part of the beliefs which constitute our accepted knowledge are readily shown to derive from *theories* rather than being entirely the product of experience. Theories are imposed upon reality rather than deriving from it.

Describing beliefs in terms of a naturally reasonable set produced by induction, and causally induced distortion, is a good example of a theoretical approach being brought to bear upon phenomena, even if it is a self-refuting one. More importantly, those general beliefs which we are most convinced deserve the status of objective knowledge—scientific beliefs—are readily shown to be overwhelmingly theoretical in character. (As this theme is developed the distinction with which it has been introduced will blur somewhat, and what started as a qualification will develop into a fundamental point about the nature of knowledge as a whole.)

Activities in established sciences are always guided by some theory about the world. For the moment, this may be regarded as a picture or a story about what the world is like; this is not derived from the world but imposed upon it. The meaning of many scientific terms can very obviously be seen to derive from their place in a theory or story of this kind. Most general beliefs in science are formulated in such terms. Such beliefs cannot be held to have arisen inductively from experience, however loosely the process is defined.

The point scarcely needs making at the explicitly theoretical level in science. Beliefs about caloric flow, molecular vibrations, lines of force, ionic dissociation, DNA helices and evolutionary connections between species do not have the character of empirical generalizations. But neither do the everyday general beliefs of the laboratory floor. The everyday knowledge of the physicist is of currents and forces and particles, not of meter readings or balanced pivots or dots on screens; operational technique could be different in every laboratory. Similarly, the chemist knows the colours of ions and the properties of functional groups. Such knowledge gives the chemist expectations of his experience, but does not derive from it alone.

The theoretical, non-empirical, character of some terms used in science is occasionally forgotten because their use has become so natural and accepted. Take the term 'light' for example. It is clear that to ask the question 'what is light?' is to expect a non-empirical answer, for it is impossible to *see* light, on present common sense or scientific uses of the term. As to light 'travelling', this is even more obviously a move into the realms of theory; Toulmin's (1953) discussion of this example brings out the point admirably.

Similarly, the use of terms like 'sense-data' or 'retinal-image', is always non-empirical. (Empiricism was, and within natural science it remains, a *theory* of knowledge.) Consider the use of these terms in the psychology of perception. There are a number of what we call 'optical illusions', which can be described as distortions perceived in figures, when they are placed over appropriate backgrounds. Thus, an appropriate background may cause a line to 'appear' curved when it is 'really' straight, or longer than another line when it is 'really' the same length. This is taken as evidence that perceptual processes must be adjusting 'the data'; something must be intervening between the 'retinal-image' and our perception of it. Hence the data itself cannot be apprehended directly; it is a theoretical assumption partly explaining our perceptions.[8]

It is easy to show the importance of theory in science, and this effectively disposes of any attempt to depict knowledge as no more than empirical generalization. Science could be treated as distortion in order to retain an inductivist view, but this move is never made. (Arguments disposing of the possibility will, in any case, appear later.) Alternatively, the situation could be saved by treating theoretical statements as empirical statements in disguise, or as convenient but dispensable tools of thought; attempts along these lines have, however, consistently failed.

All this is well recognized in the philosophy of science, and since the 'truth' of a theory is even more obliquely related to data than that of an inductive generalization, and any number of theories may explain a given set of data, important implications are recognized. In taking account of the irreducibly theoretical element in science, philosophers have become less concerned with the truth of general scientific beliefs and more concerned to inquire how theories may be rationally developed and compared. Some regard them as convenient categorizing systems for organizing facts, to be compared in terms of their simplicity. Others insist that theories should be falsifiable, and stress the role of crucial experiments in science.

In sociology too, important implications should follow. It is no longer possible to treat 'truth', or 'naturally reasonable inductions', as unproblematic baselines for explanations, and all other beliefs about nature as distortions in need of causal explanation. Beliefs about nature need to be made intelligible in some new way. It seems clear that this has been recognized to an extent; sociologists do accept that knowledge is more than a collection of empirical generalizations. Yet, there has been little attempt to face the problem explicitly. Sociologists of science have been particularly coy on the issue. They have tended to talk of scientific knowledge as 'consonant with experience' or 'in accord with the facts', as though this completely accounted for its acceptance within science, established its validity and excused it from causal explanation.

III

It is worth a small digression at this point to present and illustrate the sociological implications of the foregoing arguments. The key point is that in so far as science is theoretical knowledge there is no reason why it should not be subject to sociological causation. Facts may remain beyond the sphere of the sociology of knowledge, but the rest of science does not. Once beliefs are conceded not to derive completely from the constraints of reality no further *a priori* argument can be made against their sociological investigation. And the problem of the validity of the beliefs in question is beside the point in this regard.

It will be objected that this claim ignores the possibility of rational theory choice. Simply because theories are brought to experience rather than derived from it, it does not follow that reason and experience together cannot identify a uniquely reasonable theory, which can be treated as an unproblematic product of undistorted thought. First, scientists will choose theories which accord with the facts, and then, among those that are not thereby eliminated, they will choose the simplest theory. Thus, theory choice is fully determined by reason. There is, however, no need for the sociologist to disagree with this; he may merely inquire about the *initial* set of theories from which choice is made. Suppose we rationally show that the abnormally high incidence of disease among the working class is better accounted for by indirect oppression than by direct oppression; does this mean that our thought was uninfluenced by sociological factors? Clearly not!

The only remaining argument against the sociologist is highly contingent. Scientists, it could be claimed, are an isolated group recruited from all social classes and with interests independent of all main social groups. Since they are also highly autonomous, they will not select theories for ideological reasons; they will select them neutrally and test them in good faith without prior commitment.

Unfortunately, even if this contentious argument were accepted it would not go far enough. We must again ask where the initial set of theories comes from. If, as presumably it must be, it is drawn from, or inspired by, the scientists' general cultural resources, then the final, rationally chosen, theory may be partially determined by social factors.[9]

Imagine a man by a river, randomly picking up stones; eventually he pockets two or three particularly beautiful ones and passes on. Later, seeing his stones we note with interest that they are quartz. 'It was purely chance,' he says. 'I was merely picking up the beautiful stones.' And so he was, yet we could learn much from where he had stood, and conjecture that had he stood on the Downs, or on the Solent, doing the same thing, he would have returned with stones of a different kind.

So might it be with scientists; not their social commitments but their social *position*, or simply their *society*, may determine their thought. They may draw their ideas from a culture largely embodying the ideas of a dominant intellectual class. Or their culture may in some sense reflect the total situation of their society and contain beliefs all of a certain kind or form. Such an approach to scientific theories was developed by Veblen at the beginning of the century. It has been ignored ever since.

Although Veblen was convinced of the factual basis of science, he related its theories to social factors just as he related other belief systems and kinds of thought. His concern was not with particular theories, rather, he attempted to show how the general form of scientific beliefs changed with social context. We might say that he tried to show that in a given society only certain kinds of hypothesis or theory occurred to people, or, at least, were given prima facie consideration.

He took it for granted from the start that men viewed the facts of experience through a 'scheme of habitual interpretation' (1908, p. 40)—that is, in terms of a theory or a myth. Science could be no exception to this, for it must always take the form of a coherent system of knowledge. Veblen recognized that scientists sometimes denied this, and in reply pointed to the constitutively theoretical character of physics, its imputation of *causal sequence* to phenomena (essentially metaphysical) and its imputation of movement to the effect of *force* (essentially dramaturgical). The dramaturgical nature of the concept of force in Newtonian mechanics was emphasised by pointing to the continuing problem of action at a distance in physics, and continuing attempts to explain it away and reduce mechanics to contact forces (1908, p. 35):

> Concomitance at a distance is quite as simple and convincing a notion as concomitance within contact or by the intervention of a continuum, if not more so. What stands in the way of its acceptance is the irrepressible anthropomorphism of the physicists.

Having noted the way in which social thought and action always take the form of organized, compatible systems, practically and thematically related, Veblen went on to suggest that 'schemes of habitual interpretation' in science are likely to be congruent with, and determined by, the general 'habits of thought' in the culture in question, which in turn are determined by 'habits of life'. (Veblen's commitment to a psychological theory of learning based on the concept of 'habituation' is apparent throughout.) He illustrated his thesis first by relating the cosmologies of ancient and medieval peoples to their habits of life, and then by considering the theories of modern science.

Modern science is held to have arisen in progressively industrializing communities. 'The technological range of habituation progressively counts for more in the cultural complex' (p. 49). Early modern industry is predominantly characterized by the workmanship of the individual craftsman; this is the image that increasingly dominates the 'habits of thought'. Scientific theories, at this time, seek to order phenomena after the model of a craft process, producing a finished product (p. 52):

> The 'natural laws', with the formulation of which this early modern science is occupied, are the rules governing natural 'uniformities of sequence'; and they punctiliously formulate the due procedure of any given cause creatively working out the achievement of a given effect, very much as the craft rules sagaciously specified the due routine for turning out a stable article of merchantable goods.

Later in the industrialization process there was a swing to a machine technology which introduced into the 'habits of thought' the idea of continuous change, lacking natural points of repose (or 'inconceivably high-pitched consecutive change' (p. 54)). This, in many areas of science, 'remodelled the current preconceptions as to the substantial nature of what goes on in the current of phenomena' (p. 54). Veblen cites, as areas where this change has occurred, physics, in which field theory and conceptions of continuity in most other branches of the subject would serve to justify his claim, and chemistry, where, despite the influence of Ostwald and the growth of physical chemistry, one wonders whether it was not more astute prophecy than actual description of the discipline in 1908.

The details of Veblen's argument, and how far it might be considered justified, are of no direct interest in the present context. His work is used to illustrate how theoretical science, without any impugnment of its rational nature, can be related to socio-cultural determinants. If the theoretical character of science is acknowledged, then so too should be the legitimacy of the questions Veblen asked about its theories. It may well be that after reflection and study we would reject Veblen's theses; the scientific changes he described may be better understood in other ways; highly general sociological factors may not influence scientific culture in any systematic and interesting way.

But this does not make it any the less deplorable that his work has lain neglected for over half a century, and that sociologists of science have tacitly treated his entire approach as *a priori* invalid. At least Veblen was clear about his theory of belief acquisition, and was consistent in relating his sociological work to it. With admirable detachment he followed the implications of his position. Although no modern philosopher is more committed to science than was he, he accounted for trends in scientific theory in the same fashion as trends in primitive mythology; anthropomorphism and its modern antithesis, medieval teleology and scientific causality were equally puzzling to him. The sociological study of natural beliefs cannot proceed without some such theory, and the more explicit it is, the better. Pussyfooting and deviousness on the issue cannot be in the long term interest of the social sciences, whether in the study of science, or in any other area.

I V

So far, singular 'factual' beliefs have been treated as unproblematic; Veblen takes this for granted; theories organize them, relate them to each other, give them dramaturgical appeal, but 'the facts' themselves remain 'given by experience'. Yet, for all the natural, obvious character of this assumption, it is beset by serious difficulties. The most serious of these arise because beliefs or statements are verbal formulations; hence, for them to arise from experience, experience must be categorized.[10]

Since 'factual' statements must involve the categorization of experience, it follows that, if they are to be regarded as universally acceptable bases for further belief, there must exist a special, theory independent, naturally intelligible set of categories of experience. As Hesse (1970a) would put it, there must be an independent observation language. If there is not such a language, or at least if no natural language of observation can eventually be reduced and translated into such a language, then there cannot be a special unproblematic set of singular, 'factual' statements determined by experience alone, or uniquely reasonable with respect to experience. Accordingly the sociologist cannot straightforwardly treat variability in conceptions of what 'the facts' are by postulating one unproblematic, natural conception, and a range of causally produced distorted ones.

So it is necessary to search for an independent observation language, a language of pure description. One immediate discovery is that many of the terms actually used in statements which we loosely and unselfconsciously regard as factual cannot be included in the language as they stand. Their usage embodies some theoretical position or point of view, or else is so context dependent that it needs explication in other terms if it is to become generally intelligible.

Consider, for example, the terms 'flower' and 'petal'. Botanists use these, like laymen, as observation terms. But their meaning in botany stems from their role in explicit structural theories current among botanists. Thus, for botanists, the magnificent petals of garden clematis are sepals, the brilliant flower of the poinsettia is a cluster of bracts, not a flower at all. The layman, on the other hand, has no explicit theory. He just uses the terms in the ways that seem natural to him, given his social background or training. His usage will be different from the botanist's. If he had to convey it to others he could be in difficulties. He could attempt to convey it by a long, biographical account of how he had learned to use the terms. Alternatively he might possibly be able to think of some model which, if taken as a guide by others, would produce a usage sufficiently close to that which he himself unselfconsciously employed. This might tempt him to regard his usage as stemming from an implicit theory.

The terms 'flower' and 'petal' are not independent observation terms; their usage is intelligible only within particular contexts, or in terms of explicit theories. It is easy enough to show the same for other terms. Observation predicates function within the contexts of living languages related to particular modes of activity. 'Factual' statements are meaningful from particular vantage points or in terms of particular theoretical orientations.

Consider another example; this time a hypothetical one. A metallurgist and a bed manufacturer noticed that they used the terms 'hard' and 'soft' in different ways. They convened a conference and invited all the groups they knew of who employed these terms. It proved possible, by negotiating in shared language, to erect a common usage for hard/soft, based on, say, how easy it was to make holes in materials.[11] Foam rubber was 'very very soft', wrought iron 'hard', mild steel 'very hard', and so on. Later they found their usage disintegrating: operators of ultrasonic drills regarded foam rubber as hard and steel as soft! Belatedly, they realized that their usage depended on taken for granted assumptions about what was easy and what difficult.

Later still, another crisis occurred. Hard/soft predicates had been overwhelmingly applied to crystalline materials and all sorts of laws and rules had arisen linking hardness with composition, levels of impurities, temperature, etc. Exceptions to these laws arose, and it was found that these disappeared if the hardness of single crystals only was considered. The hardness of a substance, it was said, 'really' corresponded to the ease of penetrating a single crystal of it. The meaning of the term 'hard' was changed so that certain law-like or theoretical statements it had become incorporated into, fitted more tidily with other statements.

Clearly, during the period of this imaginary account the term 'hard' did not function as an independent observation term. Its usage changed as implicit perspectives and explicit theories changed. It was a theory-linked term. Hesse (1970a) argues that all descriptive predicates may function in law-like statements, as well as in singular statements of observation, and hence may always suffer changes of usage in the way that 'hard' did in the above account, 'no feature in the total landscape of functioning of a descriptive predicate is exempt from modification under pressure from its surroundings' (1970a, section 4).

To establish this claim with full generality is difficult, because any putative observation term shown to be theory-linked may always be withdrawn from. It can always be claimed that contaminated observation terms are being used instead of more basic, truly independent terms, for purposes of convenience and condensation. Truly primitive observation terms may always be held to be lying at some later point in an endless regress. Thus, it might be claimed that the term 'hard', as used above, could be replaced by purely descriptive predicates. Particular operations could be described which made dents x" deep in materials. Then 'inches' could be specified in terms of the 'length' of some specific object, 'length' in terms of gradations on a tightly held piece of string, and so on.

What, in practice, establishes the strength of Hesse's case is that relativity theory has manifestly altered the usage of what have always been considered our most basic observation terms. 'Facts' expressed in terms of length, mass or time, in the pre-relativistic era, implicitly embodied a perspective, a taken for granted way of looking at the world; this was put into relief by relativity theory, since these basic concepts took on a different usage once it was accepted. Moreover, relativity theory did not merely strip the metaphysics from Newton; it involved its own *a priori* assumptions about the world, notably that concerning the velocity of light. Relativity theory did not give observation terms independence; it merely changed the nature of their dependence.

Thus, Hesse is able to argue convincingly against the conception of an independent language of observation. The 'given' of raw experience does not translate naturally and unproblematically into such a language. Observation terms function in living languages, where they are always involved in general and theoretical statements as well as singular ones. Their usage can even be shown to change over time; a 'fact' does not constitute an unchanging reference point. Thus, the idea that there exists a set of beliefs, which directly and unproblematically reflect reality by pure description, and which need no further explanation, is *totally* inadequate. The sociologist must seek to understand variation in natural beliefs without this given baseline. And if he wishes to explain beliefs as distortions, he must ask anew—distortions from what? The answer which will eventually be developed here will stress the constraints of culture rather than of reality—the culture which is successfully transmitted in the socialization process, with the acquiescence of reality and the constraints of human nature.

The key point of this section has now been made, but, before proceeding, it will be useful to loosen even more the bond between factual beliefs or statements and reality. The object will not be to endorse any of the wilder, more fanciful themes occasionally associated with this kind of argument. Perhaps it should be explicitly emphasized that nothing here argued suggests that the individual may choose what he sees or experiences in a given situation, or that reality does not constrain the possibilities of human thought or belief. However, it will be valuable to reveal the social element in the definition of what are accepted facts.

The social stock of accepted facts is not, of course, a simple summation of individual reports of experiences. But neither is it a summation of *accepted* reports of experiences. Societies tend to be materialistic, and to refuse some accepted experiential reports' status as 'of the world', and hence as factual statements. Many reports of experience are highly atypical; institutionalized belief systems incorporating them would be impossibly complex and detailed. Instead, if indeed they are taken in good faith, they are labelled as 'delusions' or 'hallucinations' or even 'visions'. Persistently idiosyncratic reporting of experience may lead to an individual being labelled oversensitive, eccentric, or insane—or a brain tumour may be diagnosed, or drug addiction. Facts are collectively defined; any system of knowledge because of its character as an institution, must include only collectively accepted statements.

Moreover, even collectively vouchsafed reports of experience may be denied straightforward factual status if they contradict accepted theories, or are themselves legitimate material for explanation by an accepted theory. Our culture is well stocked with categories used to degrade the epistemological status of shared perceptions. Usually, for example, if everyone hears a musical note in particular circumstances, this is taken as establishing some factual statement like 'there was such and such a sound'. Occasionally, however, we say instead that 'the ear constructed the sound' or 'everybody hears the implied note', and so on. We do this for instance if we find that the loudspeaker or instrument we were listening to cannot normally reproduce the tone in question, or that the tone was the base of a harmonic sequence of which only the other notes occurred in our music score. Today, the event leads us to inquire, not about how sounds are produced but about the ear and aural perception. We refuse to grant that the intersubjective evidence of our senses represents experience of the world in the normal sense.

Similarly, common sense indicates that we talk of certain figures as optical illusions. And there is little doubt that if the laity ever took a general interest in psychology, terms of this sort would proliferate in the common culture (Gregory, 1966). The sociologist could ask what distorting influences make people reject some sense impressions as experiences of the world. But it is far more reasonable to assume that a *natural* requirement for a neat and tidy belief system, a cohesive and manageable story about the world, overrides any natural propensity to accept sense impressions, and results in *cultural norms* coming into operation to define what counts as experience of the world. All cultures, of course, find themselves giving special treatment to what their senses tell them in certain circumstances; spear fishermen would fare ill if they threw at their fish where they saw them !

Psychological investigations have indeed now reached the stage where they lend overwhelming support to the view that perception is never a matter of passively monitoring and becoming aware of the world. Even before perception generates belief, the perceiver and his culture have actively been involved in the monitoring process. The evidence for this does not need recounting; the ambiguous figures and illusions of psychologists are too well known; so is our propensity to see 'visual stimuli' *as* something or other.

Perhaps the main point which needs to be made in support of such work is that its plausibility and scope are easily underestimated because of the superficiality of our informal awareness of our own perceptual processes. When we come to understand the speech of a very young child, or the user of a strange accent, what happens? We tend to talk of this as learning to understand what we hear, but is it not more accurate to say that what we hear changes (cf. Scheffler, 1967, pp. 28–30)? Is it not the same when learning to follow somebody's handwriting, or to discriminate sheep, or Chinamen, or mutant Drosophila? Does a wine or tea taster taste the same taste as the layman, and merely learn to interpret it more expertly?

These considerations have led to the suggestion that sensations, (as opposed to sense inputs, which are inherently unobservable) are capable of great variation between individuals and sub-cultures (Hanson, 1958, Kuhn, 1970). The perception of the scientist, in particular, must be related to his sub-culture and the training it has offered him. Physicists look at cloud-chambers and see particles passing across them, *not* water droplets materializing, or white lines appearing. Geneticists look at cell nuclei and see forty-odd chromosomes where laymen may see only a sort of Rorschach blot. (Less happy results can be produced by expectations influencing sensations; did Newton see a spectrum of seven colours, or Treviranus a logically appealing but spurious morphology of the retina (Gregory, 1966)? See also the fascinating collection of instances in Langmuir (1953).)

Finally, it is worth noticing that the modification of perception by scientific training is not entirely, or even mainly, a matter of learning verbal categories to 'impose' upon experience. Exposure to models of 'right' perception is very important. My own very elementary training is histology and metallurgy convinced me of this. Looking at microscope slides of cells and tissue sections, or metal surfaces, one attempts to draw them with textbook illustrations available for reference; actually one learns to see the slides in the way indicated by the illustrations.

The importance of these final comments should not be overblown. They seem occasionally to produce quite needless responses of disorientation and epistemological shock. Where they are relevant is in emphasizing the role of the culturally given in science, and thought as a whole, and the lack of any clear fact–theory boundary. Thus, they underline the importance of developing a new sociological approach to understanding the wide variation in beliefs about nature.

chapter 2

The sociologist and the
concept of rationality

I

If due weight is given to the preceding arguments, no particular set of natural beliefs can be identified as reasonable, or as uniquely 'the truth'. Nothing is implied for the normal usage of true/false predicates, of course. 'True' like 'good' is an institutionalized label used in sifting belief or action according to socially established criteria. When people become convinced that 'good' does not refer to some Platonic essence, or absolute set of criteria, they do not necessarily cease to employ the term; so with 'truth'. What is implied is that a picture theory, or a correspondence theory of truth is unsatisfactory, and that the sociologist cannot single out beliefs for special consideration because they are *the* truth.

It remains possible, however, to claim a special status for some beliefs, including scientific ones, by arguing that they are held rationally. The rationality of scientific activity may be used to justify the reliability of scientific beliefs. Although the world must always be approached from some initial standpoint, and 'facts' are always more than direct sense impressions, it can still be claimed that given theories which have been tested against the experiences they partially define, or rationally refined in terms of that experience, or rationally compared with alternative theories, constitute more trustworthy systems of knowledge than those which have not.[1] To choose to adopt less trustworthy beliefs instead would be irrational and could be held to require explanation.

Various accounts of the rational comparison and improvement of belief systems might be used by the sociologist hoping to establish a baseline of rationality. He could, for example, turn to the various models of inductive inference developed by philosophers of science. These attempt to show how inductive processing may move beliefs closer and closer to reality from some adventitious starting point.

Typically, they represent present knowledge as a set of statements, each of which is given an initial probability. Statements reporting events or observations are then added, and taken into account by inductive processes, generally based upon some variant of Bayes's theorem. As a result of the inductive processes specified, the initial probabilities are all transformed to yield new values. Repeated inductive processing results in the growth of knowledge; the probabilities arising later in the process are held to be more trustworthy than those existing earlier, even though the knowledge always develops from a given starting point (the initial set of statements with the initial probabilities assigned to them) and remains dependent upon it.[2] It cannot be shown that induction must produce convergence on to a particular pattern of belief, whatever starting point for inductive processing is taken.

In practice, the sociologist who looked to this work to provide him with a model of natural rationality would encounter serious problems. He would find several models in existence, mutually incompatible yet all with arguments in their favour. Moreover, he would find that all the models are recognized, even by their proponents, as inadequate in their present forms, so that none could be used with confidence to detect irrationality. Finally, he would have to recognize that no evidence has ever been assembled to substantiate the claim that the models are plausible representations of natural rationality. The philosophers of science who have developed the models have been, on the whole, more concerned with the justification of kinds of inference than with the description of natural patterns of inference.[3]

Another account of science as rational processing has been given by Popper. In his extremely sensitive analysis of *The Logic of Scientific Discovery* (1934) he develops an anti-inductive epistemology which takes account of all the difficulties previously mentioned. Theories about the world and the problems they give rise to are central to science; scientists should proceed by taking theories and attempting to falsify them. Given a set of initial conditions, statements can be deduced from scientific theories, the acceptability of which may be made dependent on agreed tests; if these statements are falsified then, logically, the theories themselves are falsified and must be abandoned; if they are confirmed then the theory is *corroborated*, which means (loosely) that one may feel more justified in adhering to it than one did before. Thus Popper tries to gear change in scientific beliefs entirely to the indications of deductive logic, which it is surely irrational to ignore.

Unlike some deductivists, Popper does not attempt to relate theories to 'facts'. Theories are statements from which other statements may be deduced. Among these are accepted basic singular statements which corroborate the theory. Experience, although it may motivate the acceptance of a basic singular statement, cannot justify it. If this is deemed necessary then it must be done, as before, by deducing further testable statements from the basic singular statement. The resulting infinite regress is cut short simply by *deciding to accept* certain statements. These statements have the character of dogmas, but at any future time they may be tested further; they are provisional dogmas. None the less, if science is to be done, a set of such dogmas must always exist, and reflect only the capacity of scientific observers to agree on them (1934, section 30; cf. 1934, ch. 5):

> The empirical basis of objective science has thus nothing 'absolute' about it. Science does not rest upon solid bedrock. The bold structure of its theories rises, as it were, above a swamp. It is like a building erected on piles. The piles are driven down from above, into the swamp, but not down to any natural or 'given' base; and if we stop driving the piles deeper, it is not because we have reached firm ground. We simply stop when we are satisfied that the piles are firm enough to carry the structure, at least for the time being.

Thus, Popper stresses streams of deduction in science. He does recommend certain criteria for selecting the statements at the top of the streams (that is, he makes general observations about what a good scientific theory should look like), but he gives no account of how these statements arise. In an important sense, as in the preceding account, they are treated as given. The statements at the bottom of the stream are also contingently defined. They are those which scientists are willing to accept at a particular time. Popper illuminates this point by use of the metaphor of a jury reaching a verdict (1934, section 30). Clearly, the resulting theory of knowledge leaves many questions aside and gives enormous significance to what scientists, as a group, actually do; from a philosophical viewpoint it could be claimed that all the interesting epistemological questions are pushed out of sight.

On the other hand, the preceding approaches, which justify scientific knowledge entirely in terms of the rational processing which has produced it and the way it is held, have obvious sociological appeal. Work like Veblen's is clearly compatible with them and they involve no *a priori* prohibition of sociological studies of variation in definitions of experience or 'the facts'. More importantly, they can be adopted as a framework with which part of the manifest variation in natural beliefs may be explained. It can be held that the human actor normally operates rationally, both in terms of activity and the way he develops and modifies his beliefs. Where irrationality is evident, it must be the product of some cause; the sociologist and psychologist can attempt to discover what cause.

In comparison with the previous framework, this one seems very promising. The range of human belief which has to be regarded as distorted or pathological becomes much smaller. Thus, taking Popper's account as a model of natural rationality, it is only irrational to hold to a theory if a clearly recognized falsification of it is ignored. Natural beliefs are irrationally held only if they are closed to correction by awareness of the world. Human thought ceases to be endemically unreasonable.

Conversely, the framework does seem to sort out cases where causal explanation is necessary. Do we not know, for example, that in some cases where actors 'lose their reason' physical factors are present which must surely disturb psychological functioning—brain tumours, say, or high blood sugar concentrations, or the presence of drugs? Do we not need special causes to explain why some people will acknowledge contradictions when shown them, in any context but that of the Bible? Again, when a doctor with a serious cancer insists that he is merely suffering from an ulcer, or when a football supporter insists that Wigan Athletic play as well as Everton, are we not entitled to look for causes of disturbance with the normal operation of reason?

These considerations, it must be agreed, establish a prima facie case for treating rationality as natural or unproblematic and irrationality as in need of causal explanation. The sociological possibilities of the approach must be explored. One question, however, might profitably be asked now, in anticipation of later themes. What is it about the above examples which disposes us towards the employment of causal explanation? Is it really an irrational element, the presence of contradiction or logical inconsistency—or is it simply abnormality?

II

We have, then, to assess the value of dividing beliefs into those which are rationally held and those which are not. Does this enable us partially to understand variation in natural beliefs by attributing causes to the irrationally held ones? For present purposes, we need only ask about institutionalized beliefs and belief systems, and sociological causes. The problem of idiosyncratic beliefs need not concern us. We may ask whether relevant criteria exist, which effectively discriminate belief systems and their elements into rationally and irrationally held components.

It is important that such criteria of rationality should be effective discriminators. If they are never deviated from, they will be of little interest to the sociologist, at least in so far as the variability of natural beliefs is the subject in question. Simple inductive propensities, for example, are of no sociological relevance here; the previous discussion has already commented upon their universality, the lack of any institutionalized departure from their indications.[4]

Another feature, essential to any rationality criteria we use to select beliefs for causal explanation, is their plausibility in naturalistic terms. They must involve a credible conception of what is a naturally rational way of holding beliefs. Imagine an esoteric group of philosophers, who held that one could only rationally hold beliefs of the form 'It seems to me that . . .' Clearly one would not seek a causal account of the incidence of 'irrationality' on the basis of that definition, whatever arguments existed for the desirability of holding beliefs of this kind. It would simply be too implausible an account of what was *naturally* rational. We would probably want to claim that it was a 'mere convention'. The rationality criteria required in the present context must be more than conventions. They must describe natural rationality, to be of sociological relevance. The more elaborate and sophisticated models of inductive inference are often implausible in these terms.

Finally, the criteria must be objectively applicable according to readily specified procedures. They must be more than mere labels for the taken for granted evaluations of some particular investigator. It is always tempting to call explanations one agrees with 'reasonable', accounts which one easily understands 'simple', arguments in accord with one's own theories 'logical', and to assume that 'unreasonable', 'complex' and 'illogical' beliefs must be irrationally held. It is important that this kind of approach, which was discredited earlier, does not return in disguise by a back door.

With these points in mind it will be useful to consider a concrete example, where the rationality status of an institutionalized set of beliefs is examined. I have chosen the institution of the poison oracle, as found in Azande culture, for several reasons. Its associated beliefs, relating to what we would call natural events, run strongly counter to current scientific ideas; if any belief system is to be labelled irrational this one surely must be. None the less, it may be taken as typical of a large number of primitive beliefs and institutions. Finally, it has been admirably described and discussed by Evans-Pritchard (1937), and subsequently commented upon and analysed by a number of philosophers and social scientists (among others, Polanyi (1958), Winch (1964), Horton (1967), Gellner (1968)). It is, effectively, the standard example for use in discussions of this kind.

According to Evans-Pritchard, Azande used the poison oracle to answer questions on a wide variety of subjects. It carried all the authority of a major institutionalized system of beliefs and practices: 'Zande rely completely on its decisions, which have the force of law when obtained on the orders of a prince' (Evans-Pritchard, 1937, p. 260).

The 'poison' used was 'benge', an extract from a creeping plant. This was administered to a chicken, and a question answerable in yes or no form was then addressed aloud to it. As the chicken lived or died, so the oracle was held to have answered one way or the other.

Certain precautions were taken, however. The 'benge' was always tested, and confirmed as a sample which killed some chickens but not others. And important questions were always put twice, in such a way that one chicken had to live, and one to die, for the two 'answers' to be consistent.

Undiscriminating 'benge' was accounted for by a variety of possible factors, many of which depended on the notion that taboos had been breached during its preparation or storage. 'Benge' which contradicted itself could be accounted for similarly. Where oracular pronouncements were belied by subsequent events, there was again a wide range of possible explanations. Sorcery and witchcraft were often held to have influenced the rite.

Thus, whatever the outcome of the oracle, the questioning Zande always found himself provided by his culture with an explanation which did not threaten the basic validity of the institution. And the institution itself apparently provided a perfectly satisfactory basis for decision and action, indeed Evans-Pritchard himself found it an adequate means of ordering his affairs during his fieldwork.

My own response to this account, typical I assume, of most people in modern society, is that the Azande oracle is little different from the coin oracle we use to decide which team occupies which half in a football game; it imposes regularity on chance sequences. Does this mean that the Azande beliefs are irrational, and if so, in what sense? By pursuing the question in this concrete context some insight may be gained into the value of rationality criteria for structuring sociological explanation.

We may start by asking if the Azande beliefs are irrationally held in the light of experience. Although the Azande 'observation language' is rather different from our own, it is readily understood, and allows us to ascertain that the oracular beliefs are indeed 'consonant with experience'. They deny nothing we see; they assert the visibility of nothing unseen by us. Irrationality cannot be established by this route.

The obvious next step is to consider the logical interrelationships between the beliefs. Needless to say, nothing counter-inductive is to be found. Inductive justification leads to what are for us strange conclusions because it occurs in a strange taken for granted structure, not because it breaks any logical rules. For Azande, properly performed, undisturbed oracles have been reliable in the past and hence may be trusted in the future. Similarly, Azande thought parallels our own with respect to deduction. Oracular outcomes 'follow' from the premises of their explanations. Azande are generally consistent in discourse and move from rule to example, or from instance to explanation, as we do. The premises are different, the taken for granted assumptions are different, but the forms of argument are not.

Thus, neither the demands of logic, nor those of experience, give us grounds for treating the oracle as an irrationally held belief system. The two most clear-cut and easily justified standards of natural rationality are of no help to us, and we must ask what others are available. Probably the other most widely advocated standard, in sociology and anthropology, is that of efficacy; efficacious beliefs, it is sometimes argued, are rationally held, whereas adherence to inefficacious ones is puzzling, and in need of explanation. Unfortunately, Azande justify their oracle in terms of its efficacy, and are willing to cite concrete instances by way of illustration. Within the framework of Azande thought the oracle *does* work.

But the oracle does not 'really' work. Must it not be irrationally held, because of its 'real' inefficacy? This question could only be answered affirmatively if we could demonstrate inefficacy by the power of reason alone. In practice we see their oracle as inefficacious because of our *theory* of their oracle. To relate rationality to efficacy as we define it is an undercover way of giving special status to our own theories. When the trick is exposed we are left without arguments, for we cannot justify the special status of our theories by an argument which assumes it. Efficacy seems, at first, an easy rationality criterion to apply objectively. In practice, whenever social scientists use it to classify beliefs in ways unacceptable to the actors who hold them, it serves to disguise the taken for granted assumptions with which they must actually be making their classifications; talk of 'real' efficacy may be seen as a rationalization of the felt superiority of their own theories.

Real efficacy, then, has no independent use in assessing how rationally a system of belief is held. But what about perceived efficacy? Let us agree that the Azande oracle, like rain-making ceremonies and other institutionalized primitive beliefs, can reasonably be perceived as efficacious by the actors using them. On the other hand, institutionalized primitive beliefs do exist which actors themselves acknowledge to be inefficacious; cargo cults and their associated beliefs provide a good example. Do not these beliefs need causal elucidation since their holders admit they do not work? Does not their perceived inefficacy establish them as irrationally held? The answer is that even here attribution of irrationality cannot be justified. Members of cargo cults believe that their activities will work in the future. Their beliefs are held rather like (say) institutionalized theories among cancer researchers. And just as reasons are given for believing in the eventual success of promising scientific research programmes, so too are reasons given for persevering with the rites of the cargo cult; it will work when they replicate the activities of the white man who is so manifestly successful at diverting their 'cargo'.

None of the preceding criteria has actually been employed in attempts to establish the irrationality of holding the oracular beliefs. Attributions of irrationality have, in practice, been justified by their alleged lack of simplicity, their unfalsifiability and their *ad hoc* character. These features were originally held to distinguish them clearly from scientific beliefs, but recent conceptions of science have weakened the force of the contrast (Kuhn (1970), cf. Horton (1967), Barnes (1973)). As will become clear later, simplicity, falsifiability and 'ad hocery' lack the discriminating power required by the sociologist to explain the variability of natural beliefs. They also fail to meet the other requirements adumbrated earlier.

Simplicity may be taken first.[5] Suppose we regard needlessly complex beliefs as irrationally held and in need of explanation. We may ask why Azande, who have a naturalistic conception of poisons, do not apply that, simpler, viewpoint to the oracle. Two snags arise here. First, simplicity cannot be given an objective definition; one must always ask—'simple in terms of what?' Given the consistent determinism and anthropocentrism of Azande thought as a whole, their oracular beliefs could well be presented as simpler than a naturalistic account modulated by chance, which would involve, as it were, special exemption from their overall cosmology. Even making the irrelevant comparison between oracular and scientific beliefs yields no obvious distinction in terms of simplicity. Consider what a long and complex story a scientist would produce; about the concentrations of chemicals in 'benge', their stability, and the temperature and humidity dependence of this, the constitutions of chickens, the contents of their crops, and so on. Scientific explanation is only simple from certain points of view.

Second, we may query whether 'simplicity' represents a natural rather than a conventional rationality criterion. It is easy to imagine a social group defining and enforcing a norm of simplicity. Its members would, accordingly, seek continually to pare down the number of concepts they employed in their theoretical explanations, and to reduce the number of special assumptions they employed.

But to see this as naturally rational, a universal imperative in human thought, is another matter. This may be regarded as a plausible hypothesis, but no more.

Initially, the use of falsifiability as a rationality criterion seems to be a promising approach. Since Azande beliefs deal with *any* oracular outcome with equal facility, it could be claimed that they explain nothing, and hence are irrationally held. However, the same two difficulties arise here as with the preceding criterion.

First there is the difficulty of objectively establishing that a belief system is falsifiable. This is a particularly acute problem since inspection of the system itself will not normally suffice to solve it.[6] Any system of beliefs may be an unfalsifiable one, if that is how it is held. The only practicable way of identifying falsifiable and unfalsifiable systems would be to ask those professing them if there are any conditions under which they would be given up. There is no need to tell sociologists what a comedy it would be to attempt to do this generally.

This leads to the second difficulty. Can falsifiability really be regarded as more than a rationality convention? Is the requirement that beliefs about the world be falsifiable, naturally compelling to rational men? There are many grounds for thinking not. One is the existence of a very strong conventionalist tradition in the philosophy of science! What systematic bias could so have influenced reason in such quarters that the idea of scientific theories as unfalsifiable conventions was able to flourish?[7]

Closely allied to stress on falsifiability is the idea that arbitrariness and *ad hoc* extensions and additions, compromise the rationality of beliefs. Here again we have the twin difficulties: how does one establish what is *ad hoc*, and how is it established that to be *ad hoc* is naturally offensive to reason? This time let us concentrate on the first difficulty.

Ernest Gellner (1968, p. 402) has referred to the *ad hoc* nature of the oracular beliefs. He implies that they can be split into a central essential set, and an *ad hoc* set of excuses. Evans-Pritchard's account is treated as a demonstration of how the second set of beliefs saves the first set from falsification. But why should the second set (how to explain 'wrong' answers, useless 'benge', etc.) be regarded as *ad hoc*? After all, any belief system can be split into two parts to produce the effect of 'ad hocery'. Do frictional forces save classical dynamics from falsification? Does the theory of the combustion engine have to be excused every time a car breaks down? Is it necessary, whenever a drug fails to cure or alleviate, to make excuses for the theory of medical science?

In all these cases, an appearance of 'ad hocery' is produced by severing a set of beliefs into two parts (basic beliefs and excuses). Sometimes they might correspond to a natural or chronological division in the growth of beliefs. A theory might be developed to explain why a drug works, then cases where it goes wrong may be noticed and appropriate explanations for this subsequently evolved. But why should such a process be termed 'ad hocery' rather than 'development'; or 'secondary elaboration' (Evans-Pritchard) rather than 'improvement' or 'rational modification'? Without some plausible account of the difference between good and bad embellishment, 'ad hocery' is useless as an indicator of irrationality. Such an account is lacking and it is difficult to see how one could be produced which could be regarded as more than a 'mere convention'.

In summary, it is interesting to note how plausible criteria of natural rationality (consonance with experience, consistency and 'logicality', efficacy) do not distinguish science from any other institutionalized beliefs, or indeed discriminate between institutionalized beliefs at all. Conversely, criteria which offer some promise of making this discrimination prove difficult to justify as any more than conventions. Popper (1934), with his habitual sensitivity, presents most of his criteria for good scientific procedure as *conventions* to be accepted by *decision*, and not as universal rationality principles. Thus on falsifiability: 'The only way to avoid conventionalism is by taking a *decision*: the decision not to apply its methods. We decide that if our system is threatened we will never save it by any kind of *conventionalist stratagem*' (1934, section 20),[8] and, more generally, concerning his prescribed methods for the conduct of science, 'Methodological rules are here regarded as *conventions*. They might be described as the rules of the game of empirical science' (1934, section 11).

One might ask, at this point, what it is that gives Popper's conventions their appeal. In the last analysis, the answer is clear; it is that Popper is able to present what we *already* regard as great scientific achievements as being the product of conformity to these same conventions. *The Logic of Scientific Discovery* does not justify science at all; it is justified by science as Popper presents it.

Whether or not it is desirable to use science to justify epistemology we may leave the epistemologists themselves to decide.[9]

III

So far, the search for discriminating criteria of natural rationality has failed. Attempts to explain some of the variability in institutionalized natural beliefs by finding causes for irrationality cannot get under way. The attribution of special status to scientific beliefs remains unjustified.

I shall want to argue that there are no appropriate rationality criteria to be found, and that this whole approach to the variability of beliefs should be abandoned. However, it must be recognized that such a claim cannot be finally justified; all that can be done is to undermine present arguments to the contrary. Since the claim being made is an important one, with far reaching implications, it is appropriate to make its basis as secure as possible. So far, its justification has depended too strongly on appeal to one particular example; it needs a more general grounding. This can conveniently be provided through consideration of the work of Lukes (1967, 1973).[10] He has developed the opposite view and supported it with a very wide range of sociological and anthropological material.

Lukes addresses himself to the general question of whether 'universal rationality criteria' exist. A 'rationality criterion' is a 'rule specifying what would count as a reason for believing something' (1967, p. 260n.). A 'universal' rationality criterion is one that must be generally obeyed in any society. He identifies two types of universal rationality criteria:

(1) Criteria of truth, 'as correspondence to a common and independent reality' (1973, p. 239).
(2) Rules of logic, 'the concept of negation and the laws of identity and non-contradiction' (1973, p. 238).

Both kinds of criteria must surely be universal, because they both must be generally obeyed in any human group whose utterances we are capable of understanding as language. For example, how, in a society where the law of non-contradiction was not generally observed, could meaning be attributed to utterances? How could inference and argument be followed? Yet, we manifestly do find ourselves capable of understanding the utterances of all human groups, and following their inferences.

Some utterances, in some human groups, do, admittedly, appear to be contradictory, or irrational in some other way. Such utterances (which are intersubjectively intelligible in terms of content-dependent rationality criteria) need special explanation: 'It is only through the critical application of rational standards that one can identify the mechanisms that prevent men from perceiving the falsity or inconsistency of their beliefs' (1973, p. 242).

The implication is clear enough. (Universal) rationality generally needs no special explanation, irrationality does; it must be accounted for by the existence of sustaining mechanisms (causes?). Thus we may reasonably take Lukes's work as a model of the kind of explanatory scheme currently being criticized.[11]

Let us then consider his first kind of universal rationality criteria. The members of a society being studied (1973, p. 238):

> must have our distinction between truth and falsity as applied to a shared reality if we are to understand their language, for if, *per impossibile*, they did not, we and they would be unable even to agree about the successful identification of public, spatio-temporally located objects. Moreover, any group which engages in successful prediction must presuppose a given reality, since there must be (independent) events to predict.

It is important here to consider what is meant by 'our distinction between truth and falsity as applied to a shared reality'. If it meant simply our habit of using a dichotomy of the true/false variety to distinguish acceptable beliefs then his claim might be granted. All societies do this; it is difficult to see how natural beliefs could ever be institutionalized and maintained without the deployment of predicates of this kind, just as it is hard to imagine a system of roles being institutionalized and maintained without the deployment of a good/bad type of dichotomy. Likewise, had Lukes meant that all societies deployed utterances in relation to objects, or the 'lumpiness of experience', in such a way that we wanted to say that they possessed 'naming activities', again we could have agreed, and agreed also that departures from normal 'naming activity' required causal explanation.

But Lukes's concrete examples show that he meant more than this. He seems to hold that all societies, being basically rational in the universal sense, must share elements of a universal observation language. Thus, he refers to the Nuer belief that human twins are birds as irrational by universal criteria; it does not, he implies, correspond to reality (cf. 1967, pp. 262–3). The third and fourth parts of Lukes (1973) illustrate how important such diagnoses can be to anthropologists and other social scientists in the study of ideology, religion and 'unscientific' cosmologies. Hence they reveal the importance of showing how profoundly mistaken Lukes is here. Although arguments against the existence of a neutral or universal observation language have already been offered, further examples may usefully be considered.

Why should the statement, 'twins are birds', be thought incompatible with reality? Despite the popularity of the conviction among anthropologists, it is hard to see how it is grounded, and thus how it is to be argued against. Perhaps Nuer are regarded as having a definition of 'bird' which is contradicted by the equivalence with twins. What then is this definition? What indeed is our definition of bird? Alternatively, perhaps it is thought that a class of real objects exists, which insists that our senses apprehend its unity and complete distinctiveness, and compel us to use a distinct term for it and it alone. What then of bats, penguins, ichthyoni—or cassowaries (Bulmer, 1967)?

We may sometimes wish to explain the extensions of categories and patterns of taxonomy in terms of social factors. But we cannot claim that one pattern is inherently more reasonable or rational than another. We have to remember that, as was emphasized in the previous chapter, objects are categorized as alike from some *point of view*. An anthropologist understands statements like 'sparrows are birds' because he can adopt the *perspective* which makes the statement meaningful. He might have reservations about 'bats are birds', but he would be likely to see the point; he would probably not want to causally explain *this* as irrationality; he would be happy to say that it was a different viewpoint at work. With 'twins are birds', on the other hand, he may be unable to accept the Nuer perspective, or even to imagine what it could possibly be. If, at the same time, he forgot that his own usage of 'bird' embodied a point of view, and he regarded his own statement as 'pure description', he would be tempted to call the Nuer 'irrational', or implicitly to accept this categorization of their behaviour by making excuses for it.[12]

The Nuer do have a point of view from which their usage of 'bird' is intelligible.[13] They did their best to explain it to Evans-Pritchard (1956), and Lukes quotes his rendering of it (1967, p. 258)! To us, it is a strange point of view, depending on twins and birds both being associated with 'Spirit'; but subjective perceptions of strangeness are neither relevant here, nor confined to perspectives in alien societies. Scientific perspectives can take some getting used to, but we don't question the rationality of statements like 'glass is a liquid' or 'sea horses are fish', nor any longer 'man is an animal' or 'the sun is a star'.

The example here used as a basis for criticizing Lukes's views has been chosen charitably. Elsewhere (1973), Lukes refers to the ignorance of physiological paternity among some peoples and their 'magical' notions of conception; he regards these notions as in violation of objective rationality criteria without making any attempt to show why. The assumption is that simply by peering at reality the true facts come to one. Here, as elsewhere in Lukes's papers, standards, originally introduced to explain the possibility of discourse between different linguistic communities, illegitimately metamorphose into the presuppositions of a rampant inductivism.[14] As a result, it is necessary to discount the whole of Lukes's attempt to establish 'compatibility with reality' as a universal rationality criterion. In the weaker senses touched upon in the preceding, all institutionalized beliefs are compatible with reality.

Let us now turn to Lukes's second class of universal criteria, 'rules of logic'. Here, his case is more plausible; whereas one can point to examples of different observation languages effectively dealing with the world, one cannot similarly illustrate how thought may be based on totally different 'logics'. Not even pure imagination can supply examples of meaningful language within which no 'logical uniformities' are apparent. And whilst all natural languages possess high levels of consistency in linguistic usage, and actors in all cultures seem capable of recognizing contradiction, many institutionalized beliefs do actually involve contradiction or illogicality; these criteria do discriminate between beliefs.

Hence, it is reasonable to assume that rules of logic are of implicit significance in all societies; human discourse generally conforms to them, and has to conform to them if it is to be intelligible as 'signal' rather than 'noise'. They are plausibly regarded as descriptions of natural limitations on the possibilities of human thought; perhaps it is such a naturalistic conception which Lukes has in mind when he speaks of them as 'the ultimate constraints to which all thought is subject' (1973, p. 24).[15]

But, having agreed with Lukes on these points, it is necessary to ask whether we can assume, as he does (cf. 1973, section 3), that the existence of particular beliefs involving illogicality needs to be specially explained. Certainly, it seems to be a natural extension of Lukes's argument to assert this. But, strictly, it is a non-sequitur (for which I shall offer no special explanation!). And when the assertion is considered in the light of the actual incidence of illogicality and contradiction among institutionalized beliefs, it becomes very difficult to justify. (For convenience, in what follows I shall take the convenient and innocuous step of subsuming illogicality to contradiction.)

The first thing to point out is that contradiction is endemic and routinely accepted in everyday utterances, despite their high general level of consistent usage. Accepted contradiction can be regarded as a norm, deviation from which is sanctioned as pedantry; it is difficult to justify the need for special explanation of such institutionalized contradiction. The point holds for everyday discourse in the sciences, as the following (imaginary) conversation may serve to illustrate.

Scientist: Crystals have regular structures. They may be analysed into innumerable identical unit cells, in the way that a large cube may be built from innumerable small cubes.

Pedantic Colleague: But do you not accept the second law of thermodynamics . . . ?

S: Yes . . .

P: . . . from which it follows that crystals are essentially irregular.

S: Crystals are never perfectly regular, as I implied. But, for the most part, you will find the same atomic nucleus at the same point in each unit cell.

P: But, as you know, the atoms vibrate, so they will be at the appropriate point for an infinitesimally small part of the time!

S: True. I should have talked of average positions.

P: Yet as crystals always exist in heterogeneous fields of force, does it not follow that all the average positions in different cells must be different.

S: Logically, perhaps it follows, but my account is valid for practical purposes. You insistently misunderstand me.

We may ask whether the scientist, who conforms to the norms of scientific discourse, needs his deviation from rules of logic causally explaining, or whether it is not the colleague, who deviates from norms of discourse in the interests of logicality, who needs sociological (or psychological) study ! Much of the time, of course, individual departures from rules of logic are also departures from normative patterns, and we are not called upon to ask which, in particular, needs explaining.

In everyday language, contradiction which does not get in the way of function is tolerated. Mostly, it is not thought of as contradiction at all, because it is *taken in context*, interpreted in the light of shared, taken for granted, assumptions, and thus is clear. Special causal explanation is not appropriate to such contradiction. We know that everyday speech must be (pedantically) irrational to be logistically realistic. And we know that the everyday mode of speech is what people find natural and reasonable.

Yet there might be a sociological point in identifying such contradictions. They could be referred to their originators for clarification; this would enable us to see if they rested upon a 'really rational' base. The fact that actors usually are capable of response to pedants, or puzzled anthropologists, surely indicates that they see the 'strict' irrationality of their utterances. We may infer that their 'real' beliefs 'underlie' their utterances, and only contradictions in the former need be specially explained.

If contradictory beliefs are referred back to an actor, he may be able to give a rationalizing account of them.[16] The oppressed scientist previously discussed, for example, would be able to elaborate upon his everyday utterances progressively removing contradictions and difficulties, turning 'loose' statements into precise ones, articulating unstated assumptions, qualifying the scope of statements to eliminate contradiction, and so on. To do this he would dig into his cultural resources as a scientist or physicist. The more he was pressed, the more the beliefs he articulated would become congruent with the accepted structure of physical knowledge, that is with the system of culture within which he operated as a physicist. Whether an actor holds his beliefs rationally will thus depend on the consistency of the cultural system which constitutes his 'real beliefs'.

Thus, the sociologist is led to ask whether systems of beliefs established in natural science, philosophy, primitive thought and so on are consistent and hence rationally tenable. And if they are not consistent he must search for causes to explain why they are found in practice to be (irrationally) held. Unfortunately, this whole approach must be abandoned for the following reasons.

First, all belief systems, when considered formally, are inconsistent. Indeed it is easier to show this for science and mathematics than for the beliefs of primitive cultures; the contradictions are more familiar and more thoroughly explored. They do not, of course, result in the particular systems of thought involved being abandoned, nor, save at particular periods of time, do scientists and mathematicians reveal more concern with the inconsistency of their systems of belief than do primitive peoples.

Second, again considering belief systems formally, it is easy to eliminate any particular inconsistency from a belief system. Simple, *ad hoc* adjustments always suffice. Must systems where these adjustments are not made be treated as irrationally held? Should we say that Russell let irrational aesthetic prejudices delay his formulation of the theory of types?

Third, attachment to any belief system is readily made 'rational' by accounting the attachment provisional. The actor may 'use' the system rather than 'believe' it. He may explain that other systems are as inconsistent as his, so he might as well stick with his own. He may express his conviction that somebody will eventually remove the system's inconsistencies in a manner which will leave its substance unchanged. Such statements rationalize attachment to the inconsistent system. But is the capacity to make such statements an indicator of natural rationality? And is there no difference between irrationality and lack of imagination, or a scanty vocabulary?

We may agree with Lukes about the high general consistency of human linguistic usage. We may even agree, for the sake of argument, that actors find inconsistency inherently puzzling. But we must none the less resist the claim that particular inconsistencies in human belief systems necessarily require causal explanation. Inconsistency is continually appearing and being eliminated from systems of belief; it is never absent. To understand the process it is necessary to set beliefs in relation with *activity*. To consider the logical relationships between the elements of abstractly conceived belief systems is, on the whole, misleading. The sociologist should consider beliefs in terms of their functions in practical activity.[17]

D

It is clear that when contradictory beliefs are linked into practice, contradiction must be resolved. A poison oracle where death of the chicken within an hour meant certainly *yes*, and its survival for more than five minutes meant an unequivocal *no*, would indubitably be unstable, since the oracular replies are directives to action and many outcomes would indicate incompatible sets of *activities*. In practice, such illogicalities are pushed out of institutionalized patterns of activity by the modification of beliefs; belief systems evolve so that they suffice for practical purposes.

As to eliminating 'contradiction' as a whole, that is another matter. There is no guarantee that a belief system will not face new contradictions as it continues to operate in contexts of activity. Sometimes, the means of eliminating one contradiction may eventually generate a new one in another context. Contradiction is continually threatening to occur; when it does so it is immediately pushed out of the context of activity. This trend is a cultural universal; it means that contradictory beliefs come to exist only at the boundaries of systems of action, the accidental by-products, as it were, of practical thought.[18]

Of course, speculative and theoretical thought exists in all societies, and peripheral contradictions in beliefs can always become 'objects of thought'. In Western societies, the activities of a differentiated sub-culture have come to centre upon these peripheral contradictions. Philosophers spend a lot of time on them, and frequently regard it as their role to resolve them. What are contradictions at the edge of activity for most of us, are at the centre of activity for many philosophers. It is interesting to note the lack of success philosophy has enjoyed in the matter of eliminating contradiction. It has been rather like putting the lid on a tin of paint. The lid can be put roughly into place, just as beliefs roughly order activity and thought without ambiguity or contradiction. But then there is the need to bang the lid firmly home and create an airtight seal all round the edge. Imagine that as one bangs the lid home in one place it comes adrift in another and one hammers fruitlessly round and round the top of the can without getting any further. So in philosophy it has been impossible to resolve all the peripheral contradictions at once. The appalling, unresolved difficulties of philosophy do not, however, worry the layman, whose beliefs suffice for all practical purposes. He may even rely upon an explicit adage enjoining distrust of philosophers. Similarly with scientists, if their working methods are unacceptable to philosophers, too bad for them!

In summary, the *general* consistency of human language and activity is used by Lukes as a justification for treating *particular* inconsistencies as the result of external causes distorting the normal operation of reason. This is rather like claiming that since an amplifier, to be an amplifier, must have a high signal/noise ratio, any source of noise within it must be the result of a defect or of external interference. This is a useful analogy; it reveals the non-sequitur in Lukes's argument, but it also illustrates its partial plausibility—defects or external sources *can* cause amplifier noise; on the other hand, some noise is inherent in its *normal operation*.

If we turn to Lukes's concrete examples, even his own argument lacks the scope to justify the analyses he offers. In his critical enthusiasm, he assumes that his cited rules of logic are deviated from much more often than is actually the case, running away from his carefully argued general scheme into ill considered polemics. At one point, he illustrates the irrationality of 'Soviet Ideology' by citing the very elements of it which keep it, as a belief system, in conformity with Lukes's own stated rules of logic (1973, p. 243)! Despite warning against this very pitfall at the end of his paper (1973), Lukes has allowed himself to assume that beliefs he regards as obviously wrong must deviate from his universal criteria. His arguments from 'rules of logic' run to seed, just as his arguments from the necessity of 'one reality' ran to seed and produced a luxuriant top-growth of inductivism.

Consideration of Lukes's work has, then, confirmed the tentative conclusion reached earlier. We possess no rationality criteria which universally constrain the operation of human reason, and which also discriminate existing belief systems, or their components, into rational and irrational groups. Variability in institutionalized beliefs cannot be explained by a conception of external causes producing deviations from rationality. Likewise, the culture of natural science cannot be distinctive because of its rationality, in a universal rather than a conventional sense.

IV

It is now possible to make explicit the positive side of the argument, which so far has only been hinted at. The manifest variability in institutionalized natural beliefs is to be made intelligible by being set against an unproblematic baseline of *normality*, not 'truth' or rationality. It is possible for the sociologist to identify normal patterns of belief by the investigation of human collectivities in the light of existing sociological theory.

The sociologist will associate an actor with certain institutionalized beliefs and actions by virtue of the position he occupies within the social structure. For an explanation of their acquisition he must look to the theory of socialization, and studies of the process of cultural transmission.[19] To account for their persistence, he must look to the stability of the context in which they occur. To account for their change, he must ask what mechanisms, if any, can produce cultural change in a stable context, and he must identify any special influences and causes which disturb that context and modify elements within it which have served to sustain particular beliefs. Where actors or groups hold idiosyncratic beliefs as judged against some background of normality, some special cause or condition must be identified which distinguishes the actor or group from that background. (This is not to imply, of course, that deviations or departures from normality are either pathological or uncommon.)

Let us go back to the Azande poison oracle again, which, it will be remembered, was generally and unthinkingly accepted among Azande. Suppose Evans-Pritchard, in this context, had recorded the existence of an actor or group which doubted it, or had become convinced that it was false. Would the relieved anthropologist have noted that at last he had found somewhere where rationality prevailed and causal analysis was not necessary? Would he have quickly passed on elsewhere to his real explanatory problems? Surely not. The actor or group would have been of special interest because of its departure from the normal practice into which it had been socialized. It is unlikely that explicit theories of rationality and conscious theoretical preconceptions would have stifled an anthropologist's intuitive curiosity about an *abnormal* sub-group. Had it been in contact with another culture? Had it suffered through oracular pronouncements? Did it gain from its deviance? Did it think it had discovered a more reliable oracle, less susceptible to the spells of enemies?

As to normal patterns of belief and action, these must, in the first instance, be treated as culturally *given*. They are maintained as permanent institutional features through socialization and social control, and it is technically impossible to explain them via their ultimate origins. Among such given cultural patterns none is any more puzzling, or any more in need of causal explanation, than any other. The arguments of the preceding chapters can be taken as establishing that this is so. We may claim that all institutionalized systems of natural belief must be treated as equivalent for sociological purposes.

It should be noted that this is not to say that any collection of utterances at all may be treated as sociologically equivalent. Institutionalized belief systems are a special set; they are all capable of being readily transmitted in socialization. Actors are not of limitless plasticity; they cannot be socialized into operating with any collection of beliefs or utterances. Lukes's basic, very general point, that there are limits to the possibility of human thought, is doubtless correct.

We could perhaps say that natural human propensities (our manifest natural rationality) determine the possibilities of human belief. But since the sociologist always encounters existing belief systems, he can simply take natural rationality for granted. The concept has no role to play in sociology. It is more likely to be useful to philosophers and psychologists interested in natural induction, or naming activities, the discrimination and categorization of objects of experience.

It follows from this that natural science should possess no special status in sociological theory, and its beliefs should cease to provide reference standards in the study of ideology or primitive thought. The sociology of science is no more than a typical special field within the sociology of culture generally.

It also follows that the sociologist will be unable to advance his understanding of belief and action by categorizing it in terms of his own criteria of rationality, efficacy or truth. His sociological understanding must start with an appreciation of actors' normal practice as it is, and of its inadequacies as they themselves define them. He must make action intelligible through detailed and extensive insight into the nature of actors' perspectives, their categories and typifications, the assumptions which mediate their responses, the models which organize their cognition, the rules they normally follow.[20] Then he must construct theories which treat this material symmetrically. This is, as yet, the approach of a minority in sociology, including 'idealists', 'phenomenologists', 'ethnomethodologists' and some 'symbolic-interactionists'. None the less it is, essentially, a correct approach, and one which is universally applicable.[21]

These are far reaching claims which go against the assumptions of most existing work. The use of a baseline of truth or rationality is evident in most accounts of primitive belief systems, of religious beliefs in any kind of society, and of political ideology. Sociological and historical accounts of the rise of science and its success similarly make use of these crucial concepts. The following chapters should, however, reveal that the present arguments are indeed justified, and that the valuable features of the studies here mentioned are not lost when some of the assumptions which guided them are discarded.

chapter 3

The culture of the natural sciences

I

When natural science is studied simply as culture, one of the things that immediately becomes puzzling is its very existence as a category. Why should the diverse patterns of belief and action we identify as science be so identified? Why should we regard a particular part of our natural knowledge as scientific, now that it can no longer be seen as commonly validated by a uniquely rational method? Is it possible to give any sort of general account of the normal practice of science?

One possibility is to regard the sciences as embodying a single set of procedural and methodological *conventions*. This is an interesting possibility, if only because of its compatibility with Popper's work (1934).[1] As the preceding chapters have already implied, however, it cannot be justified. Belief in the real existence of a universal 'scientific method' is the product of constant idealization; it cannot be sustained in the face of concrete accounts of the diversity of science.

This is not to say that science as a whole reveals no important general characteristics. On the contrary many such features are to be found. One is the strong aversion to anthropocentrism and anthropomorphism characteristic of all scientific disciplines. This is manifested in many ways: *a priori* opposition to teleological argument and theorizing, aversion to anthropomorphic or animistic theoretical entities, an insistent differentiation of fact and value, a cosmology firmly denying man any special significance, and, finally, a tendency to reject or devalue scientific work on hypnotism, extrasensory perception or similar topics. This trend is reflected in the rites and customs of science, notably in the style and form of the scientific paper, where the passive tense is now *de rigueur* and verbs, wherever possible, are converted to nouns.[2]

Many other general features could be mentioned. There is the now universal trend to mathematization and quantification. And there is the characteristically abstract and theoretical nature of scientific knowledge, which sets it apart from common sense, or the more concrete lore of the chef or the builder.

But, although these features have methodological implications, and go some way towards describing a 'scientific approach' to problems, they do not amount to a general methodology for science, since they do not get anywhere near a full specification of how scientific knowledge claims are to be evaluated. To establish the existence of a general 'scientific method' in this sense, it would be necessary to show that scientists, as a whole, accepted and employed a set of methodological conventions or prescriptions such as, say, Popper's. Or, at least, it would be necessary to show that the acceptance of our presently constituted scientific knowledge was intelligible in terms of such a set of conventions.

Unfortunately, this cannot be done. Such has been the diversity in past and present scientific culture that any suggested convention always seems to disqualify enormous chunks of currently accepted science from enjoying this status. Nor is this merely through such contingencies as the non-experimental nature of some sciences,[3] or the fact that others deal with unobservable unique past events. It is simply because scientists themselves do not possess any shared single set of conventions, whether for procedure or evaluation.

Concern with falsifiability is often thought to be a methodological convention characteristic of science as a whole. Yet it is easy to show that this is not so. If we start by considering individual scientists, or small working groups, we find that this concern, more often than not, is absent. Instead, there is interest in obtaining support for a theory by the discovery of confirming instances.[4] The conditions under which existing beliefs would be abandoned are never specified, and often they are retained in the face of apparently strong disconfirming evidence. In many cases beliefs initially sustained in this way have eventually become unquestioningly accepted as part of our present knowledge; an instance is the theory of evolution, which at one time seemed incompatible with reliable physical estimates of the age of the sun.

If we consider the development of scientific theory in the abstract the general importance of falsifiability becomes even more difficult to accept. Very often scientific research is initiated on the basis of some simple, beautiful idea which, even if it is, in practice, treated as unfalsifiable, could easily be made subject to some agreed test. As research proceeds, qualifications, secondary hypotheses and arbitrary additions surround the initial theme; the line between explanation and rationalization becomes more and more difficult to draw.[5] It becomes increasingly difficult to think of something which could count as a test of the existing system of knowledge. For example, we may compare early formulations of the concept of valency with later developments involving variable valency, unutilized valencies, secondary valencies, and so on. Or we may examine the development of Mendelian genetics, comparing, for example, the concept of dominance with the later conception of penetrance.

Finally, if science in application is considered, the role of falsifiability is no more easy to discern. Scientific pronouncements do not become more testable when they are made in a practical context. On the contrary, the scientist enters 'outside' situations as a transmitter of expertise, not as a participant in a debate or critical confrontation. His opinion upon the mechanism of the Azande poison oracle, for example, would be arrived at by applying accepted scientific approaches to the issue, and assuming that the outcome settled the matter. He would not seek to test his views against Azande accounts. Nor would there be any point in doing so since his position would be just as unfalsifiable as theirs.

One can, of course, find examples of concern with falsifiability in science. Tests and acknowledged 'crucial experiments' are sometimes deliberately constructed. One can even find highly atypical examples (particularly within experimental psychology) where individuals have sought to compare their own theory with a competing one, and have decided that their own theory should be abandoned. But this merely reinforces the point that no single convention has guided scientific methodology, or even *ex post facto* successful scientific methodology.[6]

All attempts at general descriptions of scientific method tend to go the same way when compared with scientific practice. Scientific activity is simply unintelligible in terms of distinctive general conventions; scientific knowledge claims have not been sifted by the application of a single set of general standards. That the opposite is so often thought to be the case is a result of prior conviction, rather than detailed examination of scientific activity as it is conceived and performed.

II

Instead of attempting to construct a simple formulation of the 'essence' of scientific activity, we can adopt a more piecemeal approach based upon sociological and historical materials. On the the basis of this work we may agree that science is a part of culture, and that at the present time it constitutes a highly differentiated element of it. Restricting ourselves to academic science, we can readily identify fully differentiated scientific roles, special linguistic forms, specific esoteric clusters of activity, characteristic artefacts and so on. We know that these segments of culture have been changing rapidly over a long period of time, and sociological work on simultaneous discovery and scientific priority has indicated the coherence of this cultural change, the underlying cultural cohesiveness of the various branches of science, and the way in which groups of peers in science effectively participate to define what they count as scientific knowledge at a particular time (Ogburn and Thomas (1922), Merton (1957, 1961, 1963), Hagstrom (1965)).

Finally we know that science itself, as a culture, is very highly differentiated into disciplines and specialties. Increasingly, the scientific specialty is being treated as a relatively autonomous sub-culture with an extensively differentiated system of social control, and it is here that the process of cultural change has to be studied in the case of present-day science. That this is near enough taken for granted among sociologists is mainly due to the work of the historian of science T. S. Kuhn, and the 'Invisible College' hypothesis of D. J. de S. Price, which offered opportunities for quantitative sociological work (cf. Crane (1972)).

The sociologist must ask what it is that guides the research of a scientific specialty, what makes it a coherent social phenomenon, and what makes its rapid rate of cultural change feasible. He must seek a description of normality and change within the specialty which is sufficiently general to apply to any part of science, and which is accordingly of general use as a basis for the kind of understanding discussed at the end of chapter 2. Again, the work of T. S. Kuhn offers a promising starting point. He gives an account of scientific culture which is compatible with the diversity of scientific practice; the 'price' of accepting it is that description and justification become less firmly interlocked than before. The influence of Kuhn's work will be obvious in the following account of scientific culture, although no attempt has been made to reflect his views accurately and other important sources are freely drawn upon.

It has already been noted that the work of the scientist is always guided by a theory of some kind, and that the theory has to be seen as an independent variable, in the sense that it cannot be held to *derive* from observation and experiment. A theory was loosely characterized as a story about the world, which imposed order and coherence upon it; this is indeed the case, but its key function is to order and structure the *esoteric* experience and practice of the scientist in his scientific role.

Theories do always possess wider possibilities, and occasionally these are exploited to their limits, so that theories become of cosmological significance. Such developments (the growth of mechanistic cosmology, the dying universe doctrines based on classical thermodynamics, and so on) are only intelligible in terms of a perspective extending far beyond any narrowly defined conception of scientific debate. But, in the highly differentiated context of modern science, we can profitably focus on the relationship between the scientist's theories and his esoteric, highly specific, problems and activities. In most cases, this keeps us close to the scientist's own conception of where he may legitimately seek for the answers to his questions.

To understand the relationship between theory and practice in science it is necessary to explore in more detail the nature of a theory. The key point that must be established is that a theory is a *metaphor* created in order to understand new, puzzling or anomalous phenomena, either in terms of a familiar, well ordered part of existing culture, or in terms of a newly constructed representation or model, which our existing cultural resources enable us to comprehend and manipulate.[7] The puzzling area is subjected to metaphorical redescription in terms which are 'strictly' appropriate only in a different context. This redescription constitutes theoretical explanation; if it is accepted, our notions of propriety may change and the metaphor may submerge, or even die (cf. light travelling, the genetic code).

This conception of scientific theory and its implications are best justified and illustrated by means of a concrete example. The introduction of Dalton's atomic theory into chemistry early in the nine-teenth century is a suitable choice, being sufficiently general to illustrate most of the points needing to be made, yet reasonably accessible, and intelligible without much detailed scientific know-ledge. Since the example will be used illustratively, no attempt will be made to present details of theory or chronology with any great precision.

If we examine the situation prior to the introduction of the theory, we find that a number of accepted chemical techniques and pro-cedures were in existence, and rapidly being exploited. The most important of these techniques were the use of the chemical balance in conjunction with accepted preparative and transformatory pro-cedures such as calcination, and the resources of pneumatic chemis-try available for the study of gases or vapours.

Techniques were bound up with language and belief to form systems of action, best understood as such. Thus, the operation of weighing was related to a theory of the balance and the significance of its results, and this theory was necessary to an understanding of the observation language in which the results of weighings were expressed. Technique, theory and language of observation were intelligible only in terms of each other, and this is how they were learned. Weighing was learned as what Kuhn would call a set of exemplary procedures or exemplars (1970, Postscript).

Use of the balance generated a large amount of information upon the proportional composition of substances by weight, as expressed in an observation language built upon the terms element and com-pound. Compounds were complex substances made up of simple substances, elements, fixed in chemical combination. The propor-tional compositions of compounds were frequently treated as puzzling or problematic by chemical practitioners; they could be treated as data in need of ordering and explanation. Generalizations and explanatory models could legitimately be presented to organize or understand them. One generalization subject to much controversy at this time was the claim that any particular compound always contained a fixed proportion by weight of its constituent elements. Opinion at the time was slowly moving to the view that this was indeed the case.

It should be noted that there was nothing *inherently* puzzling about the material in question. Subjectively, many scientists found it so, but that is another matter. The data on the composition of chemical compounds could have been treated simply as information about how the world was. Very familiar elements of culture may be found puzzling by some social groups, whilst others insist that they are already perfectly intelligible and need no further explanation.[8] Often, taken for granted phenomena are illuminated by a theory and metaphorically redescribed. They are found puzzling for the first time as the answer to the puzzle becomes available. Why is there an atmosphere? Why winds? Why are diamonds hard? Why do materials differ in colour?

Suffice it, then, that the results made available by use of the balance were found puzzling, and the Daltonian theory provided a way in which they could be made intelligible. Chemical reactions could be regarded as the re-ordering of the basic particles of elements —their atoms—into new, ordered clusters—the molecules of compounds. The notion of an atom, although an idealization, was modelled on our everyday conception of a lump of solid material. To describe (i.e. to redescribe metaphorically) reactions as the cumulations of atomic events was to describe them in a way with which chemists were culturally equipped to deal; the atomic events were intelligible in terms of the rearrangement of permanent solid objects. Chemical reaction was redescribed in terms of an atomic model; this model was itself intelligible because atoms could be thought of as material particles. They were the device by which useful elements of the familiar culture pattern (properties of material particles) could be transferred to and reorganized about the puzzling events (chemical reactions). In the idealization (the atom), useless or unpropitious elements of the familiar area could be eliminated (divisibility, destructibility, etc.) and favourable elements added (propensity to small, whole number combination etc.). The result was a set of familiar cultural resources organized into a simple and illuminating story about a range of puzzling material.

A number of factors contributed to the appeal of the detailed model of Dalton.[9] It fitted well with a number of existing concepts and categories. It offered a way of visualizing chemical reaction which made a number of systematic relationships in chemical data appear natural or inevitable; the laws of constant composition, multiple proportions and reciprocal proportions, which were already gaining some independent credibility, were, in particular, easy to represent as natural consequences of the model. It accordingly gave coherence to a set of otherwise unconnected facts and coincidences. And, more generally, it offered a world view which treated all existing materials as variations on a few simple organizational themes. Natural diversity was underlaid with chemical unity.

But over and above these factors lay another more important one. The Daltonian model was perceived in conjunction with exemplary applications, which distinguished it from other models much more clearly than the above 'intellectual' criteria could do. Its acceptance was very much bound up with perceptions of what could be done with it. As Thackray has stressed (1966), the Daltonian scheme provided a calculating system for determining the relative weights of the ultimate particles of matter from potentially accessible observations. When the calculating system was studied, in terms of the concrete examples of Dalton and others, it thus indicated promising ways of deploying existing chemical procedures. The model's potential as a basis for future activity within a scientific role could be appreciated, in a way which could well have remained obscure had it been presented abstractly. We can regard Daltonian atomism as a *paradigm* in Kuhn's terms; it accords well with his observation that paradigms necessarily include concrete achievements, which can act as exemplars upon which future work in a research tradition may be modelled.[10]

Although the model was effectively incorporated into chemical practice, it created difficulties as well as resolving them. Again, this can be regarded as typical of a newly introduced theory. In this case, a vast amount of experimental data suddenly became anomalous, since it indicated the existence of compounds whose constituent elements were not combined in fixed and definite proportions. Other results became puzzling because they were at variance with the laws of multiple and reciprocal proportions. Acceptance of the model involved changing one's beliefs so that they became discordant with 'the facts' as a whole. Daltonian atomism grew in a context replete with disconfirming instances.

Moreover, the model lacked any independent justification. It was inferred, or justified, entirely by drawing from the data it was used to explain. Other areas of science, on the whole, could lend it no support. And its main features, in themselves, could apparently never be checked. Atoms were postulated as invisibly small bodies; it was assumed that they must remain, for ever, beyond the reach of observation. The model was thus doomed to remain a matter of speculation, incapable of ever being fully justified by the 'empirical' means so greatly valued in science.

Individual chemists varied greatly in their responses to Daltonian atomism. Some rejected it completely in terms of a strong and explicit positivism, others rejected it formally, whilst granting its admissibility as an heuristic device. On the other side, it was accepted by some as an 'as if' theory which could possibly be true, and by others as a real description of the fine structure of matter.

These varied responses raise the question of whether the argument so far does not stand in danger of being hoist with its own petard. Puzzling phenomena were said to be metaphorically redescribed, as scientific theories were developed and articulated, yet this does not seem accurately to correspond to actors' points of view. Some scientists were positivistic, and rejected opportunities for redescription, and it is clear that few if any actually thought of themselves as exploiting and developing metaphors. Since the danger of imposing external perspectives upon the diversity of scientific practice has been stressed, and the importance of proceeding from the actors' own definition of the situation, the present discussion clearly stands in need of justification.

This can be provided if the discussion is thought of as an account of cultural change in science, rather than as a description of every individual move an accredited scientist makes. Despite the existence of positivists and positivistic activity in science, all research traditions develop their beliefs, and culture generally, through the deployment of metaphors; long term cultural changes are metaphorical extensions, or changes of metaphor. Actors who make these extensions may not talk of them in these terms, but the present account does not *replace* actors' own accounts or necessarily devalue them; rather it draws attention to general features of scientific belief and action, as subjectively defined, which are of particular sociological interest.[11]

Let us see how this defence works with the example in question. It is clearly valid to talk of the atomic model being used for *redescription*, by those taking it as an 'as if' theory, as well as by those regarding it as a real description of matter. The model operates in the same way in both cases, only its ontological status varies.[12] By talking of *metaphorical* redescriptions, we emphasize that, when actors first employ them, they may be unintelligible, or even absurd, by conventions of normal usage; they may be *literally* absurd. (The difference between the literal and the metaphorical is, of course, a matter of social convention, of what is institutionalized and what not.) Thus, to say that a flame is the rapid re-ordering of lots of tiny particles might be thought as absurd as to say that a twin is a bird (!); only involvement in the chemical science of the day would indicate the possibilities of the statement.

Reference to metaphorical redescription also emphasizes that, however much of a realist a scientist might be, he never fully develops all the 'literal' ways of talking in his familiar system for use in the area he is explaining. Thus, many properties of material particles (conductivities, melting points, deformability, etc.) were never considered to be the properties of atoms. Indeed some of these macro properties were *explained* in terms of the simpler set of properties thought to be possessed by atoms, plus the contingencies of atomic arrangement.

On the other hand, it is important to note that models are used metaphorically and not comparatively. Scientists were not concerned merely to talk in literal language about the way in which chemical reaction resembled the re-ordering of particles. Simple comparison of the two systems was impossible; it could only begin when one was conceived in terms of the other. Furthermore, scientists were not just concerned to notice likenesses; they sought to *create* likenesses; adoption of a model was followed by a continuing increase in utilization of the cultural resources it made available. Finally, unlike a simple comparison, use of the model involved changes in patterns of accepted usage of concepts, both in the area being explained and in the familiar area of culture. On the one hand the atomic model hardened the conviction that compounds were of constant composition and modified usage of such terms as 'mixture', 'compound' and 'pure'; the everyday observation language of chemical science was subtly influenced. On the other hand, the study of reactions modified conceptions of the nature of atomic particles and of everyday particles too. The two sides of a metaphor can interact in a way inexplicable in terms of comparison; consider the claim that glass is a liquid, or the idea of J. A. Mayer that the earth is a steam engine. Doubtless there are those who would find the latter, despite its offer of insight into the nature of the hydrologic cycle, an offensive description of our complex earth; but it can do wonders for one's conception of an engine !

Thus, the view of theory as metaphor gives a good summary

account of how those who adopted it (in whatever way) used the atomic model. But what of those who rejected it? Over the best part of a hundred years the chemical atomic theory was subjected to a wide range of attacks from positivists, some of whom avoided using it, even simply as an aid to the imagination. Positivistic claims and approaches are nowhere better studied than in the context of atomism. Since models are used in all areas of science, and rarely fail to draw positivistic criticism, important general points can be established through consideration of this particular example.

Positivistic criticism stresses the unobservable or untestable elements in models and metaphors. It stresses respect for observable fact and discourages speculation. It challenges those who propound theoretical schemes to justify themselves. There is no reason to deny the value and occasional fruitfulness of such criticism, but it does not weaken claims that models, metaphors and exemplars are of basic importance in scientific change. These claims can be defended practically, at a number of levels, without recourse to philosophical criticism of positivism as a theory of knowledge.

First, and most superficially, it could be shown that scientists themselves have never placed great value on disconnected pieces of fact. It is theoretical change which has been overwhelmingly important in the cultural growth of science as scientists themselves define it. It is explicitly theoretical innovation which has won the major proportion of formal scientific awards and honours.

Second, it could be shown that the best positivistic contributions, as defined by scientists, have served to discipline and redirect ongoing theoretically based patterns of research. The valuable contributions of positivist ideology have been *parasitic* ones, which could be made only because others were sustaining a tradition which could be criticized. Good positivistic contributions have offered problems and suggestions to these developing models and metaphors.

Finally, to reinforce the second point, the practice of positivist scientists could be revealed as inadequately accounted for by positivism. In the case under consideration, for example, the weighing procedures of positivist chemists could have been examined, and shown to be 'theory-laden', or their more general scientific activity considered and shown to embody much in the way of hypothesis and speculation. Even more revealing is the long term response of positivists to atomism. As this theory developed, it tended to convince its opponents, until, just before the First World War, belief

E

in the reality of atoms was well nigh complete, many sceptics having changed their minds on the issue. Yet, during this time, the theory had (in positivist terms) become more and more speculative; ideas concerning the shape and internal structure of molecules had proliferated, as had speculations upon the strength and flexibility of the bonds between atoms. These themselves remained beyond observation. Although there were many variants of positivism, and the arguments involved were diverse and complex, it is difficult to avoid the conclusion that when positivists were convinced by the atomic theory they were, at least in some cases, responding to modes of demonstration which they had previously held to be illegitimate. We must ask whether their earlier professed criteria of evaluation were authentic, or whether they had, consciously or inadvertently, given an inaccurate account of what they really found to be persuasive.[13]

The acceptance of atomism and some of its associated interpretative and calculative procedures was an unusually long drawn out process.[14] None the less its incorporation into chemical practice was in many ways typical. As it was used, and seen to be used successfully, concern with its validity diminished among its adherents. It came more and more to be taken for granted and emphasis switched to applying it and pressing on with the process of metaphorical redescription. The theory was incorporated in what Kuhn (1970) calls a puzzle solving tradition; it helped to create expectations about the world, which scientists endeavoured to show to be justified. And it permeated the constellations of routine procedures characteristic of scientific practice; the scientist learned, as a matter of course, to prepare molar solutions, to calculate atomic weights, to operate with gramme-atoms rather than grammes and so on. Successful puzzle solving and metaphorical redescription counted as confirmation of the theory, and eventually, in many cases, merely as confirmation of the competence of the scientist concerned.

In the very process of becoming accepted, of achieving taken for granted status, the meaning of many of the statements central to the atomic model was transformed. The law of constant composition, for example, ceased to be treated as an empirical claim or generalization, and became, for the most part, a way of defining a chemical compound.[15] No explicit reformulation occurred; instead, there was a slow change in the beliefs scientists treated as in need of validation, and those which were treated as criteria for judgment.[16]

Thus, the reception of (Daltonian) atomism resulted in a change in the modes of evaluation and justification used in chemical practice.[17] The atomic model itself was transformed from something to be established and justified, into something taken for granted in processes of argument and justification. At the same time practitioners felt more and more at home with the vocabulary of atomism; its metaphorical status became less and less apparent as it became institutionalized, until today, for a chemist to point to the status of atomism as a model would be nothing but pedantry.

The example may be regarded as typifying the way in which new modes of metaphorical redescription become incorporated into ongoing patterns of scientific activity. Science may be regarded as a loosely associated set of communities, each using characteristic procedures and techniques to further the metaphorical redescription of a puzzling area of experience in terms of a characteristic, accepted set of cultural resources.

III

It has been established that the main path of cultural change is laid down by scientists concerned to utilize, extend and develop a metaphor as much as possible. The key forms of thought and argument involved are metaphorical or analogical. From a sociological point of view, this is an extremely interesting finding, for it links the pattern of cultural change in science to studies of the nature of this phenomenon in other contexts. Schon (1963) has shown the important and pervasive role of metaphorical redescription in modern Western culture generally. And many studies exist showing its central place in undifferentiated, preliterate cultures; the works of Cassirer (1946, 1953), and of Lévi-Strauss, are among the most important here. A recent remarkable review and bibliography by Shibles (1971) emphasizes the crucial role of metaphor in thought as a whole, by documenting its study and treatment within the Western intellectual tradition generally.

To show the metaphorical nature of thought is to show the culture bound nature of thought. This always creates problems concerning validity, which perhaps is why social scientists have been reluctant to extend general accounts of culture and cultural change into the sphere of natural science. Only Schon has seriously attempted to do this.[18] Others, even when their work has been comparative, and, as it were, asking to be made into a general theory of thought, have always felt obliged to insert a rider claiming special status for science. The puzzle thereby created—why is science different?—is often ignored, and never answered plausibly.

The work of Lévi-Strauss is particularly interesting in this context. From the beginning of his study of *La Pensée sauvage* (1966), he reveals profound sensitivity to the parallels between primitive and modern thought. He states his intention to stress the intellectual stature of the former, and the thirst for objective knowledge among primitive peoples. And he suggests that he will not easily be complacent with respect to his own culture, when he writes: 'Every civilization tends to overestimate the objective nature of its own thought and this tendency is never absent' (1966, p. 3).

But, despite this propitious beginning, Lévi-Strauss does not quite convert his magnificent studies of primitive myth and classification into a fully general theory of the intellect.

The myth maker is compared to the 'bricoleur', a very superior kind of odd job man. As the 'bricoleur' constructs devices for a wondrous range of purposes from a limited set of bits and pieces (whatever happens to be at hand), so the primitive intellect constructs myth out of bits and pieces of culture. This delightful image of the myth maker as a kind of plumber, who works with culture rather than piping, is entirely appropriate to the scientist. He, too, redeploys pieces of culture in new ways to perform new tasks. The only difference between the two contexts suggested by Lévi-Strauss's account is a small one. He thinks that the myth maker tends to use only those bits of culture which are, as it were, left about largely unused in the existing ways of life. Scientists on the other hand seem rarely to have had scruples against robbing existing language games.

None the less, Lévi-Strauss tries to use his account of the myth maker as bricoleur as a source of contrasts between myth and science. He thinks that it shows myth to be culture bound in a way that science is not. Myth remains 'entangled in imagery'; it is formulated in 'signs' which 'unlike concepts . . . do not yet possess simultaneous and theoretically unlimited relations with other entities of the same kind'; unlike science it knows no logical distinction between 'extension' and 'intension' (1966, p. 20).

It is a pity that Lévi-Strauss could not have introspected more about his own struggle to convey this distinction between science and myth, his inability to capture it in concepts 'transparent to reality', and the consequent growth within his text of the mass of vivid metaphor needed to convey it. To an extent, he is conscious of the culture bound nature of scientific discourse, and notes that the scientist himself 'never carries on a dialogue with nature pure and simple'. But determination to establish a difference takes the upper hand. If there is not a clear difference between science and myth as culture, there is as intended activity—scientists and engineers aim to 'go beyond the constraints imposed by a particular state of civilization', bricoleurs always remain within them. The difference between concepts and signs becomes that of intention of use : 'concepts aim to be wholly transparent with respect to reality, signs allow and even require the interposing and incorporation of a certain amount of human culture into reality' (cf. 1966, pp. 19–20).

Thus, in the last analysis, a tendency to overestimate the 'objective' nature of modern thought restricts the scope of the synthesis achieved in this important comparative work. Here is but one instance of how real insight into the culture of the natural sciences could help anthropologists to solve the problems in the comparative study of belief systems first enunciated by Durkheim and Lévy-Bruhl.[19]

IV

It could be argued that the distinctiveness of scientific culture has been systematically obscured in the preceding discussion by neglecting the procedures by which scientific theories or models are justified. A number of negative points have been made about the 'context of justification' in science, but there has been little positive discussion of it. This omission will now be remedied, but no change in the analysis of scientific activity offered earlier will thereby be entailed.

We may talk of a context of justification or evaluation in science just as we would talk of it in relation to any other sub-culture. In neither case can it be assumed that a fully differentiated set of evaluative activities exist, distinct from the production of innovations and new beliefs. What can be indicated by the term is that cultural products are always selectively absorbed into the institutionalized patterns of belief and action surrounding them. Science is more than any set of claims about nature: poetry is more than free association: myth is more than any old rag bag of culture: a recipe is more than any mixture of comestibles thrown into an oven. Utterances are evaluated as scientific, poetic, etc. by appropriate actors or collectivities. In general, evaluation occurs by actors asking what the cultural products *do*, or they are simply found appropriate to particular needs and purposes and accepted without reflection. So it is within science; evaluation depends on actors' purposes and requirements, and the way these cohere into normative patterns characteristic of different groups.

If it chanced that definitions of good work were always identical in science, then it would be worthwhile to attempt to identify a contingent set of standards definitive, in practice, of scientific judgments. Unfortunately, such homogeneity is not to be found. Taking science as we find it, we have to acknowledge that its constituent collectivities, although they may be more uniform in their judgments than is our culture as a whole, do not deploy identical general norms of evaluation.

We have already noted the way in which a particular model, and its associated exemplars, may become evaluative standards in themselves, as a discipline passes into a period of 'normal science' (Kuhn's useful term is now so well known that it can reasonably be employed without explication). But there is no uniformity either in the standards used in the original assessment of basic models and exemplars. A community involved in a crusade against the baneful influence of metaphysics upon science will adopt different standards of judgment from one hoping to obtain useful insights applicable to preventing the spread of disease. The highly aesthetic standards employed to judge fundamental innovations in some branches of theoretical physics are different again. Such variability is only to be understood by consideration of the various aims and resources of scientific sub-cultures, and the different contexts in which they work.

The greatest degree of agreement on standards of judgment in science tends to be found among the members of a single specialty. Here, models, exemplary procedures, patterns of reasoning, and background assumptions of what is plausible, what unlikely, all tend to be taken for granted. Most of the time, these act as *criteria* of good work and scientific competence. They are not reassessed against every new piece of work produced, rather the work is assessed against *them*. Work compatible with them tends to be absorbed routinely into the culture of the specialty; work fundamentally at variance with them tends to be ignored.

Of course, much ongoing research falls into neither of these two categories. Accepted procedures may yield results incompatible with existing models; models may suggest an experimental finding which stubbornly refuses to come about. Thus, ongoing research generates anomalies, and they may form the basis of much future work. As Kuhn (1970) describes, they provide raw material for the key activity in science—puzzle solving. This, when centred on anomaly, may predominantly involve deploying the resources and possibilities of a model in order to account for puzzling results, or inventing and redesigning equipment so that exemplary procedures lead to the expected results at last.

Ongoing work in a specialty (we may call it a research tradition) will always be involved with anomalies. As a culture, the specialty will always have successes to boast of and difficulties to face. Typically, the scientific specialist within the culture will simply accept its basis; generally his socialization will have been designed to produce this acceptance. In abstract discussion, the scientist may recognize uncertainty in his basic position, but he will *act* upon it in a taken for granted way. Nor is this easily criticized. It is future research, the results of which are necessarily unknown, which hardens or threatens the credibility of scientific models and inter-pretations. Taking these models for granted in the context of 'normal science' promotes future research, and is not otherwise disadvan-tageous in comparison with other strategies of belief.[20]

Real, self-conscious, evaluations face the scientist only in choice situations. An accumulation of recalcitrant anomalies may have resulted in the proffering of an alternative model or paradigm to the accepted one, or a fundamental tenet of existing thought and practice may have come under criticism for the same reason.[21]

More mundanely, different developments or interpretations of a model may be in conflict, or different technical approaches to a thematic problem of experimentation or observation. Occasionally, the question may be whether or not to adopt an approach as paradigmatic for future work, when the alternative is fairly random experimentation or parasitic criticism.

Faced with such choices, a scientist's response is not to be understood in terms of any general context-independent criteria. Of its nature it cannot be. Let us consider the sort of grounds for choice the scientist might have, assuming him to be operating in terms of what we might loosely call considerations internal to science. Perhaps the most important factors in evaluating a model or model extension are its perceived achievements and future promise on the one hand, and its difficulties and anomalous implications on the other. There is no way of converting these two opposing sets of information into common currency in order to evaluate a model. Even in deciding between models, the answer is only unproblematic if one model is judged to be superior to another on all counts. Otherwise, the problem of weighing pros and cons occurs.

For the logician, it is difficulties which would be likely to carry the greatest weight in evaluating models and theories. To be contradicted by experiment, or inconsistent between parts, would weigh heavily against a theory. But the scientist occupies a social role where he is expected to *do* science. For him, it is promise and achievement which count for most.[22] The two are to an extent bound together, since exemplary scientific achievements provide, in themselves, models for future scientific work. In ongoing science, a single smooth curve going through the 'data' is worth any number of 'failures' and 'disconfirmations'; difficulties may be expected to sort themselves out later.

This is why scientists are so extraordinarily reluctant to abandon a long established paradigm. They would cease to have anything to *do*. If they do accept criticism or adopt alternative views, this will never involve shutting off the established possibilities of *activity*. Criticism which does this, that is, negative criticism, may be opposed however strongly based it appears to be. Thus, more than once in the history of science, physicists and mathematicians have responded to logical criticisms of their procedures, or perceived logical difficulties within them, with the claim that it was *logic* which needed to be changed! In understanding the choices of scientists, it is apposite to examine their social role rather than the 'logic' of their situation.

Appreciation of the scientist's concern with practice does permit a general understanding of his evaluation procedures, but it is an understanding of their diversity. Since the scientist always has an eye to what he, himself, can do with a new model or procedure, one would expect evaluations to vary, just as the concrete practices of scientists themselves vary. Of course, because of the considerable degree of homogeneity in the activities of individuals within scientific specialties, one would expect a corresponding homogeneity in scientific evaluation within a specialty, even of work originating outside it. But science as a whole is a highly differentiated institution with large numbers of separate specialties within it, sometimes in overt disagreement and conflict with each other. The different patterns of practice in these different specialties might be expected to engender systematic differences in the judgment and evaluation of new work.

These differences are indeed readily found, and it is instructive to examine the way in which their resolution is attempted (on those occasions where there is, in fact, concern to do so). Sheer communication can be an enormous problem in such attempts with groups who see the world in terms of different paradigms 'talking through each other'; discourse has to revert from the esoteric language of specialties back into the everyday language of a shared culture. Even then, basic differences of aim and philosophy, and different tacit assumptions, together with the easy defensibility of incompatible positions, may make resolution or accommodation of views impossible. R. G. A. Dolby (forthcoming) has recently studied the controversy surrounding the ionic theory of Arrhenius and Van't Hoff with a view to bringing out these difficulties. His work clearly reveals the futility of looking for a general 'logic of evaluation', although it also reveals the contingent and contextually intelligible ways in which conflicting parties in a controversy may seek, and to an extent find, a solution for their differences. Related studies of controversy in science may be found in Kuhn (1970).

Because science is a collection of sub-cultures, which modify the perceptions and judgments of the individuals belonging to them, the remarks made here would remain valid even if evaluation in science were entirely the product of independent individual judgments. In practice, appropriate responses to new work are frequently incorporated into the normative structures of specialties, so that individuals may treat it in terms of stereotyped responses appropriate to their affiliations. This institutionalization of orientations may intensify the differences between scientific sub-cultures and prolong their conflicts; eventually, evaluations may become so strongly entrenched in a specialty and its socialization processes that they become dissociated from their original practical rationales and take on the nature of stock responses.[23]

V

Thus, we are led to consider the transmission of scientific culture. If the preceding arguments are correct, problems of transmission here are in no way different or less serious than elsewhere. Science enjoys no advantage because its beliefs are in unique correspondence with reality or uniquely rational, hence its processes of cultural transmission will be in no important respect different to those employed by other knowledge sources. Like the prophet, the astrologer and the witch-doctor, the teacher of science will have to deal with the problem of his own credibility; he is faced with the task of transmitting *lore*.

Most of the time, this is no problem at all. The sciences are accredited knowledge sources in modern society; one who transmits their culture may expect to be believed. Like astrologers and witch-doctors he may expect the respect accorded to the expert. In the past this was not so much the case; the scientist was more in the position of the prophet. And he behaved more like one, exercising a charismatic effect upon his disciples, becoming associated with the ascetic rather than the worldly virtues, and providing illustrations of his integrity and eccentricity for later amplification in hagiography and myth. Yet his problem was rarely quite so intense as the prophet's; because of the esotericity of his knowledge he rarely became involved himself, in restructuring the key collective representations of his society; his lore could be plastered over the existing common sense of his time, and left to make its effect (if any) autonomously.[24]

None the less, within science itself, devices to maximize credibility, and lubricate the mechanisms of culture transmission, have become institutionalized, and remain of interest; many of them have been discussed by Kuhn (1970). A particularly clear-cut instance, although it is no longer in widespread use, is the historical cameo found introducing the **real substance of** a chapter in a science textbook. This presents, in a page or two, an account of how alternative theories to those about to be presented were refuted in the past, and occasionally mentions a 'crucial experiment' which established the present position as valid. Humphrey Davy's experimental refutation of the caloric theory of heat, and Wöhler's experimental refutation of vitalistic stances in organic chemistry are among the many gems to be found in such contexts.

More generally and significantly, one can point to the selection of successful areas, and the suppression of difficulties and criticisms, in the transmission of models and theories. Particularly on first exposure to a theory, the student finds it presented authoritatively and in the best possible light. Experimental procedures may be utilized in achieving the presentation. Demonstration experiments, evolved over many years and representing the best that can be done in an area, may be produced as *typifications* of the relationship between theory and evidence. The selective presentation of experiments may be coupled with the claim that single experiments confirm or refute theories, so that 'proof' of the theories being imparted by the teacher may be seen to follow.[25]

In analysing these mechanisms, it is important to note that they cannot always be seen purely as responses to the need for credibility. Often they also reflect other problems involved in the transmission of culture: simple logistical demands, for example, or the technical pedagogical necessities associated with imparting model patterns of action, and a variety of competences. Thus, deliberate simplification in the early stages of science teaching, which can involve the teacher knowing that everything he is saying is, by his own standards, false, may be regarded as a response to practical pedagogical problems, which only indirectly enhances credibility.

It is interesting to note how the simplistic versions of theories first offered to students are later developed and elaborated. Only to an extent does this occur by initial definitions of concepts being withdrawn, and replaced by more exact formulations. More important is a dialectical process of refinement stemming from the interaction of definition and experience. In order to demonstrate that this description illuminates rather than obscures the process it refers to, a concrete example is required.

Consider a chemist who is first taught a definition of a compound, which stipulates that it is a substance formed, with a change in energy, from a constant fixed ratio of elements by weight. It is unlikely that he will ever be taught another definition of the term, yet for the rest of his career he will continue to encounter compounds which violate this first formulation. Loosely, we may say that at each such encounter the chemist's 'idea' or 'conception' of a compound changes. The first new conception is a 'synthesis' of the definition and the first anomalous compound encountered. The second conception is a 'synthesis' of the first synthesis and the second anomaly, and so on. The term 'conception' has been left deliberately vague. The important point is that, in general, it is not verbalizable. The experienced chemist's conception of a compound is a form of knowledge not expressible in verbal statements. It may have been constructed from a formal definition plus experience of (say) absorption compounds, intercalation compounds, hydrates, polymers, variable composition minerals, free radicals, tautomers, crystal lattice vacancies and alloys. The experienced chemist would be confident (and reasonably confident) that he knew what a compound was, yet he would be unable to construct a verbal definition which entirely satisfied him. All important scientific concepts are of this kind.[26] One of the qualities of an experienced and sophisticated scientist is his incapacity to 'define his terms'. Fetishism over definitions can be a tremendous handicap to doing good scientific work.

This analysis of the importance of definition in science may strike many as heretical. Yet it in no way devalues the importance of definition itself. The dialectical learning process must take off from some starting point; strict definitions ensure that future experience is apprehended and organized in a coherent way. No better basis could be desired for justifying their role in scientific activity.

Early socialization establishes the legitimacy of the scientific enterprise. The problem of credibility can largely be forgotten as training proceeds. In so far as it remains significant, it merges with the problem of imparting habitual modes of perception, judgment and procedure to groups of neophyte scientists. Academic training in science is always constructed with the production of future generations of researchers in mind. Transmission of the current paradigm is the key problem.[27]

To produce this uniformity in cognitive and procedural style, scientific training in the university generally remains dogmatic and authoritarian. Criticism and discussion of present views is discouraged and the materials necessary for such activities are not made available. Exemplary procedures are stressed and have to be mastered by repeated attempts to solve problems based on them. Such problems are a prominent feature of textbooks, and practice with them may be formally organized into 'examples classes' on university courses.

Mastering examples of this kind adds to the student's knowledge of science in a way about which it is hard to verbalize, but which is none the less crucial for understanding scientific activity and change. One may know what free energy is, for example, as taught in a lecture on thermodynamics. One may be able to define it 'correctly', to relate it imaginatively to a model or models or to talk about how it changes in various circumstances. But to be able actually to *do* anything with it is another matter. This is only possible, in general, when the term has been used in working through problems designed after certain exemplary models of solution. With these exemplary models the student must be familiar. Doing such problems changes the nature of the student's knowledge, making it *applicable*—whether in mundane routine fashion, or creatively and imaginatively. Such comments would apply in practically every branch of science, to mathematical theorems, mechanics, problems in chemical kinetics, thermochemistry, spectroscopy and similarly in the biological and earth sciences. Kuhn (1970) compares such practice with exemplary procedures to the finger exercises of the pianist; Polanyi (1958) has discussed it as an aspect of *tacit* knowledge. Both writers are concerned to stress how scientific knowledge is more than a compendium of statements or prescriptions, how the capacity to do science cannot be transmitted by purely linguistic means. The same is true of any set of activities within a sub-culture.

In summary then, the way in which socialization occurs in science fits well with the analysis of the nature of scientific culture offered earlier. Science is not a special kind of knowledge source; it has to face the problem of credibility, and the technical constraints facing the transmission of culture in any context. The context of scientific training comprises an interlinked system of models, exemplary procedures and techniques meaningful only in combination. There is no attempt to transmit rationality rules, indeed the scientist must assume that his students are in some sense rational already if he is successfully to teach them. Neither is there any attempt to teach a general 'scientific method'; the nearest approach to this is the prominence in some disciplines of general precepts concerning the importance of controlling experiments, and the stress in quantitative work of general techniques for dealing with errors. Even the latter tend, in general, to be taught in a routinized, cookery-book kind of way—as techniques, not general modes of thought.[28] Finally, there is no attempt at any level of training to discuss formally what makes a good theory, or what general criteria can be employed in the assessment of new work. It is left to scientists to make their judgments with a consciousness shaped by the models and exemplars of their research tradition.[29]

chapter 4

Belief, action and determinism: the causal explanation of scientific change

I

The previous chapter has indicated how the culture of natural science may be made intelligible without recourse to externally based, 'objective', assessments of the 'truth' of its beliefs or the rationality of its activities. Thus, it has supported with particular illustrations and arguments the general theses presented earlier. It has emphasized the need to treat all belief systems as equivalent for sociological purposes, and it has shown how action must always be related, in the first instance, to the meanings and typifications of actors themselves. All actors must initially be regarded as operating authentically in accordance with their own conceptions of reality.

It follows that sociological causation should not be invoked to explain beliefs simply because they are apparently erroneous or irrational. In practice, this means that causal (and functional) accounts of beliefs have frequently been unsoundly based through sociology as a whole. As critics have frequently pointed out, causal sociological analyses have, in effect, been parochial and evaluative. They have justified the beliefs of the sociologist and those he most esteems in his own society, and explained away the conceptions of others as distortions. Social scientists have lacked any real curiosity about the status of their own beliefs.

All this could reasonably be taken as the expression of an idealist position in the context of sociology. Many of the critical points made earlier are the products of idealist thought. None of the conclusions suggested so far is clearly incompatible with idealism. In the writings of Peter Winch (1958, 1964), for example, we find a stress on the actor's perspective, and on the equivalence of different belief systems and ways of life, very close to that of the preceding chapters. And nothing has yet been said to oppose Winch's well known diagnosis of the status of social science.

So it is important, at this point, to indicate why idealism must be rejected, as well as the characteristically empiricist approaches discussed earlier. Idealism is to be rejected because of its hostility to causality and determinism. The opposition, so strongly stressed by philosophers, between causes and reasons as explanations of action, is of central importance in idealist thought. Causal explanation is appropriate in natural science, but not in the human or social sciences, where action must instead be made intelligible in terms of actors' reasons for performing it. The social scientist must seek to understand the way of life of a society, and hence what counts as a reason for action in that society; by doing this he will find that he is able to understand particular actions in terms of reasons, and the contexts in which the actions occur.[1]

Now, although the particular modes of causally explaining beliefs commonly employed in sociology have been criticized and rejected, it has not been with the intention of repudiating causal explanation as such. On the contrary, the alternative suggested here would make the sociological study of beliefs more consistently deterministic than before. On the one hand, beliefs representing departures from normality are held to be in need of causal explanation. On the other hand, beliefs which are bound up in normal practice, although in a sense unproblematic, must be accounted for by some theory of socialization which will give a deterministic account of their acquisition. And the stability of these same beliefs will depend on the stability of the constellation of normal causal influences which serves to sustain them as unproblematic, institutionalized features of the overall social landscape. Thus, sociological work has been misconceived, not because it has employed causal explanations, but because it has wrongly identified the baseline from which such explanations must operate, and has not recognized the need to subject *all* beliefs and practices to them.[2]

The idealist approach is justified in its stress on the importance of actors' meanings and typifications, but its hostility to determinism does not follow from this. Despite a large body of opinion to the contrary, there is no necessary incompatibility between causes and reasons as explanations of action, indeed reasons can be listed among the causes of action. Given the general importance of this issue in the context of sociological theory, it will be worthwhile to consider it in some detail. This is greatly facilitated by the work of MacIntyre whose (1966) paper on 'The antecedents of action', offers the best point within an extensive literature from which to attack the problems involved. The discussion will show why, although the account of natural science in this volume is almost entirely centred upon actors' beliefs, purposes and reasons for acting, it is none the less offered as a deterministic account.[3]

II

MacIntyre's argument (which will be followed freely and selectively here) starts by analysing the way in which the concept of causality is used. It notes the Humean sense of cause as constant conjunction, which has received so much attention from philosophers and logicians. But it goes on to suggest that this is far from being the only kind of usage, and points to another, which is surely far more widespread and frequently employed. This is the designation of one of a set of necessary conditions as a cause, particularly when that condition is of special interest to us. The implication is that, had the necessary condition been absent (or different), the caused event would not have occurred (or would have occurred differently), given that there was no change in the other necessary conditions. This is an entirely different conception of causality from the Humean kind. As MacIntyre points out, citation of an ice-patch as 'the cause' of a road accident implies neither that 'whenever ice-patches occur there is an accident', nor that 'there is never an accident unless there is an ice-patch'.

Suppose we cite metal fatigue as the cause of an air crash. The implication is that in other relevant respects the aeroplane was normal, how we would expect it to be. Had the metal been like-wise in its normal condition, no crash would have occurred. The deviation from normality explains another deviation from normality. The background of normality forms the set of unchanged necessary conditions against which the causal story stands out and operates as an intelligible communication. The cause is a necessary condition in which we are interested; in labelling it, we define a taken for granted background of normality in terms of which our utterance makes sense. In another context, we might have said that *taking off* in an aeroplane with metal fatigue caused the crash. The implication would have been that such aircraft were not normally flown. Human interest tends to centre on necessary conditions which are departures from normality, and produce consequences which are in turn abnormal. It is these conditions which are generally identified as causes.[4]

Both the causal sociological explanation I have criticized, and that I have advocated, are of the above kind. In the first case, an abnormal biasing factor is held to produce a departure from normal, naturally reasonable belief. In the second case, special causes are sought to explain departures from institutionalized belief. In both cases, a background of stable permissive necessary conditions must be assumed.

Occasionally, interest may centre upon a necessary condition because it represents our capacity to intervene in nature. It is a condition we can control and vary. We say that we caused an explosion by pushing a button. This necessary condition of the explosion is singled out as the cause because of its relationship to our control of the explosion. Again, had not other necessary conditions remained constant the explosion would not have occurred.

The conception of cause as relevant necessary condition is important in the formulations of natural science. A spark may cause an explosion, a photon may produce a molecular dissociation. Frequently, such relationships are economically reduced to statements of the co-variation of quantities, or scientific laws. To increase the pressure of a gas causes, other conditions remaining constant, a proportionate reduction in its volume. This may be expressed as a general law; it may be said that volume is a function of pressure. This does not alter the deterministic nature of this part of science, nor must the functional language be thought of as replacing the language of causality. It remains appropriate to claim that pressure increases cause the volume of a gas to diminish, that by squeezing a balloon one may effect a diminution in its volume. Natural science as a whole may be regarded as thoroughly permeated by determinism in the important sense emphasized by MacIntyre. On the other hand, scientific formulations rarely if ever aspire to be Humean generalizations; this involves a search for sufficient conditions to determine an event whereas scientific accounts practically always apply, given a taken for granted background of unspecified necessary conditions.

MacIntyre claims that, with the sense here described, the language of causality may appropriately be employed in the context of human action.[5] We may assert, for example, that an action was caused by its initiator being given a reason for performing it (cf. MacIntyre, pp. 220–3). Told that he is cuckolded, the husband challenges the lover to a duel. Given the totality of initial conditions we may say that being given a reason caused the husband to act. Told of Einstein's interpretation of Brownian movement, a sceptical chemist espouses the atomic-molecular theory and proclaims its worth. Again we may say a reason causes an action. We may also say that the reason caused the chemist's beliefs to change.

The argument is unexceptionable. Wherever we find actions or beliefs which seem to be the consequence of some externally produced reason, piece of information or activity, it is possible to hypothesize a causal connection without in any way straining the normal usage of the language of causality. There is thus no logical or *a priori* incompatibility between reasons and causes as explanations of why actions occur or beliefs are adopted; sometimes reasons may be causes.

So far, we may come in the wake of MacIntyre's analysis. Given the stringent separation between reasons and causes generally insisted upon, it is a considerable way. Moreover, MacIntyre clears away a number of minor difficulties standing in the path to determinism. In particular, he disposes of the pedantic argument which insists that since many postulated causes of action stand in 'logical' relation to the effects they are intended to explain they cannot properly be causes. Here MacIntyre simply points out that a logical relationship in itself constitutes no argument against a causal connection. He points to the relationship between being insulted and taking offence. These two terms are internally or conceptually related, yet it is perfectly permissible to claim a causal connection between the two. Natural science abounds with such examples: adding water to a chemical system may cause hydrolysis, illuminating it may cause photolysis.

Yet, for all this, MacIntyre does not see human action in terms of complete determinism (indeed he treats 'fear of determinism' almost as though it constitutes an *argument* against conflating reasons and causes). It is possible to imagine, he would agree, an actor who was completely determined; such an actor would operate entirely in response to external prompting or stimulation. But human activity is not, by any means, entirely of this kind, and to the extent that it is not, it is not determined action.

Causes and consequences, it is asserted, must be separately identifiable events, one of which is clearly antecedent to the other. Externally derived factors, even if they are meaningful utterances, may count as independently identifiable events. *Being given* a reason may operate as a cause. But 'internal states' cannot count as causes, because they cannot be ascertained independently to be necessary antecedents of action. Thus, *having* a reason, an intention or a desire cannot be a cause for the action to which it may be linked.

This allows MacIntyre to conceive of internally generated, non-determined, intervention, into sequences of determined responses to external causes of action (p. 223):

> The more I know about possible and actual causal explanations of my behaviour the more likely I am to be able to intervene successfully and control what I do. Free, responsible, controlled behaviour is then behaviour where I have at least the possibility of successful intervention.

An unsatisfying, mongrel conception of the human condition is the result. Partly, it has resulted from examination of how we commonly use causal constructions. Partly, it has been produced by philosophical fiat. For the necessity that cause and event be independently identifiable is no part of common usage. It is an arbitrary and misguided requirement, strongly positivistic in its implications. It is the sole ground upon which MacIntyre can justify restricting determinism. And it is an insufficient ground.

Examples from natural science will suffice to establish this. Suppose we say that the spectrum of a compound is caused by electrons moving between energy levels, or by molecules changing from ground to excited states. Here the cause has to be inferred from the effect. None the less it is a perfectly good cause from a scientist's viewpoint, and involves, as usual, a set of necessary conditions (that for example electric field=magnetic field=zero). Again, consider the explanation of the break up of uranium atoms by the impact of neutrons. The impact of a neutron cannot be independently identified, but again a perfectly good causal statement is possible. One could extend the scientific examples indefinitely, for in science it is a crucial function of theoretical entities that they are invoked as causes, to explain events or phenomena. Yet if such entities—atoms and sub-atomic particles, genes, photons, forces— could be independently identified, they would lose their status as theoretical entities.[6]

Why then should we not say similarly that statements relating intention or desire or purpose to action may be understood causally? 'He fired the shot because he intended to kill the enemy.' 'He signed the contract because he wanted the fee.' 'He worked twelve hours a day in order to pass the examination.' And why not admit the causal possibilities of all our categories of 'internal' experience? 'Going over his chess game in his mind he no longer believed in the soundness of his combination.' 'He betrayed her out of jealousy.' 'He betrayed her on principle.' 'He betrayed her because he reasoned that her captors would reward him.' Can we not say that these statements offer causal accounts which presume a background of necessary conditions?

Clearly, with such a potential population of 'internal' causes, it is easy to move to a position of complete determinism. This is an excellent position for a sociologist to adopt since it encourages in the highest degree the search for pattern and orderliness in human activity. Admittedly, it can claim no more than the status of an hypothesis, but it is an hypothesis with little to be said against it.

It might be claimed that in the case of physical phenomena things could not have been otherwise, whereas in the case of human action they could have been. But one may say that in both cases things might have been different, if the constellations of necessary conditions had been different. Spectra may have been different in the presence of a magnetic field. Action may have been different if the actor had been in a bad mood, or drunk, or thinking of something else at the time or in the company of his girl-friend. Admittedly the actor is a system where necessary conditions are numerous and highly variable, so that action is less easy to predict than spectral emissions, but this is not a point relevant to the issue of the appropriateness of causal explanation.

Given the blind aversion to deterministic orientations common in many quarters, large numbers of more or less feeble objections to them always populate the intellectual scene. Much is made of the fact that an actor may change his behaviour if he learns that it is being predicted, but here the actor's knowledge may simply be taken as a necessary condition in a deterministic account of what he does. It is sometimes claimed that a successful determinist account of human action would so change the nature of discourse that society as we know it would cease to exist. That this is ever seen as an argument against determinism merely reveals the continuing incidence of the lamentable practice of making a fetish of ordinary language. Finally, it is occasionally suggested that whereas the physicist is justified in his causal language by its relation to a well established theory, social scientists should not employ a similar language because they lack such a theory. But if this injunction were taken seriously no theory would ever become well established! Language and thought would ossify (cf. Gellner (1959)). As in politics, the truth is that yesterday's treason produces today's established order.

One point which this final criticism correctly assumes is that a general deterministic orientation is related to a general theory or model. Such a model extends the possibilities of causal explanation so that it can be employed without the scope of MacIntyre's positivistic fiat. A model of the atom allows physicists to give causal explanations of spectra without observing correlations, or producing evidence of the occurrence of consecutive independent events. Conversely, commitment to a causal or quasi-causal language by physicists is bound up with commitment to physical models.[7]

Analogously, a deterministic orientation in social science may signify commitment to the development of theories concerning the nature of belief and action. This will involve metaphorical redescription in terms of models, including, perhaps, models of the 'internal state' of the actor. Such models are no more reprehensible than models of atomic structure, and if they are less well established this is no reason to object to their use. (Indeed, given that science is constitutively theoretical, and always proceeds by metaphorical redescription in deterministic terms, it could be said that causal explanation was constitutive to 'the idea of a social science'.)

It is interesting to compare this conception of the sociologist with that of Winch (1958). It will be recalled that, for Winch, sociology must not model itself upon science. It must not develop its own criteria of identity with which to conceptualize action and belief. A chemist may legitimately define certain substances as elements, but a sociologist must not seek to label actions and beliefs in the way that the chemist labels substances. Actors have their own labels, their own criteria of identity. It is these which must be used to label actions, not the criteria of identity of the sociologist; it is these indigenous criteria which make action intelligible in a society, and predictable to an extent.

In practice, Winch's critique has been very valuable. It has exposed the danger of making external judgments of rationality, and the baneful consequences of imposing concepts like 'magic' upon the practices of others. And it has stressed the way in which action must be made intelligible in actors' own terms, and encouraged detailed empathetic study of the actors' world. But Winch's critique comes far too close to being an attack on sociological theorizing as such (1958, p. 88):

> It is quite mistaken in principle to compare the activity of a student of a form of social behaviour with that of, say, an engineer studying the workings of a machine . . . His understanding of social phenomena is more like the engineer's understanding of his colleagues' activities than it is like the engineer's understanding of the mechanical system which he studies.

This statement might just conceivably have passed muster if Winch had devoted a single sentence of his work to similarities between the sociologist and the engineer. But he did not; the contrast between the two roles is grotesquely overemphasized. To be sure, the *identification* of social phenomena for study is very different from the identification of mechanical phenomena. Actions are not to be investigated by observing physical movements, but by learning the 'way of life' within which they occur (to employ the observation language of Winch's *theory* !). But from this point the engineer and the sociologist stand in close analogy. The engineer uses or seeks a model or a theory to make the manifest properties of matter intelligible in a deeper sense. Why is bridge A stronger than B in some respects, weaker in others? Probably he invokes 'forces' and the techniques of Newtonian mechanics to his aid. Similarly, the sociologist, confronted with a way of life, may ask why some elements in it change more rapidly than others, why actors are apparently inconsistent, at times, in the reasons they give for their actions, why a reason for an action is a reason, and so on. Like the engineer he needs a model to obtain a deeper understanding of what he studies.

Without a model, the sociologist can do no more than catalogue the procedures of a particular way of life. In fact, his use of models can be vindicated even within the framework of Winch's argument.

It is only necessary to examine the practice of actors within a way of life, to see the way to do this. Such actors, as Winch says, are not passive and mechanically predictable; more to the point they are never totally uncritical dopes of their culture. They are themselves given to theorizing about the 'internal states' of their fellows, and they employ their theories in assessing the professed reasons of others. Some reasons are credited, others are dismissed as rationalizations. Everyone realizes that when individuals have personal, socially impermissible reasons for their actions, they cite instead socially permissible reasons by way of justification. In speculating about the real reasons or causes underlying façades of legitimation, theories of action are developed and used. Winch must either regard these theories as within the way of life, and hence legitimate, even though they impose labels upon the actions of others, or he must subject them to external categorization in order to condemn them.

Let the sociologist claim for his models the same status as actors' own. If he is told that they have this status within his own society only, let him ask why. No critic could answer him who did not himself have a general model or theory of action, even if this was implicit.[8]

III

A deterministic attitude to belief and action can be justified by commitment to a model, or even by the conviction that a viable model of man as actor will eventually be found. One possibility, which possesses a large number of advantageous features, is to study action and belief using the metaphor of man as a programmed device. The analogue of an unsocialized individual is such a device equipped with only a very few elementary programmes; we may say that the human individual is innately equipped with hardware and certain very basic pieces of software only. Socialization involves programming and the 'filing' of information. The culture of a society may be thought of as the full set of possibilities it possesses for the programming of new actors. Every actor becomes programmed with a sub-set of the total resources which make up the culture as a whole. The individual possesses the innate potential (the circuitry, or hardware, and the basic software) to be programmed in an enormous number of ways. The general features of the programme he does acquire depend upon the way of life into which he is socialized.

From this perspective, behaviour which is mediated by a received programme is *action*; understanding it involves familiarity with the programme which produced it. As the idealists claim, action has thus to be understood in a different way from mere behaviour; responses to pinpricks are not mediated by culturally transmitted programmes, responses to letters are.[9] We can draw an analogy with our understanding of the operation of computers. It is possible to investigate the operation of a computer without any interest in its specific programme and file content. Attention may focus on electronic switches, power supplies, magnetic tapes and discs, and so on. A general account of its operation may be constructed in terms of the language of electronics and cybernetics, perhaps with the use of a few anthropomorphic metaphors to describe its organiza-tion. On the other hand, if we became interested in what a com-puter was actually *doing*—say in how it ran a power station—we would clearly need to know how it was programmed and what material was laid down in its file. A highly schematized account of the computer itself would suffice, along with the detailed exposition of the programme involved. This is the kind of account the sociolo-gist must hope to obtain from the study of action.

This particular example is also useful as a means of relating beliefs to the general model. It is often appropriate to consider a working computer anthropomorphically and talk of its knowing or believing something. We could say that a computer running a power station knew the capacity of the fuel stores, the usual varia-tion in demand for power, the most economical working rates, and so on. We might, on occasion, say that the computer believed some-thing which was not so; it might believe its stores were empty when they actually were full, due to faulty monitoring devices, or it might believe high demand was imminent because it had not been told about a public holiday.

Such statements could be replaced by statements about the state of the computer's programme and file. This would be possible because of our 'inside' knowledge of the computer as a physical system. Generally, we would prefer knowledge of the computer's 'inner state' to knowledge expressed in the anthropomorphic idiom. But this would not be to say that the latter type of knowledge was worthless, that it could not be relied upon. On the contrary, it gives us genuine insight into the computer's operation; as much, we might claim, as ascribing a belief to an actor provides insight into his actions. And there are circumstances where the anthropomorphic approach to the computer is definitely to be preferred to alternatives.

We have little or no 'inside' knowledge of the human actor to correspond with that we possess about computers. We cannot replace the knowledge we gain of actors' beliefs by an alternative description. Having inferred beliefs from action and from the actors' discourse we can go no further. Yet we can hold to the view that our knowledge of actors' beliefs stands to a pattern of programming in just the same way as an anthropomorphic description of a computer's beliefs does to the computer programme. Knowledge of an actor's beliefs is knowledge of his programming in a certain sense; it is limited indirect knowledge, but as much as can be obtained from 'the outside'. (Imagine studying a sealed computer running a power station; we could hypothesize what beliefs the computer held from outside observation alone, given of course that we were prepared to make certain assumptions about the situation. We could also claim that the hypothesized beliefs suggested some pattern of programming and some arrangement of the electronic patterns which acted as files of stored information. Given a model of computer organization we could attempt to infer programming and the state of the computer's file from the hypotheses we had initially constructed in anthropomorphic terms.)

Thus we may say that to hold a system of beliefs corresponds to being programmed in a certain way[10]—or is a gloss for this. (Ethnomethodology undervalues glosses, and hence the worth of 'folk disciplines' like science and mathematics.) This enables us to take a deterministic approach to belief and action, and to hold that in some circumstances the former can be regarded as a determinant of the latter. Just as a computer's belief that the fuel supplies of its power station were running low might be held to cause it to order fresh supplies, so might actual belief cause action in the context of social life. Even though the explaining belief is inferred from the action it explains, the deterministic relationship can be justified by commitment to the model; the plausibility of the model is the real issue.

The activities of most working programmed devices can be made intelligible either in terms of a language of reasons or a language of causes. Thus they show us how it is possible to give explanations in terms of reasons and yet retain a determinist point of view. Consider, for example, a computer which is programmed to play chess. It is perfectly appropriate to talk of the computer's moves in the terms commonly employed to refer to chess playing; the language games associated with chess playing are applicable to the situation.[11] Yet it is also possible to give a broadly determinist account of the computer's operation in terms of inputs, processing and outputs. A different explanatory scheme would be employed from those used to account for the computer blowing fuses or valves, or keeping itself cool, but it would be a determinist form of explanation none the less.

We can readily imagine an expert in computers and their programming switching into the language of reasons to talk of the device's operation; he might do this for economy of expression, or to communicate with individuals who did not share his esoteric understanding. He might say that the device gave too much priority to avoiding doubled pawns, or that it made a fetish of exchanging knights for bishops. By operating in more esoteric terms he could adjust the programming to correct these weaknesses in the computer's game; we might say that its reasons for moving became slightly different, although its moves would remain intelligible within the framework of the language games appropriate to chess.[12]

It would be incorrect to imagine that the analogy between man and working computers justifies a preference for a determinist approach to belief and action. The analogy is unfairly loaded in favour of determinism. Our 'inside' knowledge of computers persuades us that deterministic explanations of their operation are justified; we have little or no such inside knowledge of man.[13]

The metaphor of man as programmed system and the associated deterministic stance cannot be conclusively justified any more than it can be convincingly discredited. The above examples merely illustrate the plausibility of the metaphor; they can do no more. The deterministic stance made possible by the metaphor can be seen as a natural extension of scientific theorizing; it is a characteristically scientific move to make. Should it prove successful it will create its own justification *ex post facto*, as other scientific theories do. No other basic arguments can be enlisted in its support. The deterministically oriented discussion of science which follows in these final three chapters can be understood readily enough without the use of this particular model; no exemplary procedures of explanation are bound up with it. But in many ways it is apposite to employ it. It is increasingly being taken up by natural scientists in their attempts to understand man, so it is interesting to press their perspective as hard as possible, and discover what it implies for the knowledge and activity of science itself.

It is important to recognize that a large number of important and well founded criticisms can be brought to bear against the use of the metaphor. Such criticisms, however, can always be taken as showing the need for its amendment; fundamental or 'logical' criticisms, which would indicate the need to abandon it altogether, always lack firm foundations. The inadequacy of those arguments which would characterize the metaphor as a misuse of words or a category mistake has already been amply detailed. Another 'logical' objection is that of circularity. The operation of computers it might be argued, is intelligible in terms of anthropomorphic metaphors; terms like 'memory', 'reading', 'sorting', 'errors' are built into the language games associated with computers, even constituted into the thought of computer designers themselves. If we must understand computer processes anthropomorphically, surely we cannot at the same time understand man's activities in terms of a computer model. The answer is that there is no reason whatsoever why we should not; to imagine that there is springs from an inadequate conception of what is involved in explaining something. An example from natural science provides the quickest way of disposing of the point: here one may seek to understand atomic or molecular events by analogy with the behaviour of macro bodies, yet at the same time it is legitimate to explain the behaviour of macro bodies in terms of accumulated molecular events.

A number of technical criticisms of the metaphor can be answered readily enough by emphasizing that to refer to programming is not necessarily to refer to the particular kinds of device or computer which we presently possess. It can immediately be acknowledged that there is no sign of any device being produced which could serve as a concrete model for understanding human thinking. Concrete analogies may only serve to mislead: it would be inadvisable, for example, to regard transmitted culture as a set of instructions, yet this is how the programmes of computers, with their role of passive service, are frequently talked of. Similarly, few existing computers spontaneously initiate activity, yet it is essential to assign this attribute to the actor.

Other technical criticisms are more serious, since they indicate that the present theory of programmed devices is inadequate, even as a tenuous basis for understanding human capacities. What of the constitutively theoretical character of human thought, for example? How does the analogy with programming deal with the fact that we think in terms of models and metaphors, that linguistic development is a continuing process of metaphorical extension? At present it does not; it is necessary to accept that the power of the metaphor is limited and that for it to grow our knowledge of the familiar system involved must improve.[14] Similarly the human capacity to acquire any of a wide variety of languages, depending on the context of socialization, lies, at present, beyond explanation by analogy with the operation of a programmed device.

Finally, there are technical criticisms which suggest that the basic structure of the model is misconceived, or, at least, far too simple. Psychologists of some schools would claim that the actor should not be thought of as a 'finished' system which is then programmed; a better analogy is with something which is being constructed and programmed concurrently. Some aspects of construction may be responses to earlier programming. This may indeed be the case. Others might claim that the model took no account of important human characteristics which impinged upon belief and action—visual imagination, for example, or drive levels or innate aggression. But then, the metaphor is not intended as a complete representation of the actor—indeed it is clear that it cannot be; so in so far as such characteristics appeared plausible they could be taken into account. No attempt to do this has been made here, since their relevance to the present context of discussion is not great.

These are the difficulties which must be accepted if the model is to be used to incorporate the valuable elements of sociological idealism into a deterministic framework and abolish the dichotomy between reasons and causes in the explanation of action.[15] Given the absence of an alternative model it could be argued that the difficulties are worth facing, but since those sociologists who espouse a strong and explicit determinism, and those who practice the techniques of 'verstehen', 'empathy' and 'taking the actor's point of view', differ upon so very many issues, technical and otherwise, the present suggestions are more likely to be treated as a pollution of the boundary between schools of thought than as a pathway to agreement.

IV

Having exposed and justified a deterministic orientation, it can now be put back where it belongs, at the implicit, taken for granted level, whilst cultural change in science is briefly discussed. It is best to proceed as far as possible with the minimum possible consideration of 'external' influences or determinants; let us focus upon a single specialty, assumed to be fully differentiated and autonomous. Socialization into a specialty involves the acquisition of sub-programmes, which, added to a pre-existing pattern of socialization, produce the capability for a certain kind of understanding and activity.

Scientific training in itself cannot produce scientific capability, nor is it designed to do so; the training modifies and adds to basic elements of socialization found throughout the cultures in which science is based. The prerequisites for scientific training are not, however, numerous, and this point only becomes of importance when the attempt is made to introduce science into cultures profoundly different from those of modern industrialized nations.

The scientist who has been successfully trained within a specialty possesses a specific set of esoteric capabilities resulting from his overall background of socialization and training. In particular he possesses a number of routines, of acting and of thinking, which are capable of being applied in a limitless number of ways, depending upon circumstances and how these circumstances are perceived. We may make the analogy, as Kuhn does, between the scientist applying routine procedures to his problems, and the musician applying learnt routine techniques to the performance of a composition. Just as the musician can master much of a composition with routines—trilling, executing triplets, scale passages and so on —leaving only a few passages which require intense practice, so the scientist can break down much of his puzzle solving work into routine procedures.

Much of the potency of science must be related to the wide range of applicability of its standard procedures, and not to the possible deductions which can be made from its general laws. The role of deduction in science is grossly overemphasized; natural applications of techniques are insistently perceived as logical or deductive moves.

Consider our capacity to add. Most of us are, apparently, capable of performing any of an infinite set of concrete adding operations. We do this unreflectively—it could be said by going through a series of 'mental routines'. Even if this way of putting it is not accepted, it must be agreed that actual processes of addition do not involve deduction; they do not require the capacity to be 'logical'. Adding capacity springs from a training in addition; we were taught adding procedures by the use of simple sums as examples, and as problems to practice on; addition was actually *done* in a mechanical or rote-like way. Eventually powers of addition 'took off' and we knew we could add any set of numbers. The acquisition of this general capacity was the natural consequence of particular capacities, given our natural proclivities (the possibilities implicit in the hardware we possess). Our ability to add is not the ability to make deductions from a number of rules of addition; it is a natural product, an 'and so on' effect, stemming from a training.[16] We might compare it with the capacity to ride any bicycle, acquired by learning to ride one bicycle, or perhaps even with the acquisition of general linguistic skills from particular linguistic experiences.

The trained scientist finds that certain problem solutions come naturally to him; he finds them routine because of his training. A chemist might find standard techniques of synthesis, the practical and calculative techniques of quantitative analysis, standard spectroscopic operations and inferences from their results, all very much a matter of routine, even for a large number of compounds he had never encountered before. His routine problems are like those new pieces of the pianist which can be reduced to known techniques of fingering, pedalling and so on. The resources he brings to bear on these problems are generally the resources of a sub-culture; in solving them, he participates in the normal practice of that sub-culture.

The possibilities of routine work perceived by the scientist do not, however, stem entirely from the sub-culture. The chemist might note that his work routinely applies to substances found in medicine, agriculture or the food industry; the population geneticist might find parish records or birth registers constituting the data for a routine set of calculations. Moreover the typifications of the general culture constrain the progress of routine scientific work; we might say they tend to channel the flow of the 'and so on' effect. In some societies, it may seem entirely natural to extend knowledge of animals to man, just a matter of routine; in others it may involve making a startling metaphor (or a category mistake). Key social boundaries have not contained the force of reductionist science but they have made its progress more than a matter of routine.

The importance of routine activity in science, work which 'comes naturally' to the scientist, is difficult to overestimate. The sociologist must regard a large part of scientific activity as explicable in terms of the development of a sub-culture along 'natural' lines. Given the training provided by the sub-culture, the pattern of total cultural elements within which the sub-culture exists, and the context in which work is going on, such activity largely ceases to be problematic save ethnomethodologically. This is the kind of activity which sometimes prompts historians of science to say that a field is developing under an 'inner logic'. It is worth stressing a naturalistic alternative conception, if only to avoid the misleading implications of this description.[17]

Despite the importance of routine developments in scientific sub-cultures, they do not suffice to account for the overall pattern of change in science even if no account is taken of such contingent determinants as 'external' influences or chance encounters with new classes of phenomena.[18] Cultural change within science can only be understood if two other important processes are considered. One is the way in which patterns of culture may be combined and re-ordered by social processes; routines and procedures may be transferred from one sub-culture to another, or differentiation may occur and establish new clusters of normal practice. Sociological perspectives upon this kind of change have been provided by Hagstrom (1965) and Mulkay (1972).

The other is the transformation of patterns of normal practice, not by rearrangement, but by authentic creative activity. Characteristically such activity does not 'come naturally'; innovators would generally describe it as the product of effort and imagination, and this tends to be stimulated by particular kinds of context or circumstance. However, instead of discussing the social factors which favour or hinder such processes, their general nature will be considered here. The topic is, in fact, of considerable sociological interest since highly creative scientific work can always be related to the culture in which it occurs. We may say that the cultural resources of creative groups or individuals are important determinants of the nature of their innovations.

To see why this is so it is necessary to return to earlier themes. The work of a specialty must be seen as guided by key metaphors and concretely organized about a number of exemplary models of procedure. At any particular time, a scientist will find that his specialty provides him with a number of procedural and interpretative exemplars, all deriving from accepted concrete scientific achievements, and all capable of acting as models for the matter of course production of routine work. These are always bound up with overriding models or metaphors at a particular stage of development or articulation. Part of the cultural resources available from a given or familiar system of culture will have been deployed in the task of explaining phenomena in a puzzling or unfamiliar area, and part will not. Against this background, creative, non-routine scientific activity becomes intelligible as an aspect of the universal human propensity to create and extend metaphors[19]—a propensity so basic that without it not only would the existence of real cultural change be impossible but also the existence of culture itself.[20]

One important way in which creative activity occurs is by a problem or puzzle being seen as an example of an existing exemplar or model problem solution. Kuhn (1970, Postscript) has stressed the key role of this kind of event. He has used the example of the point mass pendulum to illustrate it.

The motion of the point mass pendulum may be regarded as 'understood' at a certain stage in the history of mechanics. A mass or weight concentrated at a single point in space could be conceived of as suspended from a fixed anchorage by a weightless string of fixed, unchangeable length. This was a point mass pendulum; its free motion in ideal conditions could be predicted or calculated by the application of fixed procedures and techniques. These had been validated in terms of the standards then accepted in mechanics, and hence constituted an exemplar routinely applicable to particular problems as a matter of course; a swinging weight on a thread could be treated as such a pendulum; it would be near enough 'the same' as the idealized body in the exemplar to allow routine unreflective application of the exemplary procedure. Huygens solved the problem of the motion of a real pendulum (think of a ruler swinging from one end) by imaginatively conceiving of it as a set of connected

G

point mass pendula. By imaginatively relating the exemplar and the real problem, Huygens solved the latter—and in doing so created a new exemplar. Later, Bernoulli treated the flow of water from an orifice as an analogous physical system to Huygens's pendulum, and was thereby able to calculate the speed of efflux.

In these examples the mode of thought was analogical or metaphorical, and the analogies were *created* by the thinkers involved; they invented new ways of seeing their problems which offered the promise of solutions non-existent before. As a final example, to make the point as simply and graphically as possible, we may consider the problem of understanding the forces within a horizontal beam loaded with a weight. There was no obvious, routine way of applying the techniques of classical mechanics to this problem when it was first attacked with them. For all its simplicity, no way of deducing the properties of the system from the laws of mechanics existed. The problem was first usefully investigated in a transformed state (Figure 4.1). By breaking the beam at an arbitrary point, and joining the parts with a hinge and a spring, a system was constructed much more amenable to treatment by the techniques of mechanics and the calculus. Over time the analogy was, of course, greatly elaborated, and modern solutions to the problem are incomparably more sophisticated than the first attempts (although, to my knowledge, they are still not regarded as 'final'). But the whole tradition of work on this kind of problem involves the kind of transformation symbolized by Figure 4.1, and the willingness of groups of actors to accept constructions like B as plausible representations of problems like A.[21]

The results of pieces of creative science of this kind must, of course, accord with experimental findings to some extent if they are to be accepted. But the constraint of experiment is easy to overestimate, and its role in securing the acceptance of work is never more than partial.[22] Part of the acceptability of work such as this must be related to the existence of a body of practitioners sharing the exemplars involved. The force of analogy featured in the context of evaluation of this work; it was accepted partly *because* it was imaginatively created from accepted model procedures.

Another important way in which normal practice may be imaginatively reconstituted or developed is by extension of the resources used in metaphorical redescription. Again, the point is best made by reference to a concrete example; this can be drawn from the

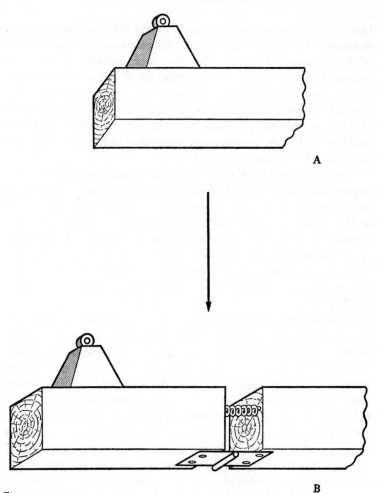

Figure 4.1

context of nineteenth-century chemical atomism which has already been discussed. The chemical atomic theory originally grew in a technical context dominated by the balance and the various techniques of pneumatic chemistry. It was mostly used to render intelligible a range of systematic weight relationships. Atoms were entities modelled on everyday particles, but the 'useful' elements derived from the metaphor were the conception of integrity, similarity/difference and mass. Our culture does, of course, provide us with many more ways of thinking and talking about ordinary material particles or objects than these, but for the most part they remained idle in the context of the atomic theory in the first half of the nineteenth century.[23] Yet they were available for use, and nothing in the overall normative structure of chemical science prohibited their use if the occasion arose. They couldn't be routinely invoked; no existing routines or exemplars could structure the use of what, in this context, were new elements of culture. But they could be, and were, imaginatively transposed and applied to emerging chemical problems.[24]

One of the problems which grew in importance in nineteenth-century chemistry was that of why materials with the same analysis, and hence the same ratio of atoms combined in them, could differ in their properties. Why did different compounds have the same chemical formula? This was the problem of isomerism. It demanded resolution if chemists were to guarantee the reliability of their work as a description of the properties of substances; as it stood, it was an anomaly. Yet nothing in existing practice could offer relevant insights.

In solving the problem, chemists increasingly made use of the idea that identical numbers of atomic particles could be arranged within a molecule in a number of different ways. What is a truism for everyday particles was assumed to appertain also in the invisible world of atoms. Initially, willingness to accept this spatial analogy varied among chemists. Some espoused it wholeheartedly; others reacted with hostility and intense positivistic criticism. Neither side could justify its views in terms of clear institutionalized norms of judgment. On the whole the spatial analogy was most readily accepted by those in research traditions where theoretical preconceptions were most readily compatible with it, and by those who found it applicable to their practical problems and difficulties; common training and related concrete practices and problems made certain groups particularly susceptible to the force of the spatial analogy,[25] and this ensured its initial adoption.

The ensuing growth of stereochemistry was a magnificently successful episode in the history of a scientific model. Large numbers of chemical isomers were distinguished by attribution of formulae symbolizing the different spatial arrangement of atoms. Optical isomerism was explained by postulating molecules which differed from each other only as a left hand differs from a right (Figure 4.2).

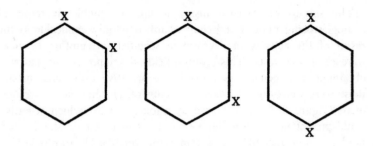

How hexagonal molecules of the same composition may be isomers

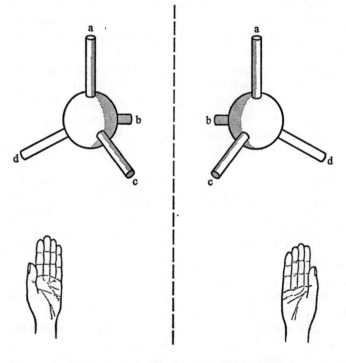

How tetrahedral molecules may be optical isomers

Figure 4.2

The success of stereochemistry is not intelligible in terms of analogies being noticed and counted up. It is only explicable as the result of the activity of a group of scientists attempting to make stereochemistry work. This group quickly developed certain patterns of atomic arrangement as central interpretative exemplars; mostly these were stereotypical kinds of tetrahedral and hexagonal arrangement (Figure 4.2). They served as *resources*, with which scientists could predict how many compounds or isomers should share a particular atomic formula (i.e. a representation like H_2O or $C_6H_4Cl_2$). If a set of isomers confounded predictions it could be said that existing exemplars did not *apply* to them, that they embodied arrangements of atoms of some yet unknown kind. Whether or not this was said, the isomers would be treated as puzzles for future work and not as disconfirmations of existing exemplars. At the same time stereochemists would look to their successful interpretations to justify their work; thus the development of the stereochemical analogies was in every way parallel to the development of the more rudimentary atomism to which it was an extension.

The preceding examples serve to typify the way in which extension of models and metaphors and imaginative transformations of existing puzzles are central to the process of cultural change in science. They show that the understanding of creative science is always bound up with the understanding of metaphor; and understanding metaphor is essential to understanding all kinds of cultural change.

Although the small number of examples cited are adequately illustrative in these crucial respects, they inevitably fail to provide a fully representative picture of creative scientific work. They are all, for example, extremely successful pieces of creative science, which have added to the cultural resources of science in an unproblematic way. But similar modes of thought may be involved in showing that an exemplar cannot apply to a particular problem, or that a model needs secondary elaboration if it is to be successfully applied. Again, all the examples involve exemplary modes of calculation and interpretation, yet there is nothing fundamentally different about the development of technique. Technical innovation can be just as much a creative activity as theoretical innovation; it is a grossly undervalued aspect of science. The design, manufacture and arrangement of lenses, electrical circuits or sources of radiation is more than a matter of trial and error, or routine rule following;

it involves the use of models and analogies, a distinctive way of seeing the apparatus, and familiarity with exemplars of good design. Finally, all the previous examples are responses to existing puzzles or anomalies. Such puzzles are indeed much the most common spurs to imaginative development in science, but their role has no necessity about it. Examples of unprovoked developments within ongoing research traditions can be found. Louis de Broglie's attribution of wave properties to matter was provoked by no existing puzzle in physics or elsewhere; it suggested puzzles and experiments.

These are, however, not important insufficiencies in the present context. It suffices here that science has been revealed as in crucial respects an enterprise of the imagination working with available cultural resources.[26] Developments under the aegis of a general model are to be made intelligible through the key concepts of anomaly and metaphorical redescription, and such developments comprise a large part of the non-routine element of cultural change in science.

The only important kind of change which is not covered in the preceding account is that which involves replacement, or at least major reorganization, of the general model or metaphor at the base of the activities of a specialty. The best known account of this kind of change is Kuhn's discussion of 'revolutionary science' (1970). Kuhn's account is not intended to apply to any kind of model replacement. It applies only to episodes involving major re-orientations of ways of seeing and doing. The point is brought out particularly clearly in Kuhn's treatment by the depiction of revolutionary science as a kind of retooling operation. It is something intimately bound up with the concrete practice of a group of scientists.

An example will serve to clarify this point. Long after the assimilation of Copernicus's cosmological scheme, the finite, bounded physical universe was replaced by an infinite one. The change seems important in the abstract, but it involved little change in concrete scientific practice. It is tempting to talk of it as an adjustment of the Copernican model rather than a replacement. The Copernican Revolution, on the other hand, involved far more than mere fiddling with the positions of the sun and earth; it revolutionized the whole approach of the times to astronomical and mechanical matters, and indeed to the study of nature as a whole. Similarly, the Bohr atom is usually considered as a replacement of

Rutherford's rather than an adjustment to it. Formally the latter description is just as appropriate, but Bohr's work established new exemplary procedures as central to the acquisition of physical knowledge, and its fundamental significance in this sense is commemorated by regarding the Bohr atom as a new model.

Another way of looking at this contrast is by considering the changes which model replacement effects in the cultural resources of the familiar system used in metaphorical redescription. A change involving major modifications in modes of seeing and doing is one which entails major changes in this familiar system. The Bohr atom, for example, made the properties of waves important elements in the familiar culture used for explanatory purposes. The transition from the Copernican to the infinite universe, on the other hand, involved little change in the cultural resources utilized to explain astronomical phenomena.

Setting aside some reservations and qualifications in his 'Postscript', Kuhn accounts for revolutionary science entirely in terms of the internal development of the specialty involved. The key concepts of anomaly and metaphorical redescription are again central to analysing the process of change; the former, in the crises leading to revolution, outrun the explanatory possibilities of the latter.

Ongoing research activity is continually throwing up anomalies, and some resist repeated attempts to dissolve them. Over time, such 'recalcitrant' anomalies may accumulate, and give rise to concern within a research community. This is a contingent matter which Kuhn does not discuss in detail, although certain points appear implicit in his account. Anomalies are particularly worrying when they are systematic and patterned deviations from expectation; this creates the conviction that some underlying systematic mistake is occurring, or that some unknown alternative pattern of order will 'work' better. They claim attention too, by being interconnected with each other, and deviating from expectation in 'the same' sort of way (although the capacity to perceive this sameness may only occur after considerable attention has been already devoted to them). Finally they are most troublesome when the resources of a paradigm are well-developed, and it is less easy than it might have been in the past to have faith that everything will turn out well in the future. (Kuhn (1957) stresses this point in the context of the decline of the Ptolemaic cosmology.)

Growth of recalcitrant anomalies can generate a situation where alternative models and metaphors are sought for, and large scale amendments to the existing scheme of things are proposed and tried out. Such activity indicates a *crisis* state, which may or may not be diagnosed explicitly by practitioners. Eventually the crisis state is resolved by the agreed adoption of a new paradigmatic framework within which the research tradition can proceed. The pattern of proceeding on the basis of accepted routines and exemplars is reconstituted.

Kuhn illustrates his thesis with several examples of major cultural re-orientation in the history of science. He cites the transition from the phlogiston to the oxygen theory; the way that the study of light has oscillated between particle and wave models, the transition from a Ptolemaic to a Copernican and then a relativistic cosmology, and the breakdown of classical mechanics in the realm of micro physics with the advent of the new quantum theory.

Kuhn's account is presented as a generalization from historical evidence; it is not supported with arguments indicating that fundamental re-orientations *must* proceed exactly as he describes. And there is indeed some suggestion that at times they do not. Geoffrey Cantor (forthcoming) points out how the wave theory of light was received and eventually accepted in Britain by a scientific community previously lacking any idea that the existing corpuscular theory was in any kind of difficulty or crisis; no speculative alternatives were being considered; no key anomalies were being intensively studied. Other work suggests that the mingling of separate research traditions may be of greater importance in the production of fundamental change than Kuhn's work would indicate. It is difficult to understand the relative importance of 'contracting-earth' and 'continental-drift' hypotheses in geology, and the sequence of research which eventually led to the 'plate-tectonic' theory of the earth's surface, without taking note of the way in which workers in the area belonged to different sub-communities with different practical concerns (cf. Turvey and Gibbons, n.d.).[27] In general, Kuhn's work reveals little sensitivity to the highly differentiated structure of science and the importance of competition and mobility between different 'schools' or specialties. It leaves us unprepared for the finding that a combination of the skills of several specialties led to the elucidation of the structure of DNA and hence the creation of a new basic model for biological investigators.

Nor does it take account of the way in which the introduction of quantum mechanics into the theory of chemical bonding was assisted by mathematicians and physicists.

On the other hand, Kuhn has successfully typified an important mode of fundamental change in science, and he has shown the way in which major changes in models, or ways of acting and perceiving, necessarily arise out of the basic flow of more or less routine activities which comprise the normal practices of specialties. Kuhn has also stressed the problem of evaluation which arises during periods of revolutionary science, but this, despite its interest to philosophers, is not of great importance here. It will suffice to note that in the competition between paradigms, which is characteristic of a revolutionary period, evaluative criteria cannot, in the last analysis, be provided by either of the paradigms involved. For one paradigm to succeed, scientists must switch allegiance or uncommitted new-comers must be attracted to it in the face of the competition of the other; either way the paradigms must be compared by standards external to both. Scientists debating from standpoints determined entirely by their own opposing paradigmatic frameworks can do little more than 'talk through each other' and convince *themselves*, but not their opponents, of the superiority of their own position. Thus, in so far as the proponents of one paradigm convince their opponents or win the most followers in 'fair' debate, the evaluative standards involved must be based in the common culture of all or most of the scientists involved. Such standards are of course no less contingent and subject to variation than those found only within the esoteric contexts of specialties (a discussion of typical criteria involved in deciding between models or paradigms has already been provided in ch. 3, section IV).

v

To summarize, the preceding section, by concentrating upon a differentiated specialty and assuming its activities to be autonomous, has revealed three kinds of cultural change which it might undergo. Routine change is produced by the matter of course application of the exemplary procedures and modes of interpretation of the specialty. For many purposes, it can be treated as the normal, unproblematic level of scientific activity, the 'what would have happened otherwise' reference for special explanations. None the less, the path it follows is not to be understood without any reference to the wider culture. Other changes are effected by the imaginative reconstruction of problems, or by utilizing new possibilities of metaphorical redescription within the compass of an accepted model. These changes are made more intelligible when the cultural resources and work situations of innovating actors are considered. We might say that, within the same general culture, actors with the same training, engaged in the same kinds of concrete practice, are susceptible to the same kinds of analogies; this explains the coherent and cumulative long term changes which can arise from a summation of large numbers of genuinely creative acts of this kind. Finally, there are fundamental changes in the way of acting and perceiving taken for granted within a specialty, associated with replacement or major alteration in the dominant model or metaphor. Again, these changes have to be understood in context, against the background of a particular set of anomalies raised by an esoteric problem solving tradition, and a set of technical resources and practical skills which members of the tradition expect to continue in use. But the common culture of scientists may also be important here, their general ideas about explanation, their 'common sense', perhaps their aesthetic and philosophical predilections.

By concentrating on a differentiated specialty and assuming its autonomy we have guaranteed that the above account should correspond with a conception of scientific change as internal or intellectual. It does, of course, differ markedly from the account of cultural growth in science which some orthodox 'internalist' historians would give. It stresses the dependence of science upon the resources of the overall culture within which it exists; it does not represent science as a peculiarly rational enterprise; and, most importantly, it is not presented as a refutation or an alternative to a deterministic account of scientific change. Indeed, the first three sections of this chapter have been concerned to show how the present account can be described as completely, perhaps even blatantly, deterministic.

On the other hand, the preceding account has given no role to those causal factors which 'internalist' historians have rejected most insistently as influences upon science—social structural changes, economic demands, political ideologies and so on. And it has clearly implied that thought or 'the intellect' has some possible degree of autonomy from such external determinants. The question is, how much? The previous section merely constructed an ideal type of scientific change within an autonomous specialty; autonomy was assumed for the sake of simplicity. How far this simplifying assumption corresponds with what is found in concrete investigation must be left for detailed consideration in the next chapter.

chapter 5

'Internal' and 'external' factors in the history of science

I

From the perspective of this volume, the extent to which scientific change is determined or influenced by 'external' factors is a contingent matter, requiring separate investigation for every particular instance. Science is a part of culture like any other. To the extent that actors define it as a bounded set of meanings, beliefs and activities with an 'inside' and an 'outside', we may enquire about the strength of the boundary, and the degree to which external determinants operate across it. There is no reason why such determinants should be regarded as absent, or as all important; indeed both extremes are incompatible with what has been said already. Neither is there any reason why the citation of external determinants should necessarily be seen as a threat to the status of scientific knowledge, or as a slight upon the skills and genius of scientists themselves. One does not criticize the painter if he is inspired by literature, or by the plight of the working class, nor is he taken to task if he allows his colours and textures to reflect the possibilities of the current technology. (And along with such influences come changes in artistic judgment.)

Thus, the matter of external determination is not of great significance in itself. What makes its detailed discussion appropriate is the extent to which it has become bound up with important historical and sociological controversies. Robert Merton's much criticized treatment of science in seventeenth-century England (1938) will be the best known of these to sociologists, but there are many others, where opposed conceptions of historical explanation, the nature of science, and the scope of sociological methods and theories have been able to come to grips over concrete issues. Unfortunately, little common ground has so far been established between the 'internal' intellectual modes of interpretation favoured by most historians, and 'external' sociologically oriented ones. There has been no happy blending of the historians' concern for fact, with the sociologists' aims of generalization and explanation. On the contrary, sociologists have displayed little theoretical sophistication in this area, whilst their carefully assembled 'data' have met with the indifference of most historians.

In considering the internal/external debate, it is important to recognize that the present treatment of science, as what actors mean by science, is not the same as that most commonly found in the controversy itself. There, science is generally treated as though its nature has been stipulated in advance of investigation, and cultural elements are divided into 'scientific' and 'unscientific' sets on the basis of the stipulation. This may be an abstractly conceived methodology, a set of more general evaluative standards or an idealization of what genuine knowledge should be like.

Making a demarcation in actors' own terms is useful for explanatory purposes. Such a demarcation is part of the actors' perception of the situation; and action is intelligible only as a response to that perception. It may be of real sociological interest to know how actors conceive the boundary between science and the rest of culture, since they may treat inside and outside very differently. Making a demarcation by external standards, on the other hand, is useless for explanatory purposes, and hence for sociological purposes. Inevitably, it divides patterns of action, intelligible as a whole as the 'normal practice' of scientists, into 'scientific' and 'unscientific' parts; natural connections in the thought of past scientists are severed, in order to facilitate praise or blame, or to construct a justification for the teleological conviction that modern science must be the culmination of all that is best in the thought of the past. Major texts like the *Principia* have to be dissected so that two heaps of fragments can be assembled in conformity with some external standard. This can serve no explanatory purpose; it merely provides material for the hagiographer, and the creator of moral fables and cautionary tales.[1]

For present purposes, then, we should not seek to define science ourselves; we must seek to *discover* it as a segment of culture already defined by actors themselves. (This is not to imply that science can be 'found' as a pure phenomenon; it means merely that someone with a sociological perspective should treat it as an actors' category.) It follows from this, of course, that the history of science very rapidly ceases to be the study of 'science' itself and becomes the study of 'natural philosophy', or 'natural astrology' or whatever other appropriate actors' category appertains at a particular time. There is, however, no great significance to be attached to this. We may regard the history of science as the history of the cultural antecedents of present science. These antecedents may loosely be themselves termed 'science', as a matter of convenience, even when the term itself is an anachronism. All that matters is that the anachronism be recognized. The historian of science tends to be interested in the history of easily demarcated areas of our present knowledge, which are also defined as science by the majority of other actors in society, and by scientists themselves. These areas of knowledge are linked with the activities of highly differentiated communities, which we generally agree are scientific ones. This general agreement can, and in fact does, define what the historian of science writes the history of (since, even if the historian is concerned only with 'genuine' science, he will not give modern physics or chemistry a personal check-over before undertaking to study its past!). In constructing his history he will encounter earlier sub-cultures of crucial importance in understanding how the present culture of science came to exist. They will embody a normal practice which may, perhaps, be set on the line of cultural change which led to some current normal practice in science today. The historian of science will have to study these earlier sub-cultures, and will often unselfconsciously treat them as 'science' too. If they differ markedly from present scientific practice the historian may be disturbed by their existence, wondering, say, how 'magical' or 'mystical' elements could occur in the history of his subject. There is no general ground for such a reaction; the cultural antecedents of science cannot be expected to bear a basic resemblance to our present knowledge however far in the past they are situated.

What follows then, will be little more than a number of straightforward remarks on how the activities of a sub-culture may be influenced by factors external to it, and may exploit resources developed outside its boundaries. Nothing very profound is involved. Yet, when the context of discussion is science and its antecedents, interesting points do emerge, since the existing controversies in this context have been so strongly constrained by entirely different assumptions. The discussion is best begun by considering the simplest problem in the internal/external dispute, which is the role of external factors in stimulating, retarding or influencing the direction of scientific change. Such *directive*, external factors may be contrasted with those which produce changes in modes of perception and interpretation, or in standards of judgment.

II

The importance of directive external factors as influences on present-day science is clear. Social, technical and economic determinants routinely affect the rate and direction of scientific growth. And in the highly differentiated institutional context of modern society they are clearly specifiable as external factors.

No exhaustive survey of external influences on current science need be given here. The task is, in any case, impossibly large. Ezrahi (1971) has made a valuable general survey of the varied causes of the political support and financing of disciplines. Many studies exist showing the importance of existing technology to scientific growth; one need only point to the relationship between computer technology and the growth of X-ray crystallography in this regard. Bernstein (1971) has explored the important influence of social factors on the organization of scientific knowledge and its arrangement in curricula.

Many more examples could be given, illustrating with different degrees of plausibility, different kinds of external direction. It is, however, cases where economic and utilitarian considerations are involved which offer the most clear-cut illustrations of this. Today, most scientists work in specifically applied contexts; the institutional location of science is preponderantly in industrial and government laboratories. Ongoing scientific culture has received many important contributions from directed work in such contexts. Within universities and academic contexts too, an enormous amount of work is explicitly applied or utilitarian: consider the great array of disciplines within medical science, metallurgy and engineering science, agriculture and forestry, computer science and cybernetics, plus explicitly applied research units in geology, ecology, linguistics, psychology, statistics and so on. Even within traditional 'pure' departments in universities, research grants from political, industrial and military sources have an effect on the pattern of cultural change, especially with the present demand for expensive resources, such as particle accelerators, in academic research. And in any case the overall research effort in such departments is related to the demand for their graduates in the economy.

It is true that much scientific change occurs despite, rather than because of, external direction or financial control. Scientists seek external support to do what they want to do anyway, cultivating the famed skills of Dr Grant Swinger to make their work appear relevant to grant-giving bodies. None the less, even in the context of disinterested research, external requirements have had *some* influence on the pattern of cultural change. Work on the exact mapping of the earth's surface over thousands of miles is of technical interest in geomorphology; the kinetics of very high speed gaseous reactions is of importance in physical chemistry. But progress in the disinterested study of both these areas has probably occurred just that bit more rapidly because of their relevance to other matters.[2]

Moreover, utilitarian and economic considerations may perhaps influence academic work in the absence of any direct specific financial connection, or explicitly acknowledged relationship. Slack (1972) has claimed that economic factors have been deeply involved in the growth of academic organic chemistry. He makes the interesting suggestion that concentration on the (atypical) single-product high yield chemical reaction is a response of some kind to the need for profitability of chemically based industries. Unfortunately, the requirements of internal chemical practice would also lead to some stress on this kind of reaction. The example is one where external and internal factors compete in the explanation of what may in fact be an overdetermined pattern of change.

It has to be acknowledged that external support or incentive cannot guarantee the attainment of a particular goal, or, for that matter, anything more than the matter of course development of the field involved. The postwar American support of cancer research illustrates the meagre returns which may accrue from the indiscriminate support of research upon a problem bearing no clear relationship to the existing 'state of the art'. However, when a scientific field exists in a mature state, with taken for granted routines and exemplars, results of some kind can generally be expected in any area to which research is directed. External factors may then become of major importance in determining the pattern of routine cultural growth. And, although creative science may be far less predictable or responsive to external influence, we may still claim

H

that the more are the opportunities for it, the more it will occur. In general, the importance of external directive influences cannot be disputed in the context of our current science; the only worthwhile questions concern the extent of their importance.

Turning to the history of science, there is, as might be imagined, no shortage of evidence suggesting that the rate of scientific change has, in a wide variety of contexts, been partially determined by external factors. Many kinds of technological, economic, and social or institutional influences are cited in Fellows (1961), Pannekoek (1961), Mendelsohn (1964), Thackray (1970), Hahn (1971), Ben-David (1971) and many other sources. However, this work is not, by any means typical history of science. Those in the mainstream of that discipline, on the few occasions that they have addressed themselves to the matter of external influences, have tended to argue against their being of any significance. Their case has been made at its strongest in the context of the Scientific Revolution, the important period of change initiated by Copernicus's *Revolutionibus* and culminating in Newton's *Principia*.

One does not expect to find the changes of this period necessarily influenced by the kind of external factor relevant today, in an entirely different institutional context. But a number of attempts have been made to relate the scientific events of the time to contiguous socio-economic changes—the rise of mercantile capitalism, the erosion of barriers between scholars and craftsmen, changing economic and military interests and changing religious beliefs. Some idea of the varied approaches of this kind can be obtained by comparing the work of Hessen (1931), Merton (1938), Zilsel (1941), Hill (1965), Kargon (1966) and Needham (1969). It is this kind of work which has been criticized from within the mainstream of 'internalist' historians; their treatment of history of science as intellectual history has been held to preclude socio-economic explanations.

According to the internalist account, the Scientific Revolution is to be understood in terms of internal, intellectual development. From the *Revolutionibus*, concerned with the technical difficulties of quantitative Ptolemaic astronomy, to the *Principia*, likewise esoteric and mathematical, internal problems alone stimulated the cultural changes taking place in natural philosophy. To describe the way that this occurred has been the objective of internalist scholarship. This reveals the continuity and coherence of the changing thought of the period and its initial dependence upon earlier scholarly work.

With the perspective adopted in this volume, it is tempting to say that the internalist historians showed science developing, as it had to develop, as a form of culture. Nor need we take any *a priori* objection to their rejection of the significance of external or non-intellectual factors. Any analogy with modern science is clearly inappropriate. Today, science is fully institutionalized; then, it was, at most, an institution in embryo. Today, science possesses vast numbers of taken for granted routines and procedures; then, it involved a massive and complex metamorphosis in a wide area of culture. We may proceed with an open mind to examine their case against the externalists.

Unfortunately, nothing in the way of a comprehensive refutation is provided. Internalists have not tried to study how external factors stimulated or retarded interest in science, or how they might have favoured one kind of study over another. They have not opposed externalism in its own terms at all. Rather they have regarded their own internal history, in itself, as evidence against externalism. And they seem to have done this because they equated externalism with positivism, and the crudest form of economic determinism.

The argument against positivism implicit, for example, in A. R. Hall's (1952) study of ballistics in the seventeenth century is clearly correct. Recent developments in the art of warfare did not stimulate a sudden interest in ballistics, which resulted in the discovery of the facts of projectile trajectories and the induction of scientific laws.[3] External factors did not operate by swinging the searchlight of science into new areas, where heaps of inert facts were revealed, ready for checking and sorting. Nor were those philosophers who constructed a scientific treatment of ballistics drawn to its study by expedient interest or external incentive. Once projectile trajectories had entered the problem situation of natural philosophy, individuals tended to pick it up from their predecessors in that intellectual tradition. Here again is the central internalist point; they wanted to reveal science as a project of the intellect, which, of course, it is.

Hall has no objection to the view that ballistics became incorporated into natural philosophy because practitioners encountered it in 'the background and experience of their age' (cf. Hall (1952), p. 160). He recognizes quite frankly that science does not exist in a cultural vacuum, that its activities may be facilitated by technological resources, that its problems may be drawn from the general context of the surrounding culture. But he recognizes it only to forget it again. It simply hasn't been of any significance for the internalist tradition.

Briefly, then, the internalist case is conceived in opposition to exceedingly crude forms of externalism, and to this extent it is a valid case, even though one might wonder at times, exactly who is being argued against. To an extent, one can understand the way in which external history has been characterized. There is a tinge of positivism about many externalist studies of the Scientific Revolution. And the work of Hessen, in particular, is certainly crude, although by no means so crude as the parodies of it found in internalist criticisms would imply. On the other hand, there is far more in the external history than the kind of interpretation criticized by Hall. Joseph Needham's detailed comparisons of Renaissance science, and its context, with analogues in the history of Chinese culture cannot be dismissed so simply, involving, as they do, thorough consideration of intellectual history. One might have hoped for more sophistication from the internalist historians, instead of a blanket condemnation of externalism, often degenerating into mere polemic.

It is this polemic which suggests that the overall rejection of externalism may have performed some kind of unacknowledged function for historians of science. Consider, for example, A. R. Hall's disparaging review of Robert Merton's *Science, Technology and Society in Seventeenth-Century England* (1938). Hall (1963) strongly criticizes a number of Merton's views concerning external influences upon Restoration science. One of these is that the socio-economic context stimulated a particular interest in physical science at the time. Hall never manages to make it clear whether he regards this thesis as false, or merely unimportant. He offers no worthwhile evidence to oppose it. Somehow, he creates the impression of refuting it, and several other claims in Merton's work, when all he really does is to make them appear vulgar.

Close inspection reveals Hall's paper to be more an internalist *credo* than a sound review of a controversy. Historians, we hear at the end, must take sides in the internal/external debate if they are to establish that their profession is 'more than narration and chronicle'. The historian of science S. Lilley, who reviewed a wide range of materials before concluding that, to understand scientific change, both internal and external factors must be taken into account, is rebuked by Hall, apparently for nothing other than threatening professional interests!

Moving back to the literature as a whole, we can only say that the role of directive external factors in the origin and progress of the Scientific Revolution remains unclear. In so far as they operated, they influenced an ongoing intellectual tradition, and expertise in intellectual history is necessary in any confident evaluation of their importance. Given what really amounts to a lack of interest in external factors on the part of most historians, this cannot be expected to emerge for a considerable time. Even in ideal circumstances, it might prove impossible to resolve some of the key issues in the debate. The social context of sixteenth- and seventeenth-century natural philosophy and the ethos within which important figures worked may prove impossible to reconstruct. The gap between internal and external history may prove technically unbridgeable.

Even so, confidence in the necessity of some kind of external history can be retained. There are many questions which cannot be treated by an internal account and which demand systematic explanation. The social and temporal distribution of the seminal figures in internal history cannot be fully explained by that history. Neither can the parallel and independent changes occurring in several branches of knowledge at the same time be left as a matter of coincidence, especially when some of these changes occurred against an internal context of knowledge and technique which had changed little or caused little dissatisfaction for a considerable preceding period. Such a constellation of changes invites explanation in terms of some large scale generalization, such as that proposed by Joseph Needham.

T. S. Kuhn clearly perceived the need for more than internal explanation in his study of the Copernican Revolution (1957). Recognizing Copernicus's work as an innovation within the context of technical astronomy, he none the less perceived that the intellectual history of that narrow segment of culture offered no insight into the timing of the innovation: 'Any possible understanding of the Revolution's timing and of the factors that called it forth must, therefore, be sought principally outside of astronomy, within the larger intellectual milieu inhabited by astronomy's practitioners' (p. 132).

There seems no particular reason why Kuhn should not have

referred to the institutional context as well as the intellectual milieu.

III

The debate over the Scientific Revolution also provides a useful context for considering the problem of the identification of science, and establishing a demarcation between it and surrounding culture. We may approach the question via standard internalist interpretations of the Revolution. Its history is part of the history of the intellect. Earlier traditions of thought are essential to its understanding. Medieval thought, to an extent, prepared the way for it.

Yet the very excellence of internalist scholarship has exposed the problem of how much internal continuity did exist, and to what extent a real break occurred in natural philosophy at the Renaissance. The revealed pattern of cultural change is not a logical one in the pedantic sense. Indeed, internal history reveals that identical, logically formed arguments concerning, say, the size of the universe, the existence of a vacuum, or the naturalness of a form of motion, may carry different weights in different sub-cultures at different times. Inevitably, in their detailed investigation of the process of cultural change the internalists demonstrated its lack of necessity.

As to whether the cultural changes from Copernicus to Newton were the *natural* outcome of earlier thought and procedures, this is more controversial. Some stress continuity very strongly, typically basing their views on the history of mechanics and its link with medieval theories of impetus. More often, internalists acknowledge a real intellectual revolution during the Renaissance, pointing to the mathematization of mechanics, the important changes in astronomy and the general decline of Aristotelianism. One such was Alexandre Koyré for whom the above-mentioned changes are associated with the re-emergence of Platonism, a new metaphysics.

Koyré explains specific (scientific) cultural changes in terms of another more general shift in culture. As to whether Platonism is internal or external to science, he is equivocal. Clearly it is a philosophical development, yet philosophy and science are not fully separate traditions at the time—at least science and this philosophy are not. Beyond this Koyré is not concerned to go.

Other historians, however, see Koyré as providing a complete explanation of the Scientific Revolution in terms of internal history. A. R. Hall (1963) quotes Collingwood (pp. 11–12):

> the Renaissance philosophers enrolled themselves under the banner of Plato against the Aristotelians, until Galileo, the true father of modern science, restated the Pythagorean–Platonic standpoint in his own words by proclaiming that the book of nature is a book written by God in the language of mathematics.

For Hall, this is to assert with Koyré that 'modern science is of its own intellectual right fundamental and absolute'. Slightly earlier in his text Hall has made the point in another way : 'the history of science is strictly analogous to the history of philosophy'. Perhaps one could distinguish historical and sociological attitudes by whether these two formulations are regarded as prima facie equivalent or contradictory !

For the moment, the details of Koyré's argument, and its plausibility, can be set aside, in order to concentrate on how far it is to be regarded as an internal account. For this purpose, it will be useful to compare it with some more recent accounts of the role of philosophical influence in scientific change.

In an extensively documented historical study, Paul Forman (1971) has attempted to demonstrate a link between philosophy and physics in the cultural context of the Weimar republic. Condensation of Forman's long and careful argument invites disaster, none the less I shall attempt to distil out essential points for use in the present context. If their sketchiness and subjectivity provoke the reader to examine the original text, so much the better.

It is well known that the development of the quantum mechanics of Heisenberg and Schrödinger in the late 1920s was (and is) presented as a major break in the development of physical theory. The new mechanics was interpreted as *acausal*; it was thought to imply a breakdown in strict determinism. Forman has shown that this mechanics occurred after a period when criticisms of strict determinism and fully causal science had become prevalent in Weimar culture, and had gained currency among scientists themselves. He suggests that this prior inclination of physicists to acausal positions lubricated the introduction of the new mechanics, may have influenced its presentation and interpretation, and might even have been constitutively involved in the ways of thought which created it.

Acausality is straightforwardly presented as an *external* influence. *Lebensphilosophie* and antagonism to the alleged strict determinism of science are shown to grow in the postwar intellectual milieu in Germany. They find expression in the philosophy of Oswald Spengler, whose writings provide one route by which they are carried into the community of scientists, and whose diagnosis of physics is to find an echo in later comment and speculation by physicists themselves. The acausality of the scientists is derived from the acausality dominating the wider milieu; it occurs later than the latter, and as a response to it.

Thus, both Hall and Forman are confident that they can identify the 'inside' and 'outside' of the science of their period. But one finds a philosophical influence operating within science itself, the other describes philosophy playing an important role as an external influence. Turning next to the work of Robert Young (1969, 1971, 1972) on Darwin and the evolutionary debates, we find yet another possibility.

Young has been concerned to show that Darwin's work, and his subsequent defence of it over a long period of the nineteenth century, cannot be seen entirely as a technical controversy, turning on how well the available biological and geological materials fitted into the evolutionary framework. For example, he shows that Darwin's own position is unintelligible save in terms of a dogmatic and unyielding uniformitarianism. Faced with an immense number of theoretical objections and alleged counter-instances, Darwin made a number of important and far reaching concessions to his critics over the years. But one thing he would neither abandon nor qualify was his commitment to the complete uniformity of nature; so it was with some of his supporters.

This finding, along with many others in Young's work, casts doubt upon standard internalist accounts of nineteenth-century biological science, with their hagiographic flavour, and their strict separation of the 'genuine' science of Darwin and the less reputable thought of others. Young is concerned to emphasize the common context of nineteenth-century thought about man's place in nature, and the continuity between aspects of it which we are now inclined to separate; 'science', 'social thought', 'natural theology', and so on. Uniformitarianism frequently features as an assumption in all these areas as we now define them. This is one of many indications that it is futile to attempt to separate off 'genuine' biological science at this time. It contributes to Young's general case for setting aside the internal/external dichotomy in the historiography of science, a case which can be readily accepted since it is made against those who deploy their own standards to identify what belongs within genuine science and what does not.

Here then are three examples in the light of which we can explore the possibility of drawing a boundary around science, and hence separating internal and external elements in its growth. In all three cases the postulated influences are 'philosophical', and all may have influenced the criteria of evaluation of scientists. Thus, they are well suited for comparison.[4]

Clearly, it is Forman whose task is the easiest. He is able to identify a well differentiated community of physicists, perceiving themselves as a separate group of practitioners, and being perceived in this way from 'the outside'. The fine structure of the disciplinary boundary might not be perfectly clear, but its general geography is readily ascertained. In such a case it is possible to distinguish separate groups of cultural elements as follows:

(1) esoteric cultural elements peculiar to the particular sub-culture in question;
(2) general cultural elements, widely distributed, but essential to the esoteric normal practice of the sub-culture, and defined as legitimate by it;
(3) general cultural elements, wholly or partially accepted within a sub-culture, yet not part of its esoteric thought or practice, and not defined as legitimate;
(4) esoteric elements peculiar to the activities of other sub-cultures.

The overall culture in question may be regarded as analysable into these four parts with respect to any sub-culture it contains. For a scientific sub-culture, matter of course development and some kinds of imaginative development are intelligible in terms of (1) and (2). From our present standpoint these are 'internal' changes. Forman, on the other hand, postulates what must be an external influence, originating in sub-cultures outside physics (and 'science' generally) and subsequently penetrating into it. Acausality like any category (4) element is clearly external.[5]

With a fully differentiated sub-culture, only class (3) elements present any difficulty. They form no part of the definitive esoteric normal practice, yet they are not external. Consider, for example, the explanation of optical isomerism in terms of the 'handedness' of molecules. This depended on taken for granted ideas of parity, general throughout European culture, and not until then involved in the normal practice of chemistry. Chemists just happened to share beliefs about parity because of the general culture in which they lived. This made Van't Hoff's model intelligible to them. But the beliefs did not come in from outside; the chemists had them all the time.

Perhaps these kinds of shared cultural elements should be called internal, but it is important to recognize what is involved. Imagine a specialty studying genetics, or behaviour, where all the practitioners 'just happened' to believe in the potential equality of capacities of all humans, or in the inherent mental superiority of white over black. When the specialty turned to study humans, these 'internal' factors would assume some importance. And this is not to deny that they might then be tried and tested by accepted procedures of the specialty. Again, imagine a specialty of neurophysiology where everybody 'just happened' to believe in 'freedom of the will'. As the human brain was successfully investigated by specialty techniques, one could imagine this 'internal' factor too becoming of some importance. One could even imagine the members of the specialty being unaware that they shared this common 'philosophy', until some key event precipitated and perhaps institutionalized their mutual commitment.

On the whole, it is probably best to treat cultural influences of this kind as a distinct and characteristic group. It could perhaps be suggested that where they arise from model extension they should be regarded as 'internal', and otherwise as 'external'. This would mark Van't Hoff's work on optical isomerism as internal, and the later hypothetical examples as external. Again, one might find specialties which rigidly defined their boundaries in terms of general principles. Everyone might share a 'philosophy' yet be enjoined to keep it out of their scientific work. When it crept in, it could then be regarded as 'external' in actors' own terms. Such matters of mere terminology are, however, of no real importance and will not be discussed further.

Moving back from Forman to Young's work on evolutionary theory generates a far more complex problem. Scientific sub-cultures in this period were only partially differentiated. This makes it impossible to analyse them simply in terms of insides and outsides. Yet neither can they be regarded as mere fantasies, illegitimately projected onto the wholeness of nineteenth-century culture.

Generally recognized procedures for data collection and classification existed in areas we would now call biogeography, comparative anatomy and geology. So did recognized observations from the practice of plant and animal breeding. Routine, matter of course work was possible in these areas. But, although they were recognized in actors' own categories, and communal agreement as to the importance of their materials existed, they did not fully define the range of activity within a sub-culture or sub-cultures. And they certainly did not define the range of considerations within which the worth of the evolutionary hypothesis was 'scientifically' assessed.

To fill out the range of relevant considerations it is necessary to refer to more controversial taxonomic procedures, to the range of general theories deployed at the time, and to the various conceptions of the nature of scientific explanation and evaluation. This exposes a whole range of cultural elements which cannot be labelled as internal or external, because no agreed judgments of actors themselves can be appealed to in justification of such labelling.

Belief in the uniformity of nature illustrates this. Some urged that to be uniformitarian was to *be* scientific; it was a taken for granted part of science for them. Others saw it as an empirical claim to be judged in the light of evidence; in so far as it was dogmatically held it was an intrusion into scientific practice. Darwin himself never explicitly claimed that uniformitarianism was a metaphysical position beyond concrete justification; he was, on the contrary, continually presenting data to establish it. Nobody laid more weight on the accumulated data of naturalists and other observers than he.[6] Yet, according to Young, through a long line of concessions to his critics touching, over the years, practically every substantive point in his initial position, the one thing which remained intact was Darwin's unrelenting uniformitarianism. Moving on from his period, it seems plausible to suggest that the conflicts between uniformity and interventionism, purpose and cause, design and evolution, were not resolved in terms of other criteria. As the life and earth sciences differentiated about their various technical cores, uniformitarianism, in amended and diluted form, simply passed into them as a permanent presupposition.

It is clearly inappropriate to attempt to identify uniformitarianism as an external or internal factor. Actors' categories provide nothing near enough to a consensus on the matter. Nor were the evolutionary debates uniformly conceived, at the time, to be relevant to the particular narrow range of objectives we relate them to now, in our differentiated system of knowledge. Actors' aims made uniformitarianism an important principle in a wide range of areas—scientific, religious and political, nor were these strictly separated into distinct contexts of discourse. There were not fully distinct scientific, religious and political language games.[7]

Turning to Koyré's period, one expects an even less differentiated situation. Subject to the correction of historians, actors' categories seem insufficient to delineate a specific scientific sub-culture, or to define with reasonable consensus the cultural resources appropriate to the study of physical phenomena. Galileo's work, for example, does not seem to be intelligible in terms of any one preceding tradition of normal practice. Hence it seems reasonable and appropriate for Koyré to present his work as the general history of the intellect, without too much concern for distinctions between science and philosophy. Having made the case against socio-economic determination, the idealist Koyré has no further use for the internal/external dichotomy.

Yet one wonders whether the undifferentiated intellectual context did not simply disguise some of Koyré's commitments. Would he have admitted the possibility of thoroughgoing Hermetic influences on the 'science' of his period?[8] And would this have been an 'internal' or an 'external' influence? It is difficult to know how Koyré, conceiving his task as recording the history of our present 'rational' thought, would have treated intellectual, yet for him irrational, elements among its cultural antecedents.

Perhaps Koyré got the right answer for the wrong reason, treating science in parallel with other strands of culture, not so much because it was undifferentiated from them as because he regarded them also as 'rational'. In any event the result was good intellectual history. Nor is it improved by defining neo-Platonism as part of the 'science' of the time, and defining intellectual as internal history.

IV

Whether 'philosophical' influences are best defined as internal or external in themselves may matter little if they are in turn determined by other, more general, social or cultural factors. Work such as Koyré's cannot be used to show that science is insulated from the wider social context without a theory of how 'philosophical ideas' come into prominence. If they are, for example, mere reflections of class interests, then science becomes linked to social structure *through* the connections established by internal history.

This is a point unsatisfactorily dealt with by intellectual historians. Occasionally indeed, they leave the impression that a text has only to be dug up or translated, for its contents automatically to have an important and widespread influence. Ideas take on such autonomy, such power in themselves, that one wonders at the lack of impact of the Dead Sea Scrolls, or the deciphering of Linear B. The differential impact of 'philosophical' ideas poses a major dilemma for intellectual historians. If it is a matter of random fashion, then science makes major advances by taking lucky rides on current philosophical bandwagons, a plausible diagnosis, but scarcely in the spirit of rationalizing internal history. On the other hand, if the differential impact is rationally intelligible, then different ontologies and metaphysical positions must be in some way subject to rational comparison.

One can imagine an attempt being made to account for the impact of Euclid in terms of 'inherent worth'.[9] But in matters of ontology and metaphysics it is much more difficult to imagine laymen or scientists making 'rational advances', especially as positions on issues like determinism are known to oscillate between long standing alternative rationalizations. The only alternative is to postulate an esoteric research tradition in philosophy, which makes rational progress and influences others through its most recent developments, which represent 'genuine advances' on earlier work. As this alternative has never been properly developed to buttress the intellectualist position, it is best ignored. We may claim that when acausality waxes and strict determinism declines, or when Aristotelian metaphysics succumb to the criticisms of the neo-Platonists, intellectual history is barren of explanations. All it can do is to treat metaphysical changes as random, and challenge other historical traditions to explain what it cannot.

It cannot be said that this challenge has been answered altogether successfully. Attempts to relate ideas to social structure and social context have had only very limited success, although it is this approach which must eventually explain their differential impact. Probably the main limitation of existing work in this vein is a tendency to make a one-to-one correspondence between a belief, or set of beliefs, and a particular type of social class or interest group. Thus, deterministic mechanical philosophy is seen as characteristically bourgeois. If others believe it, or if the 'bourgeois' espouse other philosophies, this is an anomalous state of affairs. The philosophy is the logical one for the class. Such imputations lack credibility because of the great amount of 'pathology' they need to account for.

A better approach is to regard ideas as tools with which social groups may seek to achieve their purposes in particular situations. Ideas suit purposes not because of any logical relationship, but because they are naturally suited to particular kinds of use within an existing system of beliefs and norms. Hence, ideas are related to social structure by examining the perceived situation of actors in particular collectivities, and their perceived problems and aims. Beliefs which 'work' in one situation may be quite inappropriate in another.[10] The connection between interests and ideas is contextually mediated.

Paul Forman explicitly treats opposition to determinism in this way. Intellectuals in a defeated nation used it to express their criticisms of the science and technology associated with the war effort, and to point to the traditional presuppositions of German philosophy as fountains for spiritual renewal. Scientists espoused it, and began to present their activities in terms of it, as a response to a hostile intellectual environment. (In so far as scientists could recreate their image successfully, opposition to strict determinism would become an increasingly redundant position for groups concerned solely to undermine the credibility of science and the power of those who sustain and use it.)

Nineteenth-century philosophies of nature cannot be so succinctly related to actors' purposes, but it is still very easy to argue that conceptions of natural law, uniformity and evolution could perform important functions for the beneficiaries of the emerging competitive, industrial order, and that this is why they became prominent. Uniformity proclaimed the impotence of a God which had been the creation of the declining ruling class; with the emasculation of religious institutions, uniformitarianism has passed from the intellectual scene as an explicit idea. There is no more work for it to do.

There is no reason to assume that the 'new philosophy' discussed by Koyré cannot likewise be related to underlying social and economic factors. Indeed, we find Veblen attempting to do something very close to this in the work already discussed in chapter 1. His thesis is in no way opposed to the narratives of intellectual history, nor can it be discredited by them. Its worth has to be judged in the light of more general, essentially comparative, studies.

It is pointless to attempt to discuss here the merits of particular accounts of the changing world view associated with the Scientific Revolution. The issues need prolonged debate in the context of detailed historical scholarship. Yet I shall record agreement with one point upon which both Koyré and Veblen are in accord. They both recognize that no minor cultural change is involved; they are dealing with a revolution in our overall modes of thought, and both, in their different ways, treat it as beyond the scope of explanations based entirely upon the esoteric technical activity of narrow sections of culture or society. The rupture of the cosmos and the demise of teleology demand broader explanations if they are to be explained at all.

In my view, these changes are best linked with the general decline of anthropomorphic and teleological beliefs in Western culture, manifested also in the disappearance of witchcraft beliefs, the (partial) demise of astrology, secularization, and the rise of impersonal explanatory models. To explain this constellation of changes in general terms we must look to the particular mode of social differentiation which has occurred in the West, involving the stabilization of differently based and conflicting foci of power. This has restricted the possibilities and narrowed the basis of communication which is in any way based upon moral consensus (cf. Douglas (1966, 1970a), Horton (1967), Barnes (1973)). We might suggest that, in the general context of post-feudal Europe, teleology had to decline. More specific historical studies and comparisons with other civilizations are required only to understand what replaced it—the mathematization of natural knowledge and its suffusion with craft lore.

v

'Philosophical' or metaphysical influences on science must change scientific practice to be of significance. They may encourage the development of new models and procedures, or alter the existing evaluative context within which models and procedures are condemned or justified. Their effects are thus very general and difficult to demonstrate; it can always be claimed of procedural changes that they would have happened anyway. This is especially easy to do when a 'philosophy' is introduced together with a set of new techniques and procedures, and in practice, procedures and metaphysics are frequently associated in this way. Paracelsianism, for example, involved therapeutic technique and anthropomorphic, antirational philosophy; Archimedean techniques became disseminated at the same time as Archimedean neo-Platonism.

The argument which denies metaphysics a role in scientific change is found at its best in E. W. Strong's *Procedures and Metaphysics* (1936), which develops a detailed criticism of E. A. Burtt's (1932) analysis of the place of neo-Platonism in the rise of modern physical science. Here, a detailed case study is combined with a general vision of science, which has it developing through the extension of methods and procedures in the context of practical activity. The study has been criticized for limiting itself to the mystical strands of neo-Platonism, but, whatever the justice of this, the general approach remains. One could readily imagine a case being constructed, after Strong, against the more speculative themes of Forman's study. Whatever the metaphysical trimmings, it might be said, matrix mechanics would have developed and been accepted via the natural development of methods and procedures within the context of physical practice. Vague revulsion for strict determinism could have taken no part in the rise of the new quantum theory.[11]

It is no part of my present purpose to defend the thesis in Strong's much underestimated work. But it does highlight the point that philosophical influences upon science need establishing, and this has not been attempted. Indeed, the work cited in the foregoing is justifiably controversial. It remains possible to present science as an internally developing constellation of methods and procedures effectively isolated from other influences.

The easiest way of disposing of this possibility is to present counter examples. Recent work by Cowan (1968, 1972) convincingly shows how the development of new methods and procedures may be influenced by social factors. She has determined how the mathematical and biological themes and techniques of Francis Galton's work emerged from his political, eugenic concerns (concerns which can be clearly related to his milieu and the position he occupied within it).

Galton's anticipation of the theory of germ plasm does not command a secure place in a teleologically conceived history of science, so we can concentrate on his development of the techniques of regression and correlation, which do. Cowan makes it clear that these techniques emerged because Galton was trying to do unprecedented things with his data. New questions were stimulating him to treat them in new ways, to look for new kinds of pattern in their graphical arrangement, to apply new forms of computation to them. And these were the questions Galton had to answer if he were to learn how to implement his political programme (questions which could compel the devoted attention of a powerful but largely unsupported intellect only in certain kinds of social situation).

Besides shaping and stimulating the scientific imagination, the external culture may provide it with its raw material. Many cases exist where a scientific sub-culture utilizes beliefs or images generated elsewhere to produce some new procedure or scheme of interpretation. Increasingly, however, it is other scientific sub-cultures that are being drawn upon for resources in this way, with physics and mathematics, in particular, being exploited by specialties in chemistry and the life sciences. As science has incorporated into itself more and more of the cultural resources of the societies in which it has thrived, so it has become more internally self-sufficient, with cross-fertilization between specialties replacing 'fully external' inputs in the process of cultural change.

It is still possible to find external culture being actively incorporated into science, as examination of some of the key metaphors in modern biology readily reveals. But for clear-cut examples it is best to look backwards. The imaginative processes by which Clerk Maxwell arrived at his equations of the electro-magnetic field offer tempting illustrative possibilities, involving as they did the whole of space being filled with interlocked gear-wheels. But a still better example can be found in the history of thermodynamics, and in particular in the work of Sadi Carnot.[12]

It is a commonplace to state that the growing use of engines during the industrial revolution stimulated interest in heat, and in the relation between natural power and its mechanical effects. It is also abundantly clear that this development, however much it may have been influenced by 'science' (and that is a matter of con-

I

troversy), cannot by any definition be regarded as 'internal' to science! The way in which this external factor produced new scientific procedures, however, can only be understood in terms of the cultural resources it provided for the scientific imagination. Carnot's treatment of the work cycle of a heat engine transformed these resources to initiate the production of a series of exemplary procedures, which became firmly incorporated into narrowly scientific practice (Carnot (1960), cf. also Cardwell (1971)).

Essentially, Carnot obtained his results by using an analogy between a heat engine and a water engine, employing the caloric theory of heat. Hydraulics and the theory of water engines was well developed, and this analogy had been made before by engineers. The key to Carnot's results lies in the particular idealization of a heat engine he employed. This is a highly abstract conception made of perfect conductors and perfect insulators, perfectly smooth and perfectly shaped in all its parts, working infinitely slowly with infinitely small temperature gradients through completely reversible cycles—but a thousand times simpler for theoretical treatment than any concrete engine. We want to say that Carnot distilled the essence of a heat engine.

Yet this essence was clearly distilled from the properties of concrete engines. The raw material for Carnot's imagination was the problems and artefacts of power engineers. Cardwell (1971) has noted how Carnot adopted the principle of expansive operation used by Watt, and has also suggested that the separate condenser of Watt's engine was (imaginatively) transformed into the 'heat sink' of Carnot's idealization. Even more convincingly, T. S. Kuhn (1961) has revealed a remarkable series of parallels between Carnot's idealization and the heat engine of Cagnard Latour; as this engine would have been 'seen' by Carnot, it would have suggested key features of his idealization to him.

Thus, although nobody better than Carnot reveals the history of science to be the history of the intellect, nobody reveals more clearly how that history has to be understood as partially determined by general socio-economic factors. The lineage of our present scientific culture cannot be traced back endlessly through group after group of disinterested natural philosophers. It is possible to write pure history of ideas, but that history does not entirely explain itself. We might say that more than this is needed if history is to aspire to be 'more than narration and chronicle'.

VI

The time has now come to attempt to pull together the various strands of argument and to summarize the conclusions that are indicated. Four main points emerge:

(1) Simply because science is *culture* and grows and changes on the basis of its cultural resources and possibilities, it does not respond simply to material or social influences and stimuli. Matter of course scientific work may sometimes be directed fairly predictably by such influences, but more imaginatively based and unpredictable kinds of research cannot be. None the less it is perfectly reasonable to hold that general stimulation of scientific activity and direction of talent towards science will, on the whole, favour scientific change of all kinds. Historians who oppose this claim have failed to bring any kind of evidence against it.

(2) Scientific workers have increasingly become differentiated into clearly demarcated sub-cultures, where actors have tacitly agreed to conduct research for narrowly defined purposes, using a well defined range of cultural resources. Clear boundaries have emerged between scientific culture and that of society as a whole, and between different groups of practitioners within science. These boundaries are defined explicitly or implicitly by actors themselves. They permit a distinction to be made between external and internal factors in scientific change, although not in the sense normally implied by the terms. External cultural elements may become incorporated into a scientific specialty, thereby changing the purpose and standards of evaluation of its practitioners, or providing the imaginative resources for the achievement of some existing purpose, by means acceptable in terms of existing evaluative standards.

(3) As one passes back into the history of science one finds it (or, if preferred, its cultural antecedents) less and less differentiated from the general culture. Internal/external distinctions become more and more difficult to deploy on the basis of actors' own definitions; boundaries become more and more nebulous. At the same time, actors' purposes become less and less narrowly defined with respect to a particular part of their thought, and this thought becomes less and less recognizably like that of our present science. As we press history back into more and more anthropocentric cultures our science becomes related to a more and more alien cultural ancestry.

Historians may (perhaps quite rightly) insist on the impersonality of much of the 'scientific thought' of *their* period and its separateness as a cultural tradition. Nothing fundamental is at issue here, but merely matters of timing.

(4) Only tacit agreement may limit the range of cultural resources employed in defining and solving scientific problems. And this agreement, when it exists, does not preclude the use of external resources, but merely restricts its extent. In the last analysis there is no strict separation between the history of science and the history of culture or ideas.

How science is held to relate to socio-economic factors accordingly depends on one's theory of the relationship of ideas and social structure. For an idealist, the virtue of the history of ideas is that it saves the intellect from socio-economic determination. For others, the history of ideas may *reveal* the way in which ideas actually are influenced by social structure. The history of ideas itself cannot provide grounds for choice between such theories, although it can indicate the weakness of particular variants of them (positivistic conceptions of socio-economic determination for example). I have tried to indicate reasons for profound dissatisfaction with idealism and have suggested that theories relating ideas to social structure have a promising future.

It will be noted that no mention has been made of scientific progress; indeed the concept would seem to be irrelevant to sociological investigation as here conceived. Strictly, this is indeed so; how we apply such a vague and evaluative term to the history of science is not of interest here.[18] If we choose to see sociology as an extension of science, we might put our tongue in our cheeks to make a stronger claim; the last redoubt of teleology lies in the concept of scientific progress, hence in the interests of scientific progress we must eradicate the term.

Yet, when we look at the history of science, this very term forces itself upon us; quite apart from arguments. Without allowing ourselves to be seduced by such feelings, we may still take them as a guide that there is 'something there' to be understood. We should not assume, however, that what is there is a movement of scientific culture into closer and closer correspondence with some unspecified and unspecifiable reality. (This can never be more than a profession of faith.) It is likely that we are responding to a much more straightforward teleological progression, consisting in science's increasing capacity to fulfil particular aims and purposes defined by actors themselves.

Such progress is easy enough to demonstrate in the work of the individual scientist, spending a lifetime in the partial achievement of particular aims. Doubtless, it also occurs throughout the periods of activity Kuhn calls 'normal science'. Nor is there any reason to believe that there is insufficient continuity in human ends and needs to construct conceptions of progress much more generally meaningful, and applicable over far longer time spans. Yet, there is a need for caution.

The virtue of conceiving of scientific progress in relation to actors' aims and purposes is that it becomes genuinely problematic, and needs genuine justification and not complacent affirmation. Actors' aims and purposes change, and perhaps are changed by science itself. Actors' capacities to achieve their aims may be decreased as well as increased by the possession of scientific knowledge. And this remains the case if one thinks solely in terms of 'practical' aims. Thus, the existence of long term, unidirectional scientific progress is by no means easily established in these terms. Some of the difficulties may be pointed to by an analogy.

Consider the long mainstream tradition of musical composition in Europe from the early Renaissance to its final disappearance in the mid-twentieth century, when an excess of knowledge and technique finally destroyed composers' capacity to write music. Here we can see actors striving to shape their resources into fulfilling more and more closely their goals and aspirations. We can see the work of individuals becoming more and more competent and assured, the efforts of the young composer leading to the fully realized achievements of his later works. It makes sense in actors' own terms to say that composers' work improved as they matured.

We can see too how composition developed in traditions, with younger composers building upon the work of their elders, and in many cases sharing the same musical ideals and standards. We can see how technique changed over the period, how composers learned to use more and more intervals, devised new methods of modulation, constructed new forms while retaining their capacity to use old ones, and discovered more and more ways of balancing and contrasting instrumental timbres.

Finally we can note the effect of technology and economy on music.

These gave the composer an ever widening range of tone and timbre and ever growing resources of men and instruments for his orchestra. And they gave performers superior and more readily tamed instruments, as well as providing more and more of them with the time to perfect their technique, and to bring performances of particular works to hitherto unheard of standards of execution.

Yet, if we want to talk of the progress of music over this period, we no longer do so with the arrogant self-confidence of the nineteenth century; it is perfectly respectable, in our less assured age, to prefer Palestrina to Tchaikovsky. Nor would we automatically assume that the latter was the finer technician, or even that he possessed all the resources of the former plus a host of new ones.

It is, of course, reasonable to point out that science and its cultural antecedents have been expected to fulfil ends less variable and less variously evaluated than those associated with music. The basic point however remains: we lack a satisfactory account of overall scientific progress. It deserves treatment as a problem not an assumption.

chapter 6

Science and ideology

I

'Ideology' is a notoriously vague term, lacking anything approaching an accepted usage. None the less, in concrete sociological and historical work, it has frequently proved valuable to deploy it, and to adopt or imply a fundamental distinction between ideology and science. The case for making the contrast is a strong one, well made, for example, by the literature on the history of the concept of race. So, when it is noted that the arguments of the preceding chapters have eroded the usual bases upon which the distinction is made, a real issue arises. It becomes necessary to discuss in detail how we are to deal with the problem of ideology and its relationship to science; we must ask whether any real alternative to existing viewpoints exists. These will be the concerns of this final chapter.[1]

On present usage, both descriptions and evaluations may be referred to as ideological, although the sense is slightly different in the two cases. In a nutshell, values are *described* as ideological, whereas descriptions or empirical claims are *evaluated* by the designation. A set of values or a professed ethical code associated with an occupation may be termed an ideology, perhaps because of its connection with the communally defined aims and purposes of the occupational group. This does not imply that the values are inadequate, unnatural or wrong. When empirical claims are termed ideological, however, it is generally implied that they are incorrect, or at least ungrounded.

It is the latter usage that will be of most relevance here, given that natural science is at the centre of the discussion. None the less, it is worth pointing out that scientific knowledge is very far from being totally non-evaluative. Moreover, in so far as science is found to celebrate or embody values in the content of its knowledge, it is open to criticism. Since science is expected to be descriptive, evaluations within it may *masquerade* as facts or neutral statements. The practically universal and not entirely undeserved reputation for disinterest enjoyed by scientists may give spurious legitimation to values which are incorporated within their knowledge claims. For the most part, however, this effect although significant, is not of great importance.[2]

Overt prescription is mingled with description in a great deal of bona fide science, although the practice tends to be frowned upon in most academic work. Usually, it is harmless enough, with no question of masquerade, and no difficulty being involved in separating out evaluations. None the less, even in academic contexts, work in medicine, metallurgy and many other fields may be written in such a way that attempts to pick out discourse free of the explicit evaluations of the writer will be futile. Even so, the evaluations will be easy enough to perceive, and the reader can easily allow for them. On the whole it is in semi-popular writings and in marginally scientific areas that even overt evaluations can become insidious. 'Pop' ethology and ecology spring to mind here, and fields like psychiatry and criminology.

Scientific work may also be evaluative as a result of its terminology. Important concepts may be used wherein description and evaluation remain undifferentiated; observation languages may be very far from being neutral and antiseptic. Pathology is the label of an entire scientific discipline and an important taxonomic term. Clearly, it is an evaluative concept which discriminates physiological phenomena in a way the 'purely scientific' function of which is far from clear. Moreover, the kind of evaluation it embodies permeates observation statements in human physiology and anatomy and, for that matter, in related areas of biophysics and biochemistry too. Yet the point must not be pushed too hard. Evaluative observation languages are observation languages for all that. The statements in textbooks of physiology and pathology may legitimately be held to be factual or genuinely descriptive. And the values they embody lack the significance of those bound up in terms such as 'the free world' or 'extremist' or other favourites of the mass media. We do not seriously discriminate, exploit or rank-order in terms of heart conditions or ingrowing toe-nails, neither does the terminology of biological science currently abet social processes of stigmatization. Most of the evaluative elements in established scientific disciplines are similarly innocuous and lacking in social function; again, it is in what may politely be called marginally scientific disciplines and writings that undifferentiated terminology most deserves suspicion.

Terminology may also be suspect if it is incompletely differentiated from everyday or common sense vocabulary. The much maligned use of jargon and esoteric modes of discourse does at least decouple natural science from social influence. Where terms are used both in science and the common culture the two contexts of usage influence each other, yet will tend to be slightly different. 'Neutral' scientific statements may appear to be evaluative to laymen; common sense evaluative connotations may subtly influence the thought and practice of the scientist. Terms such as sane/insane, alive/dead, healthy/sick, male/female, neurosis, drug and addiction serve to illustrate the point, and perhaps to excuse to a certain extent specialists who construct grotesque and unutterable expressions with the aid of Greek lexicons. In some specialties of course, outside interest makes it difficult to maintain the autonomous status of technical terminology.

Within the traditional hard sciences, on the other hand, differentiation of terms has taken place to a remarkable extent; concepts have arisen practically devoid of evaluative connotations, and employed entirely in the context of a single discipline or specialty. So differentiated is the language of physics and mathematics that very ordinary terms can be given specialized usage within it without danger; the effect is faintly humorous as with 'strangeness', and 'catastrophe theory'. Thus, in these areas it is very difficult to make out a case for the existence of latent evaluation, or to demonstrate that values are being subtly legitimated. Such positions are not totally untenable, particularly if one is prepared to claim that even the use of such terms as 'high' and 'low' may profoundly legitimate and support an hierarchical social order, but such an approach will not be taken seriously here. The evaluative component in science will be treated here as significant but not of great importance, and as *eliminable*. This analysis comes close to what scientists themselves might, on reflection, acknowledge; it is content to use the fact-value distinction much as scientists and their surrounding culture might use it; the distinction is being treated as an actors' category.

II

The main question then, is not about the incidence of values in natural science, but concerns the relationship between its non-evaluative knowledge claims and ideology. We must ask what is presently implied when knowledge claims are characterized as ideological, why the imputation is made—or what work it can be put to, and what aspects of the current conception of ideology may profitably be preserved within the perspective advocated here. (Needless to say, in line with the earlier stress on the sociological equivalence of belief systems, any aspects which are preserved will be relevant to scientific beliefs as much as to any others.)

At present, if knowledge claims are to be characterized as ideological they are normally expected to comply with three requirements. First, they must perform some social function or accord with the interests of some social group. Second, the claims must be false, incomplete, insufficiently grounded, or in some other way discordant with reason or reality. Finally, the point which binds the first two requirements into a coherent pattern and justifies the use of the overall term ideology, the social function or interest associated with the claims comprises the cause of their unsatisfactory nature; ideology is thought which is distorted or adversely influenced by social factors.

The first point stands untouched by the approach taken here. Beliefs do have social functions, and they do seem to be related, in many instances, to the interests and social positions of those groups which propound them. Thus, all that need be done here is to recall an important but neglected point concerning the functions of beliefs. At risk of emphasizing the obvious, it is worth explicitly stating that, since a belief is ideological by virtue of the way in which it functions, it makes no sense to talk of its being essentially ideological, or ideological in itself. This point is sometimes forgotten in practice; beliefs or types of belief may be characterized as intrinsically ideological with the implication that they logically or automatically legitimate particular practices or states of affairs. In sociology, for example, 'functionalism' is often criticized as ideological and inherently conservative. Now it is certainly plausible to argue that many enthusiasts for functional explanation have been concerned to legitimate existing institutions in their work. But it is wrong to claim more than this; one cannot impugn a class of beliefs by pointing to the motives of their users. Nor is this a pedantic point; Marx was a great master of functional explanation !

A belief may take on social functions in particular contexts if it naturally leads actors with their given, pre-existing beliefs to adopt certain evaluations or courses of action. In other situations, or with different actors, the same belief may function quite differently. A belief or a knowledge claim must be seen as a tool, adaptable to a variety of functions in different situations; perhaps its origin and design were related to one particular special kind of task, but a spanner, on occasions, may make a good cudgel.

At risk of labouring the point, which is perhaps little more than an injunction against committing the naturalistic fallacy, I shall give another example, more relevant to science. Consider the belief that all individuals are born equally endowed with talents and abilities. It is easy to imagine this belief being used to justify a highly hierarchical and exploitative social order. It is a perfect tool for a repressive meritocracy. Those at the bottom of the system have the same talents or potential talents as others. They are not prevented from succeeding by any innate lack of capacity, for which they cannot be held responsible. They must have failed through laziness, indifference, lack of ambition and so on. Since their failure is their own fault, their plight at the bottom of the system is of their own making and they can be left to stew.

In practice, of course, the belief in question has been associated with egalitarianism, and most commonly held by liberals and those to their left. It was a belief used to criticize existing institutions. The differential amount of success of different individuals and groups cannot relate to different innate capacities, 'therefore' it must relate to discrimination and unfair selection institutionalized in the social system. The point is that such 'therefores' have any force only in the context of particular beliefs and norms. The study of the social functions of beliefs is an important branch of sociological investigation, but it reveals nothing about the form or status of the beliefs themselves. Any belief may be made to serve interests; given an appropriate overall pattern of culture, any particular belief may be made to serve any particular interest. (For another example, related to that above, which brings out this point beautifully, cf. Rosenberg, 1966.)

The study of ideology is occasionally presented simply as the study of the functions of beliefs. A belief is held to be ideological by virtue of possessing particular functions; the adequacy of the belief is not considered relevant. There seems little point in this. It is interesting to study the social functions of beliefs, and especially to reveal unperceived or unacknowledged functions, but to call this the study of ideology is otiose. Our beliefs about the biological nature of paternity perform social functions. Belief in the lethal possibilities of the weapons of troops and riot control squads may also do so. It is in the interest of physicists that their beliefs are accepted as correct—by repute among the public, in detail by students. Nothing is to be gained by talking of these as ideological functions.

Thus, the second element in the traditional definition of ideology proves not to be entirely unjustified. Only if the term ideology implies unreasonableness or a clash with reality, does it do any real work. Then it can be used to characterize beliefs which, despite their unsatisfactory nature, persist in particular contexts because of the social functions they are performing therein. The social functions are cited in an attempt to understand the persistence of these beliefs; they cannot be regarded as incidental to them, as with the preceding examples.

None the less, it is this requirement which must be rejected here; for the possibility of finding external standards with which to identify such inadequate beliefs has been denied. The problem thus arises of how social factors do influence beliefs, given that the prima facie case for such an influence is overwhelmingly strong. If they do not operate by causing deviation from truth or rationality, how then do they operate?

III

The first stage in attacking the problem must be to recall that in the earlier chapters causal explanation has been invoked to explain departure from normality rather than truth or rationality. In all communities, including scientific ones, beliefs are judged as valid or well founded according to culturally established precedents. These may vary temporally or between communities, but in a given community over a given period they are generally maintained by mechanisms of social control, and transmitted successfully to new members. Normal practice is practice in accordance with them, and, in a sense, may be treated as unproblematic. Departure from normal practice needs specially accounting for, and among the factors which may be invoked as causes of the departure are social influences and requirements. Instead of asking how social factors produce departures from truth or rationality, i.e. how they distort belief, it can be asked how they produce departures from normal practice. Social factors are one kind of determining influence which may produce such changes.

The difference between this view of the social determination of beliefs and the previous one is that now there is no critical function necessarily associated with the attribution of social causation. Certainly, when unacknowledged, concealed or illegitimate determinants are shown to be influencing beliefs, this *may* be regarded as a criticism, or a reason for withholding credibility from the beliefs in question. There is a parallel here with the limited or particular concept of ideology as beliefs resulting from unconscious, illegitimate motivations (Mannheim (1936)). But it is questionable whether the term ideology should be employed in this changed situation, since it implies that the illegitimately determined beliefs are necessarily inadequate ones. Here, the sociological task of causal explanation is held to be separable from epistemological and evaluative concerns.

It follows from this approach that concealed social influences upon the culture of science can be sought and examined just as they would be with any other culture. If such influences are found, that does not imply that the beliefs involved are erroneous, or 'unscientific' in some context-independent sense. This remains the case, however blatant or crude the illegitimate influences may be. In so far as they have produced departures from normal belief and action such influences help us to understand how cultural change has occurred in science; in themselves they do nothing more.

The preceding points stand in need of concrete exemplification and it will be worthwhile to consider a particular case at some length. The recent controversy engendered by the work of Arthur Jensen on the variation of intelligence in human populations will serve very well. Although there is danger in using contemporary issues with which one's audience may be involved, there is the parallel advantage that they are likely to be well known. This means that the controversy itself can be treated briefly in a way which does no more than provide illustration for the points in question. Inevitably, this will involve loss of precision and some neglect of the fine but important qualifications protagonists have attached to their basic claims or hypotheses, but without some willingness to do this, consideration of any important scientific controversy would require a book in itself. In this case, the inevitable dangers of brevity are offset by the ready availability of the literature, and its reasonable intelligibility to the sociologically trained reader. Thus, the Jensen controversy is particularly appropriate for consideration here. The only remaining disadvantage which its use involves is the indelicacy of taking a deterministic attitude to the work of living individuals, and in view of the professional aims and approaches of these individuals, who are essentially doing much the same thing themselves, this may be set aside.

Jensen's notorious paper (1969) argued against environmentalist theories of IQ variation both within populations and between different social and ethnic groups. It suggested that this variation was best accounted for largely in terms of an hereditarian hypothesis, and supported the claim with an extended literature review. Naturally, Jensen's claims and findings aroused intense opposition, and, among other things, they were rapidly stigmatized as ideological; Jensen's social views, commitments or unrealized prejudices were, it was implied, biasing his scientific judgment.

The evaluation of this claim is made slightly more difficult by the fact that Jensen's (1969) is more than a dispassionate presentation of a scientific hypothesis. It includes overtly prescriptive material and practical suggestions for educationalists. Indeed, it is very close in form to many recent British educational policy documents: it contains next to nothing on the general aims of education, sketchy justification of particular prescriptions, and page upon page of 'data' not clearly relevant to them.[3] None the less, it is probably closest to the author's conception to treat his paper as a contribution to science, with prescriptive elements, rather than as a policy document. It is Jensen's scientific position which has caused controversy among scientists and laity alike, not so much his prescriptions. And it is his scientific position which Jensen has defended and developed. Indeed, Jensen has increasingly defended his work in terms of the traditional (value) ideology of pure science, tending to forget that, if his paper was a piece of disinterested science at all, it was a heavily polluted one (cf. Jensen (1972)).

Thus, attention can reasonably be focused on Jensen's findings and hypotheses. It must first be asked if they can be set within an existing pattern of normal practice. With qualifications, the answer would seem to be 'yes'. His work combines two kinds of cultural resources, those of intelligence testing and the tradition of psychological testing generally, and those of population genetics. The combination in question is not new; in Britain it is found in the work of Burt and many others; in the USA also it has been much used, guiding, among other studies, well-known work on the intelligence and attainment of twins. Both sets of resources, separately and in combination, have proved capable of being routinely transmitted in academic contexts.

Jensen's background seems to have included a straightforward initiation into the problems and techniques of psychological testing. His interest in genetic approaches to the explanation of test variances is less simply accounted for; according to Jensen (1972), it arose from attendance at a lecture of Burt's in England, some years before he made any active use of genetic models and techniques. It might be argued that Jensen's interest was somewhat idiosyncratic in the USA context and hence in need of some kind of biographical explanation, but these genetic techniques, although neglected, had not been criticized in themselves by any significant body of opinion, did not in themselves imply a genetic hypothesis with respect to variation in any particular population trait they were used to study, and involved very general assumptions close to those implicitly accepted within the psychological tradition in which Jensen participated. Thus, on the whole, Jensen's esoteric training and intellectual background do suffice to explain why he should find it natural to deploy the approach found in his 1969 paper; and certainly there are no grounds for assuming that racism must have played a role in determining it.

It remains to ask how the approach was applied. Having located Jensen within a pattern of normal practice, his work can be assessed by the standards of that practice. Judged in these terms, is it 'good' as scientific papers go, or does it reveal distortions and important idiosyncrasies?[4] The answer is that Jensen's (1969) is without any doubt a 'good' paper, and one without important idiosyncrasy. It contains remarkably few straight errors for a paper of such a length. It is carefully argued and carefully qualified. It avoids many pitfalls involved in the use of terms such as 'environmental' and 'heritability' (although the use of these terms does occasionally become loose or take too much for granted). It is reasonably secure technically, given a primary competence in psychology and a secondary one in genetics. Thus, considering the scope of the subject treated and its unsettled nature, the indefeasibility of the paper is beyond dispute.

It does, of course, involve a persistently hereditarian emphasis. It is not the work of one who stands outside all theories and dispassionately compares them. Jensen is arguing the case for the hereditarian hypothesis. He stresses its compatibility with his evidence; he shows how additional hypotheses can increase that compatibility; where a range of possible interpretations are available he makes sure that hereditarian ones are fully considered and their merits understood; where anomalous material is encountered he ensures that its weaknesses are brought to light and the need for its replication is perceived.

There is nothing idiosyncratic in this. Scientists are expected to argue the merits of the theories and approaches they use; this is normal procedure. Models are judged by what they can *do*; their advocates are expected to show what they can do. Within the framework of appropriate norms and precedents scientific papers make out cases; they argue the possibility, probability or overwhelming likelihood of particular interpretations. This is what Jensen does; his work even reveals that tendency to low key expression, and slight understatement, so much admired as stylistic felicities by the scientific community.

Thus, Jensen's (1969) does not represent a departure from normal practice; it can be seen as the natural product of somebody working in a certain area with particular techniques and cultural resources. Hence, it offers no grounds for the contention that particular interests or social convictions were influencing his judgment when he proposed his hypotheses and presented his findings; in this sense, there is no evidence for social causation. Perhaps the same could also be said of some of Jensen's critics, but one or two of these have made contributions which offer interesting contrasts with Jensen's own.

The work of W. F. Bodmer (Bodmer (1972), Bodmer and Cavalli-Sforza (1970)) makes a particularly interesting contrast, since, on the whole, its argument accepts and uses the same set of concepts and exemplars as Jensen's.[5] The major difference between the two is one of emphasis. What Jensen finds suggestive, Bodmer finds inconclusive. Where Jensen sees a need for future study, Bodmer perceives almost insurmountable difficulties which make such study of little point. Where Jensen spends page after page presenting evidence for the hereditarian view before modestly suggesting that it is 'not implausible', Bodmer spends page after page pointing out its limitations before equally modestly stating that he does not 'exclude the possibility'.

Bodmer's work is appropriately related to the same standards as Jensen's. By these standards it is in no way unsound or incompetent. Yet, judged as a piece of science alone, it is unusual. One could not imagine Bodmer writing in the same way if his subject were wheat or rats; with Jensen one could. Bodmer is particularly concerned to suggest that work on the origin of racial differences in IQ is pointless because there is little chance of its succeeding. He is trying to limit the scope of a model which he himself uses, by taking an insistently pessimistic view of its possibilities in a particular area. The norms of scientific specialties, on the other hand, generally encourage the extension of models and exemplars and their use in new areas; they generally encourage investigators to treat technical difficulties as challenges. Thus, there is a prima facie case for viewing Bodmer's work as a departure from normal practice, and its style of interpretation and emphasis as partially caused by the nature of the external social situation.[6]

It would seem likely then (although only a much more thorough analysis would lend any real weight to the suggestion) that external social influences have more explanatory value when considering some of the responses to Jensen's work than in the context of that work itself. That is not to say that one set of work is more reliable than the other, or closer to the real state of affairs. The causal analysis has no such evaluative connotations (although it might suggest to opponents of the hereditarian hypotheses that they examine and criticize the assumptions bound up in the traditions of psychological testing or in polygenetic models of inheritance, instead of seeking ammunition in an individual biography). Assessment of the controversy itself need not be affected by the preceding account.

Neither is anything implied about the motivations or interests of Professor Jensen himself. Because nothing in his 1969 paper suggests that he is a 'racist', it does not follow that, in fact, he is not. Anyone working in the same field with the same esoteric background, and proceeding in ignorance of, or complete indifference to, the general social context, might have produced something very like Jensen's findings and hypotheses. If these happened to suit him very well, then unidentifiable overdetermination occurred.

Thus, quite apart from any individual considerations, Jensen's findings lend themselves to being defended in terms of a pure science

K

(value) ideology. Taken out of context, and suitably purified, they can, in a sense, be represented as the products of a disinterested (or indifferent) 'search for truth'. Hence, it is not inappropriate that a number of well known scientists have compared the social response to his work with that accorded Galileo's theories.[7]

The role of social factors as causes of departure from normality has been illustrated with what, in the context of the Jensen controversy, is a trivial example. None the less, the mode of analysis illustrated is far from trivially significant. It illuminates a large proportion of the literature concerned with that particular controversy, and is generally of great relevance whenever a socially sensitive area is the subject of esoteric debate. In such contexts one may expect and find actors' normal conceptions of proof and plausibility being modified or set aside, realists becoming positivists, technicians philosophers; accepted limits for speculation may be stretched beyond recognition, the accepted spectrum of citable authorities may broaden, established demarcations between assumptions and findings may blur. At the same time, credit-worthy studies, and findings inimical to particular points of view, may be omitted from consideration, or presented in a way which obscures their significance.

It will be clear from this that to establish departure from normality *may*, in practice, destroy pretensions to validity. This is not necessarily so, of course; the previous example was designed, among other things, to reveal that there is no necessary connection here. But many norms and standards are so generally accepted that the credibility of a knowledge claim will always be effectively undermined if it is shown to result from a breach of them. And if social causation is successfully invoked to explain the breach, the general, ongoing credibility of the knowledge source involved may be seriously weakened or even destroyed.

There are, for example, clear and strong norms of procedure and evaluation shared by those who seek causal explanations of disease and other pathologies, on the basis of surveys, written records and statistical materials. Here, to be conclusive, or even strong, evidence must derive from correctly ascertained cases properly controlled and appropriately treated by statistical techniques. Where the effects of some substance are under evaluation, double-blind administration is advocated and replication of results. Subjective involvement in experiment is regarded as dangerous, and *ex post facto* interpretation is highly suspect. Thus, knowledge claims in this area are subject to clear and detailed norms of evaluation which are generally accepted and never challenged in themselves; sometimes it is suggested that they are inadequate and in need of supplementation, but they are not regarded as dispensable. These norms of evaluation constrain the relationship between presented concrete medical and scientific findings, and what is regarded as established or known in the field. They do not strongly constrain the publication of concrete findings themselves. Uncontrolled findings, and even experiments, are often published in the area, as are unusual and suggestive individual cases, which in themselves, provide no grounds for any sort of conclusion. Suppression of such material would hinder the actual process of research. (Consideration of the thalidomide affair should suffice to indicate the importance of placing no restraint upon merely suggestive findings.) Norms of evaluation operate when knowledge claims are made on the basis of concrete material. They guide individuals and groups in formulating what we know. In this particular area, they provide a clear, detailed and agreed guide.

By reference to these norms, it is possible to criticize or 'expose' knowledge claims. A significant proportion of the numerous popular and 'educational' writings on cannabis, for example, represents our knowledge of the toxic and 'harmful' effects of that substance in a way which cannot be justified by the norms. Such claims may be held to be scientifically unfounded, and, since the lay public trust accepted scientific and medical practice in the area, the claims can be effectively discredited in terms of that practice. Since also, no alternative system of interpretation exists in the area, and the popular literature in question professes respect for scientific and medical standards, the knowledge claims in that literature can meaningfully be treated as departures from normality and the departure may plausibly be attributed to social causation. There is a strong prima facie case for suggesting that social factors making for hostility to cannabis use have biased the popular presentation of our knowledge of its toxic and 'harmful' properties.

It is equally likely that these factors have biased some of the reviews and reports in the serious scientific and medical literature, although the effect lacks the comical extravagance of the statements to be found elsewhere—particularly in edifying pamphlets of American origin. None the less, the difference is merely one of degree, and it has to be borne in mind that the literature itself exhibits no clear demarcation between 'popular' and scientific; there is a broad and irreducible border area. By recourse to its own normal practice, scientific work can itself be criticized and, if one insists on putting it so, revealed as ideologically determined. This can certainly be done with some of the literature on the toxicology of cannabis and with some of the more wide ranging pharmacological and psycho-physiological material on the substance.

It is sometimes suggested that clear-cut statements of a scientific position upon socially sensitive areas cannot be hoped for, that scientists can never separate out the 'ideological' element from their work in such situations. Given its usual interpretation, this claim is a gross overgeneralization, which is just as well. Although the claim is often made in the well intentioned attempt to weaken the present ritualistic and all-embracing trust in science, it may provide a blanket excuse for sloppy assessment, or for those who indulge in wish fulfilment in their interpretation of material. In terms of currently accepted norms in the area, it is perfectly possible to produce a reasonably unambiguous statement of the state of scientific knowledge about the effects of cannabis. It has been possible at any time since the subject received serious interest. Such a statement would, of course, have to include our knowledge of what we did *not* know, and indicate the tentative nature of many hypotheses. But that is beside the point. The norms in the area are sufficiently strong for a best representation of the existing state of knowledge to exist. However old fashioned it may sound, the field of cannabis research is not best considered as irreducibly 'ideological'; it is an area where agreed scientific norms exist, and where, as a result, bad faith and concealed determinants can be identified. (For bibliographies of the literature on cannabis see Advisory Committee on Drug Dependence (1968), Kalant (1968), Waller and Denny (1971), Palmer (1972).)

Given that hostility to deviant groups and their ways of life is the main relevant social factor in the above example, it is perhaps worth pointing to the much larger amount of scientific investigation which has been concerned with the deleterious effects of socially accepted drug use; the connection between tobacco addiction and lung cancer, in particular, has been the subject of some splendid pieces of scientific work. (One might suggest that the most powerful, current (1973) science-based argument against cannabis use is that it is normally taken in conjunction with a pernicious carcinogen.) Here again, with all the past controversies over the issue, one can still claim that the evaluative norms relevant to the field were always sufficiently clear and strong for a reasonable consensus on the state of existing knowledge to be obtained. Here again one may reasonably talk of good work, and work involving bad faith or concealed determinants (one may also note that the latter were more difficult to avoid if the scientist concerned worked for a tobacco company!). Moreover, such an ideal consensus would have been sufficient for many practical purposes, even in the late 1950s. The arguments advanced at that time to the effect that smoking was not established as a cause of lung cancer may perhaps be held to have lain within the permissible range of scientific opinion; none the less a legend stating that 'smoking is correlated with the incidence of lung cancer' could have been printed on all cigarette packets. This would certainly have had to be counted as established knowledge at the time, and it could hardly have been less effective as a warning than the euphemism currently displayed in Britain by order of the chief beneficiary of tobacco trafficking.[8]

IV

Where normal practice exists, social influences may be identified which cause deviations from that practice, or the natural 'and so on' pathways we would expect to follow from the practice. On occasion, causal explanation of this kind may readily be employed in criticism. It may indicate that beliefs are being advocated in bad faith, or that an unacknowledged and illegitimate factor has partially determined scientific work.

This kind of causal analysis goes some way towards explaining how social factors may influence the content of scientific knowledge, but there are many circumstances where it cannot be applied. Where systems of normal practice are created, or extended along unprecedented lines, or where one of a number of permissible moves is chosen in preference to others, different kinds of explanation are needed.

In these cases no baselines exist from which to erect causal explanations, no standards with which to define deviance and abnormality. Yet there is every reason to assume that the kind of factors which produce departures from normal practice may also be involved in its creation and maintenance. Unacknowledged social determinants must presumably influence the latter processes as

well as the former. Beliefs which are taken for granted within
some collectivity merit special treatment in some ways, but their
creation and institutionalization cannot arbitrarily be set outside
the scope of causal explanation.[9]

In fact, the main difficulty involved in extending the analysis is
a technical one. It is, in general, easy for investigators to agree when
a departure from normality has occurred, and in what respects a
piece of work differs from normal expectation. To be sure, they have
to be themselves proficient within the system of normal practice in
order to understand what counts as departure from it, but given
this proficiency the task rarely presents practical difficulties. Thus,
when illegitimate or unacknowledged causes are cited in this context,
it is to explain clearly and unproblematically identified effects—
differences between actual cultural products and the form they
should 'ideally' have taken. With more fundamental, 'creative' types
of innovation this is not the case. A much greater demand is placed
upon the empathetic capabilities of investigators, and any conclusions they may produce are subject to serious and irremovable
uncertainties.

The construction, acceptance and evaluation of such innovations
will take place upon lines lacking clear precedent. Actors themselves will give accounts of these processes involving only legitimate
elements. Innovations will be represented as responses to accepted
problems or puzzles which draw none of their plausibility from
impermissible considerations. If the complicity of unacknowledged,
illegitimate causes in these processes is to be suggested, it is first of
all necessary to establish the insufficiency of the accounts of the
actors themselves. The investigator can only hope to do this to
his own satisfaction through empathy. Putting himself in the
innovator's place, he must bear in mind his cultural resources and
the knowledge he initially accepts or would admit to accepting; he
must then examine the problem which is allegedly being tackled and
the process of constructing or selecting a solution to it, according
to the actor's account; he must ask whether the solution makes
sense given the context, and the background resources and assumptions of the actors, and whether it seems the most attractive or
plausible solution. If the investigator feels that the actors' account
does not make sense, he may try imaginatively adjusting the situation with which he empathizes until the innovative process makes
sense or appears 'reasonable'. In this way unacknowledged causes

may be brought to light. A theory of inheritance, which appears arbitrary and unappealing as an attempt to fit the facts it professes to uphold, may seem well conceived and aesthetically attractive, when considered as a response to the problem of justifying a hierarchy, or mode of discrimination. A new taxonomy of human characteristics may appear contorted and *ad hoc* when viewed from the perspective offered by actors themselves, but it may appear well organized and even inevitable if some additional rule, like 'whitey must always come first', is added to the set of constraints surrounding the innovation.

There is no need to stress the difficulty and unreliability of such investigations. It is impossible to be sure that the appropriate background of culture and knowledge is accurately known, and it is impossible to be sure that the investigator has been able to set aside irrelevant aspects of his own knowledge in judging the appeal of an innovation. Moreover the whole process is irredeemably subjective. The relative attractiveness of an innovation has to be assessed intuitively. It cannot be done in terms of rules or principles—even those professed by actors themselves. With unprecedented, fundamental innovations the principles and standards advanced in justification are part of what needs to be understood; one has to ask how far they would naturally carry weight with the actors in question. The use of empathy is the only way we presently possess of investigating whether the factors cited by an actor with a given background would in fact suffice to generate a natural propensity for him to construct or accept an unprecedented innovation.

For a concrete example, we may turn to Paul Forman's work again (1971). He tentatively postulates a correlation between the political attitudes of physicists during the Weimar period and their views on the role of causality in physical change. In a period when a repudiation of causality represented an accommodation to the general intellectual milieu, it tended to be conservative and reactionary physicists who held out against the trend, whereas those who were relatively more 'progressive' were more likely to espouse acausality. Views about the place of causality in physics can be held to have been of real, practical relevance, since they featured in the evaluation of the new quantum theory and in controversies concerning its interpretation and significance. Nor can the possibility that the construction of the theory involved prior acausal assumptions, or even that it was in some ways a response to the problem of improving the image of physics, be automatically dismissed. Thus, here is a case where an unacknowledged factor may have been involved in the generation and evaluation of fundamental, highly creative, pieces of physics. And for many actors, at least, the unacknowledged factor would have been an illegitimate one. (Forman's fascinating quotations preclude the stronger generalization which I would otherwise have confidently made !)

Further study would be necessary to check whether this factor was in fact involved, and in what way it was involved. Were there legitimate indications of acausality arising within physics, which failed to register only with those few reactionaries whose determinism was externally sustained? Or did illegitimate social influences result in accepted physical knowledge, with its deterministic character, being set aside by those who developed the new physics? Or would an investigator who immersed himself in the cultural resources and accepted knowledge of the German physics, but remained in studied ignorance of the socio-political context, have found himself unable to choose sides in the relevant controversies? Were acknowledged factors underdetermining the situation?

Clearly, an answer to these questions has to come via a deep understanding of the contemporary physics, an enormously demanding requirement, even for someone with a modern training in the subject. Moreover, an answer cannot be obtained by considering what was known at the time, and then looking at the opposed arguments and seeing which were 'best' according to some set of rules. Actors themselves were doing this; it was part of the actual debate, but it did not settle it. The different attitudes to the same arguments evinced by different sides in the controversy have to be explained by something other than the arguments themselves. Nor is it a matter of going 'deeper', to more basic levels of judgment;[10] one may wonder where 'deeper' is in this debate. What has to be settled for is an intuitive assessment of the natural appeal of different positions, given different hypotheses about the determinants of actors' judgments.

Thus, it is possible to search for unacknowledged, concealed or illegitimate determinants of unprecedented scientific change without assuming that such factors are causing diversion from 'the truth', or, necessarily, any other inadequacies in the resulting knowledge. Unacknowledged social factors may partially determine such changes, just as they may partially determine departures from normal practice; it is just that with unprecedented changes it is very much more difficult to establish the determination. In both cases, the causal story told may be much the same as that which would stem from existing conceptions of ideology as distorted thought (the particular concept of ideology). Unconscious social and political purposes or assumptions may be invoked in a similar way. The difference is that the present approach avoids the need for sweeping assumptions about 'reality' or 'rationality', and does not insist upon conflating explanation and evaluation. Simply as an approach to the causal explanation of beliefs, it comes very close to the views of Engels (1893):

> Ideology is a process accomplished by the so-called thinker consciously indeed but with a false consciousness. The real motives impelling him remain unknown to him, otherwise it would not be an ideological process at all. Hence he imagines false or apparent motives. Because it is a process of thought he derives its form as well as its content from pure thought, either his own or that of his predecessors. He works with mere thought material, which he accepts without examination as the product of thought, and does not investigate further for a more remote source independent of thought; indeed this is a matter of course to him, because, as all action is *mediated* by thought, it appears to him to be ultimately based upon thought.

The present discussion differs from Engels's mainly with respect to the nature of non-ideological thought. A small point is that Engels regards the generation of ideology as an unconscious process, whereas, here, unacknowledged determinants and motivations have been grouped together whether they are discerned by the consciousness or not. There is surely a continuum between influences and objectives which are deliberately concealed from an audience, and those which are not discerned by participant actors themselves. We can identify its extremes easily enough: beliefs may be developed to serve concealed purposes with full self-consciousness, or they may be produced entirely without reflection whilst still being, like facial expressions, determined responses to functional requirements. Intermediate states remain ill conceptualized, although they clearly exist, and an extensive repertoire of terms such as hypocrisy, self-deception, half-awareness, and so on, is available to describe them.

There is no reason to believe that concealed social determinants have been largely eliminated from the production of natural knowledge. Indeed, theories and models of interpretation bearing upon human nature in the broadest sense, are always deservedly suspect of these influences (as are claims that they are ideological!). The probity of such theories is always worth vetting, whether or not they are professed to be, or regarded as, scientific. Those advanced in the recent past, but which none the less can be studied with the benefit of changed perspectives, clearly reveal such determination, and one cannot be sure that the situation is qualitatively different today.

Enough has already been said to indicate that concrete illustrations here would have to be developed at prohibitive length to carry conviction. Two such examples will, however, be mentioned. If one considers the theories of human heredity, evolution and eugenics which grew in Britain from the time of Galton until, say, 1914, it is difficult to understand them as nothing but attempts to describe and predict phenomena, or to apply a biological theory in a new area. Actors' accounts of their own 'scientific' activities fail to convince in some respects. The taken for granted assumptions which guided work do not appear natural in the light of accepted knowledge or legitimate aesthetic considerations; comparisons of different social classes are curiously confident and uniform, given how under-determined they are by the indications of the situation. By attributing some significance to unacknowledged functions, the same theories become more intelligible, naturally appealing, and, one might even loosely say, logical. This is the case, for example, if one holds that the theories were, in part, developed as reassuring fables for members of a declining social class.[11] Similarly, early eugenic calculations and prescriptions may, in many cases, prove more intelligible as responses to the practical problem of eliminating the inconvenience or 'threat' of the London destitute.[12] Since these unacknowledged functions, besides making sense of the theoretical innovations, help to account for the social distribution of their credibility, and reflect the every-day (if formally irrelevant) preoccupations of eugenists and social Darwinists, there is good evidence for their causal role.

The 'scientific' classification and explanation of racial differences provides the second, related, example. If this is considered, for example in the USA throughout the course of the nineteenth century (Stanton (1960), Haller (1971)), it is again apparent that unacknowledged factors must be involved. The attempts of some writers to relate pallor to superiority *in every conceivable respect*, generate too much strain, even within the modes of thought of the contemporary milieu; whereas the way these 'scientific' arguments are persistently related to questions arising from slavery, imperialism, and the politics of disfranchisement makes the identification of concealed determinants no difficult task.

On the other hand, it is by no means clear that, in the absence of these determinants, racial theories would have been *fundamentally different*. Given the cultural resources and accepted knowledge of the times, investigations carried out in meticulous conformity with actors' professed standards of scientific work would still have pointed to racial differences, and confirmed hereditarian explanations of them as the most plausible. Indeed, it could be argued that a small amount of such bona fide work does exist. In any case, claims that real racial differences were never more than superficial, or that the concept of race was a spurious construct corresponding to nothing tangible, lay quite beyond the cultural horizons of anyone in these times. It is incongruous to 'expose' the writings of the period simply as 'racist', since this set of conceptions fitted naturally and securely in the taken for granted world of the time.[13]

v

This raises the question of whether the preceding discussion has not been too limited. It has talked only of illegitimate or unacknowledged determination, but do we want to claim that science where everything is 'above board' has not been influenced by social factors? Surely, the foregoing has implied that science as a whole is influenced by the *Weltanschauung*; cannot it then be included within a theory of 'total' ideology, in the sense defined by Mannheim? The answer offered in the following accepts the first premise above, although it suggests that nothing is to be gained by talking of 'total ideology'. None the less, the measure of its agreement with many of the substantive points made in *Ideology and Utopia* (1936) should not be overlooked because of what is, in part, a terminological difference.

Let us start by schematically reviewing the kinds of socio-cultural determination to which scientific investigation is subject, and making as strong a case as possible for their importance. Imagine a scientist or group of scientists seeking to explain a puzzling area of experience without the resources of an established research tradition. Interest in the area might be explicable by immediate social factors, but that would be beside the point. What matters is that an explanation of the unfamiliar area is sought, and must be provided through some form of metaphorical redescription. For this to be initiated, some familiar set of cultural resources must be settled upon, and organized as a model. Clearly, at this stage, the grounds for adopting a particular model are not likely to be clear cut; none the less, however tentatively it were held, a model or metaphor of some kind would have to be adopted and used, otherwise the attempt at explanation could not proceed at all.

Model creation is like bricolage. The scientist must select from his repertoire of available cultural resources, just as *le primitif* selects bits and pieces of his culture to create myth. In modern differentiated societies, however, choice is not limited to the cultural detritus characteristically employed, according to Lévi-Strauss, by the primitive bricoleur. Organized, functioning systems of culture may prove more attractive to the scientist. Indeed, the repertoire of possibilities worthy of his practical consideration may contain no idle or functionless elements. Choice may have to be made from resources, all of which are already tied in to central aspects of social life. And it may be that any particular choice will inevitably generate a feedback effect tending to influence the performance of existing social functions. The use of a model by accredited scientists may increase its plausibility as a representation of reality; familiar beliefs may thereby find their credibility reinforced, and their potency as legitimations of particular modes of social organization or stratification. (This may occur however strongly scientists emphasize that the model is merely an 'as if' theory in the process of being tried out.) In general, however, it will be taboo to take these secondary social considerations into account when building or selecting a model.[14]

Typically, judgments of the *a priori* plausibility of possible models may legitimately depend upon aesthetic standards, subjective assessments of their practical possibilities, and references to the corpus of knowledge already generally accepted by scientists. Thus, there are two ways in which the initial selection or construction of a model, and its institutionalization, may be related to the social context. First, the stock of available cultural resources is a function of the milieu and the range of actors' experience within it. Second, what counts as a part of accepted knowledge or an accepted standard of judgment will again depend on the milieu, and may depend on actors' social roles, and the concerns and interests of the groups to which they belong. It is impossible to generalize about the importance of these latter specific factors; their influence is mediated by too many features of the particular contexts involved; it will, for example, vary according to the pattern of recruitment into the scientific field, and how far it is confined to particular groups or strata.

These sources of determination may continue to be significant as a research tradition gathers momentum. The metaphorical extension of models may be discussed very largely in the same terms as the initial generation of a model; so too may model replacement, although of course the internally developed standards and precedents of the research tradition will constrain the situation, narrow the range of plausible new cultural resources, and supplement and replace formerly accepted 'everyday' knowledge. Finally, in routine work, the general pattern of the culture will determine the flow of the 'and so on' effect. (As was mentioned in chapter 4, routine extension of the study of animals to the study of man may depend on the nature of the culturally defined boundary between the two, routine extensions of chemical theory may be channelled by general cultural distinctions between the living and the non-living.) Thus, scientific knowledge, for all the internal standards and procedures which become relevant to its growth, will never shake itself entirely free of the effects of the culture within which it arises.[15]

The arguments are unexceptionable; they do little more, after all, than recap themes discussed in earlier chapters. It must be acknowledged, in particular, that science always operates within a framework of existing cultural resources, and in that sense is contingent knowledge. But such contingency does not, in itself, justify the claim that science is ideologically determined and forms part of a 'total ideology'.

This last concept, which binds up the mode of determination of belief or knowledge with its nature, and carries inescapable derogatory implications, generated the tensions in Mannheim's sociology (1936). He equivocated between 'relationism' and belief in the possibility of completely valid knowledge because he could not fully reconcile the implications of his concept of total ideology with his faith in the potency of reason. The best he could do was to argue that some beliefs are less ideological than others, depending upon the social position of their holders. He was then able to move from demonstrating the favourable social circumstances of the *freischwebende Intelligenz* into granting him access to really valid knowledge —an unsatisfactory finale to a penetrating and courageous work. In all of this, of course, Mannheim had moved away from problems of sociological explanation. His concept of total ideology was a tool of his *epistemology*.

For the sociologist to use this concept, he must be prepared to conflate sociological explanation with epistemological judgments. Without arguing against Mannheim's epistemology as a whole, it can still be suggested that teasing apart sociological and epistemological considerations, at least in the first instance, produces useful clarifications. Similarly, it can be argued that to talk of all knowledge being ideologically determined may be misleading. The only use of this formulation is to remind us of the intimate and necessary connection between knowledge and society, and this can easily be done in other ways, which do not carry evaluative or epistemological overtones. Unlike the particular conception of ideological determination, which does distinguish a particular kind of social determination of belief (illegitimate determination), the general conception can do no work for the sociologist since it applies to all beliefs identically. Mannheim's exemption of mathematics and science from its ambit was misguided (cf. also D. Bloor, 1973b).

This is not said to discourage the critical appraisal of bona fide science, or, for that matter, to weaken criticisms by making them appear to be mere expressions of personal opinion. By pointing to acknowledged influences in the growth of science which we would no longer regard as legitimate today, it is, in practice, possible to call into question aspects of our present natural knowledge. In any case, the concrete sequence of cultural changes comprising the antecedents of a presently accepted body of knowledge may include moves which were illegitimate even when they were made. Thus, today's legitimate innovation may be being made on the basis of accepted knowledge which is partly the product of illegitimate causation in the past. Or scientists may be doing disinterested work in complete good faith, using models initially developed with illegitimate social purposes in mind.

The effects of particular social influences upon a body of knowledge are, however, likely to be damped over time. It is easy to see why this should be so if we think of scientists as possessors of a special set of intellectual tools. These may have been designed and constructed according to specifications which took account of purposes other than their own. They will, however, put them to their own purposes, and may well be led to adjust and adapt them to serve those purposes better. Such refashioned tools they will pass on to others.

When scientists participate in a research tradition, any secondary, social purposes which they might insinuate into their work will vary, especially over the long term. In a differentiated society, over time, the legitimate aims of recruits to a tradition will tend to produce coherent cultural change, whereas illegitimate idiosyncratic aims will tend to cancel out or interfere with each other. In the long term, the effects of particular illegitimate factors will tend to be smoothed out,[16] although it cannot be assumed that the overall effect of this class of determinants is bound to decline. New illegitimate determinants may start to influence a tradition of research. And, as critics of Western society as a whole would doubtless want to point out, some illegitimate social influences may have persisted over long periods without their effects being mitigated by countervailing tendencies.

Opinions are likely to differ as to the importance of such determinants. Perhaps they should not worry the scientist, who need not know how his tools were created, and who will automatically lessen what are, for him, their defects simply by doing his work as best he may. On the other hand, they may be thought important if a broader view is taken. In particular, if knowledge is regarded as an autonomous and direct determinant of social change (or its failure to materialize) then illegitimate influences in its development are likely to be regarded as highly significant and to be urgently sought out, because of their close connection with the practical credibility of knowledge.

Strangely, belief in the direct power of scientific ideas is becoming more and more common on the left. Increasingly, in this quarter, science is condemned as ideological and charged with buttressing the structure of capitalism by legitimating its institutions and patterns of exploitation. Moreover, it is held that abstract criticism of existing natural knowledge and the development of alternative ideas may, in itself, bring about social change.

In my view, the proponents of this position were unwise to stray quite so far from the tenets of their traditional materialism. Particular abstract legitimations and rationalizations of institutional arrangements, whether they appeal to science or not, do not greatly add to the stability of these arrangements; that stability will reflect the aims of different social groups, their boundaries, and the distribution of power between them. If scientific change should incidentally undermine the legitimation of some key institution, a new one may always be erected. If one aspect of nature does not make the institution necessary, another one will be invoked which does; and should nature prove altogether too unfriendly to the cause, there are, as Mary Douglas says (1970b), always God, time and money to fall back on instead. (In any case, nature never is too unfriendly, as the dentists in the USA who have refuted several thousand distinct practical objections to the fluoridation of drinking water may have realized by now.)

Similarly, if allegedly scientific knowledge is mobilized by intellectuals and used to attack the legitimations of institutions they seek to undermine, opposing pressures will be generated. Their own mythology will be attacked in turn, and that of their opponents will be elaborated, supplemented and more heavily defended. Such intellectual jousting can never result in any 'real' outcome, determined by the 'inherent worth' of the ideas involved and the positions defended, or by what 'science really says'. The most that may be produced by a battle of ideas in itself is a certain amount of linguistic differentiation and meaning change. Liberal pundits may feel called upon to strengthen the distinction between 'equality' and 'sameness', to sustain the legitimations of their egalitarianism; scientistic conservatives, rejoicing in the universality of human aggression, may be obliged to acknowledge that what they mean by aggression isn't quite the same as what everybody else means. The possibilities of such processes are infinite. (As we all now know, there are lies, errors and inoperative statements !)

Of course, in practice, the credibility of particular legitimations can be weakened. And intellectual jousting might be justified by the claim that if one side ceased to participate the other side might make some headway. This, however, is just the point; groups participating in social conflict are practically always proportionately represented in intellectual controversy according to their power. In general, there is no evidence that scientific knowledge can directly generate changes in our institutional arrangements so as to skew them out of correspondence with the social contingencies which they normally reflect. Whatever appertains in esoteric, scientific contexts, we may expect the nature of our key institutions to continue to be determined by other, let us say more basic, factors. And because of the processes touched upon here, so too will our everyday common sense knowledge.

Epilogue

The ontological and epistemological implications of the foregoing arguments have so far been set aside. Indeed, they have been studiously avoided since the issues they raise are so vexatious that they could have impeded the execution of the main task of the monograph. Since, however, they are not entirely irrelevant to the concerns of the practising sociologist, they are considered very briefly here apart from the main text.

It could well be claimed that logically there are no such implications. All that has been discussed is variability in belief and how beliefs are maintained or changed. Nothing necessarily follows from this about validity, about what we should hold to be true, or what is the best way of evaluating knowledge claims. Philosophers and laymen may continue to evaluate beliefs just as they did before. Ontologies and theories of knowledge may be constructed and set on top of the present discussion, not connected to it in any way but simply, as it were, balancing. Philosophers may insist upon a complete separation of questions of belief and questions of knowledge.

Such a distinction cannot be argued against. None the less, it does threaten to emasculate philosophy, since it makes theories of knowledge appear arbitrary and dogmatic, and it tends to result in their being drained of function and left idle and inoperative alongside wide ranging and potent theories of belief. This is what happens in Pierce's philosophy (cf. the discussion in Ayer (1968)).

Accordingly, it might be thought better to admit that theories of belief suggest theories of knowledge, even though they do not logically imply them, and that such suggestions must be taken seriously. Given this, it becomes important to ask with which ontological and epistemological positions the present discussion of belief has the most natural affinity.

There are two kinds of possible answer here. One is obtained by asking what assumptions and what kinds of taken for granted knowledge are built into the perspective of the book itself. This perspective has been presented as a characteristically scientific one, and its credibility has been argued for by reference to natural scientific knowledge. Thus, it could be said that a materialistic or naturalistic ontology has been assumed and advocated. Similarly with epistemology, the implication has been that knowledge of how we know may be acquired by unselfconscious scientific or 'empirical' study, and that there should be no hermetically sealed off, autonomous area of 'conceptual' philosophical inquiry lying 'under' or 'beside' this.

On the other hand, nothing in this volume *justifies* the above position. This leads to the second kind of answer. In arguing that all belief systems must be treated symmetrically for purposes of sociological explanation, many traditional ways of justifying belief as knowledge were incidentally undermined. It transpired that one perspective can only be shown to be preferable to another in expedient terms, which means that the perspective adopted in this volume is itself a contingent one. Thus, the epistemological message of the work could be said to be sceptical, or relativistic.[1] It is sceptical since it suggests that no arguments will ever be available which could establish a particular epistemology or ontology as ultimately correct. It is relativistic because it suggests that belief systems cannot be objectively ranked in terms of their proximity to reality or their rationality. This is not to say that practical choices between belief systems are at all difficult to make, or that I myself am not clear as to my own preferences. It is merely that the extent to which such preferences can be justified, or made compelling to others, is limited.

The account of knowledge offered here must accordingly claim no special status for itself; it must be fully reflexive. It has been claimed that knowledge grows through the development and extension of models and metaphors, that the process can be understood deterministically, and that claims to validity throughout remain contingent, since any 'context of justification' must always rest upon negotiated conventions and shared exemplars. It follows that all this must be the case for the present knowledge claims and the way they have been developed.

With regard to the first point there is no difficulty; no attempt has been made to conceal the metaphors upon which the argument depends, or to suggest that what is being advocated follows logically from some unproblematic starting point.

Neither does the second point present any problems; a deterministic account of the creation of the arguments presented here is perfectly possible and acceptable. Even if that account cited 'external' social factors, this need not influence the evaluation of the knowledge thereby explained.

It is indeed plausible to represent this work as very much the product of its time. Until recently, it has been difficult to write of scientific knowledge without either seeking to justify it or assuming it to be justified. In the last two decades, however, the study of natural science has undergone significant and parallel changes in a number of academic disciplines. In philosophy, traditional forms of empiricism and the idea of a neutral observation language are coming under attack, together with the orthodox deductivist accounts of science. Historians of science are tending to discard current knowledge as a yardstick for the evaluation of earlier work, and are finding it possible to proceed in their field without deploying external standards of 'truth' or 'rationality'. In sociology, the institution of science is no longer held to maintain general norms of 'scientific method', nor are autonomist theories assumed in describing its relationship to the wider society. In all disciplines, there is a trend away from regarding science as the earthly embodiment of some Platonic universal; instead it is being treated more and more as a human activity like any other, or as a sub-culture routinely interacting with other areas of society. At the same time a number of academics have become actively hostile to science; it has become the subject of a rapidly increasing critical literature. This covers a wide range of positions, from those which express highly specific fears and objections, to the kind of overall condemnation found in the work of Marcuse and the Frankfurt School.

These changes might be regarded as independent developments, and, certainly, plausible 'internal' accounts can be given of their rising influence. But it seems unlikely that such piecemeal accounts should give a complete answer, especially when it is noted that many of the points now used to illustrate these recent analyses have been recognized for a long time, but have been given a different significance in the past. We might suggest that social factors have caused the resources of academic traditions to be deployed in different ways at different times.[2]

Perhaps changes in the general image of science have influenced its academic study. There can be little doubt that this image is far less favourable than it was; scientists themselves have recognized this, indeed it may be that some of them have been too sensitive to the change.[3] There can also be little doubt that social factors must be invoked to explain the change, although it is more difficult to be sure what the precise explanation might be. One possibility is that real changes in the institutional base of science lie at the root of the matter. Since its purchase by government, industry and the military, it has become impossible to combine hostility to existing major institutions, or to capitalism as a whole, with an entirely positive evaluation of science. A minority opposed to science has thereby almost automatically been generated, and this may suffice to explain the change in question.[4]

Whether or not this is so need not matter here. The point is that 'external' social factors may well have influenced academic approaches to science and hence may to some extent make intelligible the views expressed here. This need make no difference in evaluating the claims which are made. Any merits these might have when they are evaluated in a given way, will generally remain after their history has been understood.

It is the third element of reflexivity which is likely to be found the most troublesome. Why, it will be said, if the preceding account makes no claims to being the best account we have in a fully objective sense, should anybody accord it credibility? This, of course, is the classic argument against relativism in a slightly different guise.[5] The answer is easily given; this whole volume is crammed with proffered reasons why its main tenets should be accepted; its justification lies within itself.

The point is that this can only hope to count as a justification to those within particular forms of culture. What the range of forms might be I am far from sure; hopefully what has been said will carry weight among some of those engaged in sociological activity and related fields. Perhaps it is sufficiently congruent with the common sense of our general culture to be thought plausible or even compelling over a wider field. But just as there is always an uncomfortable gap between any large integer and infinity, so will there always be a gap between justification according to particular conventions, and justification in an unqualified sense.

If one insists on talking of justification in this latter way, then the gap thus opened by one's imagination can be crossed by no set of beliefs whatever. Whether this is of any epistemological significance depends on one's view of epistemology. But it is certainly significant in a slightly different way. It solves what have been regarded as the epistemological problems of the sociology of knowledge.

1 THE DIVERSITY OF BELIEFS ABOUT NATURE AND
THE PROBLEM OF EXPLAINING IT

1   In this connection, it is useful to regard acceptable forms of
    functional explanation as merely inverted causal explanations;
    cf. Gellner (1962).

2   Fortunately, it does not much matter for present purposes how
    philosophers would deal with such an *a priori* objection. Perhaps
    some would simply accept a naturalistic definition of truth, even
    though this might dangerously blur their distinction between
    epistemology and psychology. Others might try to show that their
    critic was misusing the word 'truth' or the expression 'truth about
    the world'. In the last resort a sociologist might be sent for to
    examine the critic's cultural background or religious views. We
    might imagine him, at the last, being carried off to an asylum
    raving about the distorting effect of the Western materialistic way
    of life upon Western epistemology!

3   I shall pass over the problem of whether 'the same' belief can be
    expressed in different ways or in the context of different languages.

4   I would not seek to argue that the alternative approach, *a priorism*,
    has nothing to offer. On the contrary, a naturalistic reading of Kant
    is extremely suggestive, and indicates an approach to the problem of
    knowledge which cannot be neglected or superseded.

    But Kant has been relativized, and his followers produced a whole
    range of *a prioristic* theories between which it was impossible to
    choose, and all of which were arbitrarily grounded. At present, we
    cannot use a Kantian scheme to discriminate classes of belief for a
    programme such as that described in this chapter.

5   From some points of view, of course, this statement would be
    illegitimate. But I shall continue to develop a smugly materialistic
    ideal-type.

6   Anthropological studies have never revealed the existence of

counter-inductive inference in any culture. Some apparently counter-inductive moves are best understood as insufficiently careful induction; the 'gambler's fallacy' is an example. The gambler's pattern of inference may be compared with that of a peasant who, every day that the monsoon does not arrive, becomes the more convinced that it will arrive the next day.

7 One may induce cautiously or recklessly. The beliefs induced may be provisionally or dogmatically held. Contradictory conclusions may be induced from different sets of facts. How does one narrow possibilities down to one naturally reasonable set of beliefs without being arbitrary?

8 And very good psychological theories these are too! To see how these theoretical terms assist the development of a scientific account of optical illusions and 'visual pathology', and, much more important, of the process of visual perception as a whole, see Gregory (1966).

9 Many philosophers, with interests almost entirely centred on choice between theories, take the origin of potential theories far too much for granted; they assume that ideas grow on trees. In fact theory production is a difficult and highly constrained process; it is quite extraordinarily difficult to have a new idea, let alone a promising, potentially effective one. And the capacity to produce particular kinds of new idea is strongly related to cultural background, as well as to 'innate gifts'.

Popper, with his claim that one can always, whenever desired, break out of the constraints of any framework of beliefs and ideas, is one of the philosophers who takes least account of the sources of theories. In the terms of his early work (1934), one might say that he replaces the bucket theory of the mind with a tap theory!

10 Cf. the discussion in Popper (1934, section 23). The best accounts of the issues touched upon in the following are in Hesse (1970a) and Scheffler (1967). Other interesting discussions are to be found in Feyerabend (1958) and Kuhn (1970).

11 We may thereby symbolize the fact that observation languages, like other languages, are created, sustained and modified in interaction processes by negotiation in the sociological sense.

2 THE SOCIOLOGIST AND THE CONCEPT OF RATIONALITY

1 One of the ways in which the force of the arguments of the preceding chapter might be exaggerated is by taking them to imply that rational comparison of scientific theories is no longer possible. This

does not follow, or at least it would only follow from extremely demanding definitions of 'rational comparison'.

Hesse (1970a) quotes a delightful example, taken from Feyerabend, of Aristotle and Anaximenes profitably comparing their theories of motion, even though they used different observation languages.

2 Some philosophers tried to assign initial probabilities on the basis of a principle of indifference, but this proved unsatisfactory. The current trend is to use *what is presently accepted* as the source of these probabilities. This fits very well with the stress in this volume on the necessary culturally given component in science. For a brief discussion of other ways of treating these initial probabilities see Salmon (1970).

3 I shall argue later that inductive models of natural rationality will never be of assistance to sociologists seeking to discriminate different kinds of belief. This does not, however, imply criticism of the models themselves. On the contrary, my own feeling is that they could eventually prove of great interest, although as (psychological) models of elements of thinking, not (philosophical) models for justification and validation. It is hard to see why such models are specifically related to science. The work of, for example, Carnap and Hesse could just as well be related to everyday inference in different human cultures, or even to the thought of children. Hesse's work on induction, in particular, almost begs to be treated as speculative psychology.

4 Is this lack of relevance inevitable, or a mere accident, something which may well change in the future? This depends on one's theory of what general constraints underlie thought and action, and whether one accepts the possibility of psychological or even physiological models of their general structure. The obfuscations of linguistic philosophy have tended to remove problems of induction, deduction and the categories of thought from the sphere of relevance of contingent scientific investigation (cf. Strawson, 1952). The connection needs to be reasserted; the circularity of such work is not harmful.

For my own part I would opine that it is possible to give a determinist account of the non-existence of counter-inductive thinking, and I would look to speculative psychology and models produced in related work for my support. It might be said that we are always free to think counter-inductively if we so wish. The reply is that we are not free to *believe* on a counter-inductive basis. We might inversely induce the benefits of poison but our actions would betray us when offered some. It makes sense to regard ourselves as inducing devices.

5   Simplicity is generally a very conservative rationality criterion. On most definitions, it has to be estimated by application of the categories of the estimator to an account or theory. Hence theories involving new categories appear complex, whereas, *ex post facto*, they come to be seen as simpler than their predecessors.
  Popper's definition of simplicity, which links it to *falsifiability*, is a different matter.

6   A belief system which specified the conditions of its own abandonment could, perhaps, be accounted falsifiable 'by inspection'. Unfortunately, no institutionalized belief systems are of this form, although a few philosophers profess such systems.

7   That many conceptions of rationality are the subject of philosophical controversy is surely evidence for their conventional nature.

8   'Conventionalism' within the quote refers, of course, to an approach within the philosophy of science which stresses the simplicity rather than the falsifiability of scientific theories. Popper believed that theories could be endorsed as false; conventionalists regarded them as neither true nor false.

9   The erection of conventions of rationality creates an interesting dilemma (cf. McMullin (1970), Bloor (1971)). A convention may be erected and used to define rational belief and action, in science, as elsewhere. Or it may be treated as a description of good scientific practice, and judged by how well accepted scientific work conforms to it. Philosophers of science usually present themselves as concerned with the justification of scientific knowledge, and not with the description of science as it exists. They suggest conventions of the first kind in the process of justifying knowledge. Thus, one should expect philosophers to take a courageous, critical role, putting the claims of science to the test. In practice, the literature reveals that philosophers are almost universally pusillanimous in this regard. They recognize that accepted science provides the test for their conventions rather than vice versa. And, instead of submitting their conventions to such a test, they tend selectively to draw from current science those bits and pieces which conform with their conventions, allegedly to provide typical illustrations of their operation. As a result, the notion that general standards of method or evaluation permeate all of accepted science tends illegitimately to be perpetuated. Philosophers have been insufficiently conscientious in preventing their general *prescriptions* from being taken as *descriptions* of science. And they have thereby helped to sustain unwarranted and misleading conceptions of science and rationality within the social sciences.

10   For an interesting alternative way of presenting and justifying
     Lukes's rationality criteria, cf. Hollis (1967).
11   Lukes does make the point that *any* belief can be causally instilled
     or sustained. But with a determinism which treats all beliefs
     identically sociology need take no interest in validity, whereas Lukes
     clearly regards validity as of major sociological importance. His
     concrete examples make clear that special causes of irrationality
     should be identified to account for beliefs which are invalid or
     illogical. Perhaps we could say that, for Lukes, irrationally held
     beliefs are unstable in the absence of special sustaining causes,
     whereas rationally held ones are not.
12   There is probably no need to call attention to the relevance of
     Wittgenstein's later work in this general context (Wittgenstein
     (1953, 1964)).
13   That Nuer do not employ the category 'bird' but a category
     rendered by anthropologists as 'bird', merely reinforces the import of
     the present argument.
14   Perhaps the key to the way Lukes's argument gets out of hand lies
     in the acknowledged influence of linguistic philosophy upon its
     development. This might very naturally connect the ideas of one
     reality and one observation language, and obscure their difference.
     Once this equation is made, belief in one reality opens the flood-gates
     to inductivism. Hesse (1970a) provides abundant illustration of the
     value of making a radical distinction between language and reality;
     let us agree that we all live in 'the same world' without taking this
     as a statement about language.
        The pitfalls of arguments based on linguistic necessity are even
     more apparent in Hollis's (1967) development of Lukes's ideas. He
     tends to assume that to understand a belief system or way of life
     it must be translated into one's own language, i.e. into English. He
     ignores the way belief systems and ways of life are manifestly learnt
     and reflected upon without any translation process at all.
15   There are, of course, other ways in which this can be interpreted.
     The present discussion, however, will remain linked to a naturalistic
     conception of the constraints of logic. The difficulties of reified or
     Platonic conceptions of logic have been brilliantly expounded by
     Wittgenstein (1953, 1964).
16   Would we want to diagnose irrationally held beliefs where their
     holder could not do this?
17   We could say that our understanding of beliefs as a whole must be
     based upon a functional metaphor and not a pictorial one.
     Wittgenstein's work helps us to make this change. But although the
     pictorial metaphor and the correspondence theory of truth are no

longer defended, their implicit influence remains, as in Lukes's work.

18 Thus, according to Evans-Pritchard (1937) Azande believe that a man may be proved a witch, that witchcraft is inherited through the male line, but that the other members of a witch's clan are not necessarily witches. When Evans-Pritchard claimed that if witch substance was inherited through the male line all of a witch's clan were necessarily witches, the Zande saw 'the sense of this argument' but did not accept its conclusions. They had 'no theoretical interest in the subject' and situations wherein they expressed their belief in witchcraft did not 'force the problem upon them'. (Had activities forced the problem upon them, perhaps Azande would have distinguished 'manifest' and 'latent' witches! This simple strategy would have removed the inconsistency without involving any significant change in belief.)

19 Hopefully the reader will not equate socialization and conditioning, or imagine a passive, zombie-like actor being filled with a repertoire of verbal responses. My own preferences are for theories which give a much more positive role to the actor being socialized, as in symbolic-interactionist and ethnomethodological accounts, but I shall press no particular point of view here.

20 This does not mean, of course, that actors' professions only should be studied, let alone that the sociologist should believe everything actors tell him! Laughter and tears may provide more significant and reliable indications of meaning that professed utterances.

21 A sociological theory which has to make a special exemption of a particular institution or sub-culture, like, for example, natural science, deserves to be treated with the greatest suspicion. This was, unfortunately, the case with Mannheim's work, although recently D. Bloor (1973b) has shown that Mannheim needlessly exempted mathematics and science from his theory of knowledge.

3 THE CULTURE OF THE NATURAL SCIENCES

1 Popper did not regard his conventions as embodied in the practice of the whole of science. He presented them prescriptively. He did, however, consider them to be followed by the best or most successful pieces of research.

2 It has been argued that this characteristic of scientific knowledge is increasingly permeating the wider society, 'rationalizing' its institutions and constituting a major impetus to secularization. In my view this is a false picture; it produces the intractable problem of why such a characteristic should initially develop within 'science',

and it ignores evidence that a parallel independent change occurred in culture as a whole as societies took on a 'modern' form.

It seems much more plausible to argue that the differentiation and industrialization of modern societies produced important shifts in the overall character of their knowledge. Anthropomorphism and teleology are modes of communication which rest on shared conceptions of value and legitimate order. Such modes become unstable in differentiated societies, with their institutionalized conflicts between different bases of power, and their diverse yet co-existing moral codes. Universally meaningful communication necessarily becomes impersonal in such a context. And natural knowledge, as an institutional form within a differentiating society, becomes impersonal too. (For comparisons of science with the natural knowledge of undifferentiated societies cf. Durkheim (1912), Lévi-Strauss (1966), Douglas (1966, 1970a), Horton (1967), Barnes (1973).)

3 Experimentation has, of course, played a very important role in the development of natural science; its importance is none the less overrated, even within the 'experimental' sciences. Cf. Kuhn (1962), Koyré (1968), Fisher (1936).

4 Thus, observation that the XYY chromosome complement tended to be associated with above average adult height has led overwhelmingly to a concentration upon tall members of the population by those seeking to understand its incidence and effects. Any number of similar examples could be cited.

5 Cf. the development by philosophers of the initial hypothesis that falsification plays an essential methodological role in good science.

6 Feyerabend (1970) has advocated a methodological convention untouched by the above arguments: it is *anarchy!* Note that this, unusually for a philosophical prescription, is a recommendation which no single individual can follow. Feyerabend is advocating a *social* arrangement. Those philosophers who enjoy telling scientists what they ought to be doing could well follow in this direction. To advocate that a specialty investigate a probable hypothesis with 70 per cent of its manpower, and a less probable one with 30 per cent, would make a change from individualistic conceptions of what is the most rational thing to do !

7 Metaphor will be considered here only in so far as it relates to the practical concerns of this volume. A general theory of metaphor is, however, of crucial importance to all studies of culture, and the reader is referred to Black (1962), Schon (1963) and especially Hesse (1963, 1964, 1970b) for expositions of the view of metaphor which is being assumed here.

8   Ordinary language philosophy is particularly prone to insist that common sense knowledge needs no further supplementation. On this basis D. Bloor has recently argued that it is an anti-scientific philosophy (1973a).

9   For a readable account of the reception of Dalton's theory cf. Nash (1948). Thackray (1966) and Nash (1956) relate the origin of the theory to its reception and acceptance. For later development of the theory and criticisms thereof see Knight (1967, 1968).

10   Stress upon scientific knowledge as practical or craft knowledge is important in the work of Polanyi (1958). Cf. also Ravetz (1971).

11   We may say that the sociologist metaphorically redescribes theoretical accounts as metaphorical redescription. This is a necessary and satisfying reflexivity.

12   A successful model in science frequently moves from the status of an 'as if' theory to a 'real description'. From here it may develop into a cosmology, before eventual disintegration into a mass of techniques and procedures, wherein what were key theoretical conceptions become mere operators, the ontological status of which is scarcely given a thought (cf. force, temperature, frequency).

13   It might be suggested that as scientific activity is institutionalized, and the maximal utilization of skills and techniques becomes an expectation within a scientific role, pressure is automatically put upon constraining positivistic standards.

On the other hand, when a controversy between two scientific theories becomes intense there is often a tendency for the language of positivism to be employed in attacking the other side, the implication being that the theory defended is closer to 'pure description'. As one side starts to 'lose' the controversy its polemic may become increasingly positivistic and critical, and embody less and less concrete work of its own, since positivism affords an impregnable position from which to snipe at the enemy (cf. Cantor, forthcoming, Dolby, forthcoming). Unfortunately those who do the sniping gain little credit for any value it has. Armstrong, for example, criticized the ionic theory from the start for treating solutions in a way which exaggerated the role of the solute and neglected the role of the solvent. Later modifications of the ionic theory took account of this, implicitly acknowledging he was right. But from the point of view of recognition Armstrong had been right in the wrong way (Dolby, forthcoming).

14   Some chemical procedures suggested by the atomistic viewpoint were very widely accepted when translated into a positivistic form. Once a theory has suggested a relationship, and this is 'discovered', it is

always possible to translate it back again into a 'mere regularity' or 'generalization'.

15 But cf. section V below. This change of meaning parallels the more frequently discussed case of the laws of classical mechanics, which imperceptibly changed from claims about how forces did in fact influence bodies, into schemata for discourse about the motion of bodies.

16 Cf. the concluding remarks in Hesse (1970a).

17 The term 'Daltonian' serves to emphasize the distinction of his atomic model from earlier ones which could not be so readily bound into chemical practice. Even as it was being accepted the model was changing, so that the preceding account cannot be taken as referring to the reception of Dalton's actual postulates. The atoms of twentieth-century chemistry differed from Dalton's in practically every property which he postulated that they possessed !

18 Perhaps Durkheim (1912) should also be credited with doing so.

19 For further elucidation of the relevance of such an insight to the problems of anthropology cf. Horton (1967) and Douglas (1970a).

20 Philosophers often try to assign probabilities to scientific beliefs in attempts to rationalize or provisionally justify them. This can be criticized as a misguided attempt to convert *uncertainty* into *risk*. For a discussion of this distinction, and its neglect, in a different but related context, cf. Schon (1966).

21 Often, in science, there is no hard and fast way of distinguishing model replacement from model development or adjustment. An alteration to a model may be perceived as so large that, essentially, it destroys the 'essence' of the former way of looking at things. Thus Bohr's model of the atom is never referred to as 'merely' an extension of Rutherford's. Other factors making it difficult to distinguish the replacement and development of models are indicated in Brush's (1970) study of the wave theory of heat.

22 Again, it is difficult to be critical of the scientist for having an eye for future promise. Regarding theories as models in a state of development brings out the point well. We might parody it by noting that it is better to use a horse and cart than a car without the sparking plugs. One never knows how additions might improve a model !

23 Thus, stock arguments against, *inter alia*, 'Bayesian' statistics, 'introspective psychology', 'valence-bond theory' and 'group selection' have been accepted by cohort after cohort of students with no more reflection than that with which they came to believe in the seven colours of the spectrum in secondary school.

24 This point, that scientific culture always overlays previous

socialization and indeed is always transmitted with the aid of the resources of previous socialization, will be discussed in more detail later. For the moment we may note that science still intrudes little into the culture of the kindergarten or primary school.

25 Ironically, it is in modern teaching programmes, such as the Nuffield schemes in British schools, that this exploitation of experimentation is strongest. These programmes have stressed the heuristic element in science and have, in part, represented a reaction against dogmatic, authoritarian methods of teaching. Yet, they face the same problems of cultural transmission as any other system of teaching. The credibility lost by refusal to exploit to the hilt the authoritative position of the school teacher has been regained, to an extent, by the sheer artistry with which experimental programmes have been designed. Of course, key models, concepts and procedures must still be imparted. Where this is not done authoritatively, by practical book instructions, or by teacher's towering figure at the blackboard, it is done subtly by teacher at the child's elbow offering the little touch of insight needed to make sense of everything.

26 Those sympathetic to the conceptions of meaning advocated in Wittgenstein's *Philosophical Investigations* (1953) will find nothing strange in this.

27 In informal conversation with a physics professor current forms of scientific training were justified to me as follows. The first degree is dogmatic, 'concerned with getting across basic essentials', with equipping the scientist with the tools of his trade. Then, in the second degree there is time for reflection, for thought and criticism, for getting on top of one's training and improving on it. The result is a true education, not just a training. (No mention was made of the fact that the majority of students left after their first degree.)

28 It is tempting to suggest that general methodological concerns only proliferate in disciplines where practitioners find little of great significance to do. In productive natural science practice is never outrun by methodology; method and theory are so intertwined as to be indistinguishable.

29 We could say that scientists come close to operating a system of precedent law; philosophers, on the whole, would wish them to adopt some kind of Roman law.

4 BELIEF, ACTION AND DETERMINISM: THE CAUSAL EXPLANATION OF SCIENTIFIC CHANGE

1 This would seem to be a reasonable account of Winch's own position, although it is not absolutely clear that he would rule out all kinds

of causal explanation of human action (cf. 1958, pp. 89–90). None the less, he does oppose deterministic approaches to human action (pp. 91–4), his only accounts of causal sociological explanations are critical ones (pp. 66–94, 103–11), and he stresses as strongly as he can the difference between social and natural science.

2   It is worth repeating here the warnings advanced at the end of chapter 2. First, to use normal practice as a baseline for causal explanation does not imply that stability is an inherently more common or usual state than change, or that departure from normal practice is in any sense a pathology. Second, to relate 'normal' belief to the socialization process does not imply a conception of the human actor as passive and initially empty. Nor does it imply the kind of cultural or normative determinism so well criticized by the symbolic interactionists.

3   Often, imagined contrasts between 'free' and 'determined' action, or familiarity with particular unsatisfactory forms of determinism, which represent the actor as an elaborate piece of clockwork, or a passive entity blindly responding to external forces, generate hostility to determinism in general, as a mode of thought. Indeed, because of the stereotype of determinism current in the social sciences, it was tempting to conceal its presence here and frame the arguments in less contentious terms. This would have been easy enough, but instead, out of perversity, I have laid the emphasis the other way.

4   Conceptions of normality do not, of course, necessarily correspond with what is usual. Rather, they are culturally defined. Most aeroplanes could have metal fatigue, and most flights result in disaster, without the form of causal explanation changing. It might contingently change, of course, as people became more interested in how aeroplanes managed to arrive safely at their destinations.

5   He also claims that good Humean generalizations can be constructed to refer to human action, but this can be passed over. We could perhaps regard Humean generalization as extreme (and rarely achieved) forms of the more common kind of causal statement discussed above.

6   Philosophers have sometimes made excuses for this kind of causal explanation in science, but it needs none.

7   The peculiar properties of certain theories of modern physics do not require any reformulation of these claims.

8   For a very rough indication of Winch's own model cf. Gellner (1959, 1968). The weaknesses of modern philosophy, with its stress on ordinary language, have been analysed and criticized in many ways. One way of explaining them is as the result of an attempt to avoid and discredit the use of models and metaphors; they are the

result of a positivistic prejudice. Linguistic philosophers often regard their exorcisms of metaphor as advances on the confusions of earlier philosophers, rather than pointless and arbitrary limitations of the possibilities of thought. In fact, philosophy has missed its way since the good old days of Hobbes and Descartes.

There is, of course, a tension in ordinary language philosophy between making judgments and 'eliminating confusions' on the one hand, and 'leaving everything as it is' on the other. Wittgenstein was a thinker of far too great a stature to miss this point; it led him to develop his (basically finitist) conception of mathematics with great delicacy, knowing as he did that mathematicians were given to proceeding in ways contrary to its indications. None the less his *Remarks on the Foundations of Mathematics* (1964) do not satisfactorily resolve the tensions in his position. In Winch, there is no awareness of this tension, let alone an attempt to resolve it.

9 The boundary in question is extremely tenuous and difficult to draw. In particular, very few human responses are entirely independent of the 'meaningful' element : vomiting, blink rate, blood pressure, muscle tone and most such variables are all responsive to factors significant only in terms of cultural programming.

10 The idealist's point that the meaning of terms or statements is only to be understood in terms of the overall role they play within a way of life is interestingly paralleled in the context of computer programming. We could say that the way a particular part of a programme contributes to the running of a power station by a computer can only be understood by grasping its significance within the overall programme. The same piece of programme can play different roles in different contexts.

11 Computers have been programmed to play passable chess, and the language games associated with chess are acknowledged to be appropriate to bad play as well as good.

12 It is interesting to consider the analogue of MacIntyre's partial determinism. It would be possible to make causal generalizations where, for example, the computer always relieved a check with its next move. It would also be possible to talk of opponents' moves causing responses of a particular kind : denuding one's king might cause the computer to attack in certain situations and so on. But, where no good grounds for causal generalization exist, one would be required to fall back on reasons as explanations of the computer's play. A simple feedback device, which enabled the computer to learn from experience how to improve its play, would take most of its moves beyond the scope of causal explanation as delineated by MacIntyre.

13 But perhaps one is entitled to suggest that conceptions of man's nature should not, today, treat the existence of several thousand million neurons within every human skull as a complete irrelevance.

14 Perhaps it will be possible eventually to regard metaphorical redescription as the transfer of an important and complex set of programmes, *en bloc* and with only minor adaptations, to the processing of a new set of inputs completely different from that with which it originally dealt.

15 This is to make nothing of the heuristic and speculative possibilities of the model, which are not negligible. Thus, there are an infinite number of ways of programming a computer, yet there are none the less important limits on what can operate as a programme and all programmes share certain general characteristics. Analogously, one could hypothesize that within the great diversity of culture important universals exist and are worth searching for; culture cannot take on any form. Perhaps logical rules should count as such universals, rather in the way that pre-twentieth-century philosophers thought of them; this would be plausible in terms of the computer analogy. As another example of the speculative possibilities of the model, it is worth considering how much it could contribute to the long drawn out, inconclusive dispute over methodological individualism.

16 Wittgenstein (1964) is, of course, the source of this, although he developed the point with a different purpose. Wittgenstein wanted to debunk a number of methods of justifying the ways we normally and naturally make inferences. His view was that with inferences like adding, or indeed most kinds of mathematical inference and many others besides, one should simply say 'this is what we do' and leave it at that. For him, in effect, accepted institutional forms were bedrock, beyond further justification or even explanation. This was so even when the institutional forms were those of mathematics.

Thus, it is completely alien to the spirit of Wittgenstein's work to attempt to explain beliefs in terms of a model. Wittgenstein always tried to undermine thought based on models. None the less Wittgenstein's work, suitably misunderstood, is a splendid source of insight for somebody with a naturalistic point of view. And his explanation of why institutions like counting and adding have evolved and been preserved can be accepted without reservations; they have persisted because they have paid off.

17 The term is often used loosely and informally. None the less it does serve to sustain a misguided conception of science, and would be

best discarded. Much the same could be said of the term 'situational logic', sometimes used by philosophers studying thought and action generally.

18 Unexpected, serendipitous discoveries or findings are, of course, of enormous importance in science. Experiments may yield totally unlooked for side-effects; explorations, or programmes of observation, may throw up new entities to challenge taxonomists and theorists in the natural history sciences and fields like astronomy.

   This factor is not discussed here, since its inherently unpredictable nature makes it of limited interest in the present context. For a study of conditions which increase the sensitivity of scientists to serendipitous occurrences, cf. Barber and Fox (1958). For a detailed exposition of the role of unexpected observations in the development of a scientific specialty, cf. Edge and Mulkay (forthcoming); this thorough study of the growth of radio astronomy offers an account of the role of the unexpected in scientific change which it would be pointless to repeat, and difficult to improve upon.

19 Or, if the formulation is preferred, a product of the capacity to shift programmes elaborated in the context of one set of inputs and outputs so that they come to govern another set.

20 We might say that the triumph of the idiosyncrasy platitude would be the triumph of silence! (The idiosyncrasy platitude being the assertion that 'Everything is what it is, and not another thing'.)

21 Too strong a distinction must not be made between routine and imaginative extensions of cultural resources. In particular, a routine extension cannot be thought of as one where problem and exemplar are 'exactly the same'. The distinction is between an extension which appears natural or matter of course, and one which necessitates conscious imaginative transformations.

22 Cf. note 4, ch. 3.

23 As before, since the example is being developed for illustrative purposes no attempt at full documentation will be made. Pasteur's work offers an obvious and important exception to the above, but this does not affect the argument.

24 The universe of possible actions can never be exhaustively divided into permissible and impermissible, or right and wrong, sets by rules or social norms. I. Lakatos's (1963) brilliant discussion of cultural change in mathematics provides a marvellous illustration of this. For discussion of the general point, cf. Barnes (1972).

25 Response to new kinds of analogy or metaphorical argument can be generally related to what is naturally acceptable because of training and the concrete problem situation. These factors make some actors feel the force of analogies more strongly than others.

Wislicenus, commending the early stereochemical ideas of Van't Hoff, noted how he had been 'forced' by his work on paralactic acid to seek explanations in the spatial properties of molecules (Van't Hoff, 1967, p. 7). The reception of the theory of ionization of Arrhenius provides another example. Van't Hoff himself immediately advocated Arrhenius's theory, which accounted well for anomalously large vapour pressure lowerings and osmotic pressures in aqueous solutions, both of which were being practically investigated by Van't Hoff. Other scientists responded negatively to Arrhenius, again in ways clearly related to their concrete concerns or their training (Dolby, forthcoming).

26 It is interesting to ask what sociological factors are conducive to imaginative scientific work. Two sets of necessary conditions are required if it is to occur. The cultural resources necessary must be available to the innovating actor, and the actor must possess the capacity to generate the imaginative development from the resources he possesses.

In many cases, an innovating actor has possessed unique access to necessary cultural resources and thus it is immediately intelligible that he alone should have made the innovation in question. Often the unique access has resulted from a move between scientific specialties or work situations. The development of nuclear magnetic resonance spectroscopy by Felix Bloch followed a move from work on nuclear magnetism to war work involving contact with techniques of radar and radio detection. The cultural resources of the two situations were combined in Bloch's innovation. Similarly, Bohr's model of the atom is partially to be understood as the imaginative combination of skills and exemplars derived from his earlier Ph.D. study, with the results of Rutherford's school at Manchester and Rutherford's conception of atomic structure. Bohr was the only person at the time with the equipment to make his innovation (Heilbron and Kuhn, 1969).

In other cases the cultural resources necessary to an innovation are the common property of a large number of actors, and it is difficult to explain the unique success of one particular actor contextually. In such situations the sociologist may have to pass the problem to the psychologist, or even admit the possibility that individual differences in the capacity for creative thought are not entirely intelligible in non-genetic terms. (For an example of the psychological biography of a prominent scientist, cf. Manuel, 1969.)

27 Here is an excellent illustration of the role-linked nature of knowledge. Different beliefs about the same thing can be seen to have been sustained among separate groups by the different

activities of the groups and the different purposes for which knowledge was required.

5 'INTERNAL' AND 'EXTERNAL' FACTORS IN THE HISTORY OF SCIENCE

1 Lakatos (1971) has surveyed the external criteria most commonly used to define 'genuine' science. For an approach to the history of science close to the one developed here cf. Kuhn (1968).

2 Milton Leitenberg (1971) has presented an interesting argument for expecting military requirements to have little biasing effect on the distribution of research effort. He points out that now the military is interested in everything!

3 We could expect to find some wonderful things in aboriginal mathematics if this were how science progressed!

4 Ideally, it would have been desirable to control out the social context and the intellectual presuppositions of the historians too! For present purposes, however, this may be regarded as a fine point. Perhaps some future anthropologist will see fit to divide the present professional community in history of science into 'polluters' and 'purifiers'. The division would not simply follow the boundary between intellectual and institutional history. Joseph Ben-David would certainly qualify as a purifier, whereas clear polluters like Rattansi (1963, 1964) and Young belong in the history of ideas tradition.

5 Such an element may, of course, be drawn from another accredited scientific sub-culture, as we have already discussed. It would be external to the sub-culture [discipline, specialty] in question, but internal to 'science'. Inputs from [say] psychoanalysis into scientific sub-cultures might be described as 'internal' or 'external' by different investigators, depending on how they weighted different actors' categorizations of psychoanalysis. But the process of cultural change described would be the same either way.

6 It is unfortunate that Young's work gives no insight into the real flavour of, say, the *Origin*, with its vast arrays of organized concrete material. On the other hand, as Young points out, Darwin's opponents didn't lack the encyclopaedic touch.

7 The use of modern vocabulary itself tends to distort the issue. It tends to imply a culture where entirely scientific bits and entirely religious bits are mixed up together. This is, of course, an impression due to *ex post facto* analysis.

8 This possibility has recently been given serious consideration by historians of science, following the work of Frances Yates (1964).

9   I would argue that even with Euclid the conception of 'inherent
     worth' needs qualification. Mathematics can be understood in the
     kind of terms being developed here in connection with science. For
     an indication of what is involved see D. Bloor's (1973b) discussion of
     'Wittgenstein and Mannheim on the sociology of mathematics'.

10   An interesting case, where attitudes to hereditarian explanations of
     behaviour reversed polarity to maintain continuity of social function,
     has been discussed by Rosenberg (1966).

         The tenor of the above argument has been against a Marxist
     approach, which instead of ascertaining actors' perceptions delineates
     externally defined social classes. However, some excellent work within
     the Marxist tradition has related metaphysics to social structure
     very convincingly. I have in mind particularly Lucien Goldmann's
     study of Jansenism (1964), which in practice is sensitive to actors'
     perceptions, and makes interesting points about unconscious
     determinants of them.

11   It would indeed be a delightful exercise to use Strong's comparison
     of the 'philosophical' and the 'scientific' Kepler as a model for
     comparing the technical contributions of the German physicists with
     their airy fairy philosophy, as quoted by Forman.

12   I have sought examples from physical science here, although biology
     provides more and simpler illustrations. For a valuable and very
     readable illustration in this latter field cf. Miller (1972).

13   Indeed, strict separation of description and evaluation is more
     important in the discussion of science than in almost any other
     context. 'Science' is one of the few terms in modern highly
     differentiated societies, which combines descriptive and evaluative
     usages of comparable significance. It is often impossible to know
     whether it is being used to indicate the activity of a particular role,
     or activity in conformity with certain ideals, whether it means
     universally valid knowledge or what is currently to be found in
     books and journals. This lack of differentiation is a sign of sacredness.
     It is also a source of pitfalls for the unwary thinker (cf. Gellner
     (1962, pp. 41ff)). This may be brought out by an analogy with the
     term 'Christian', which insists on referring both to those who
     profess, or have joined, a Christian faith, and those who act in
     accordance with good principles. This enables the modern Christian,
     if he so wishes, to establish himself within the confines of a
     monumental complacency. He may bask in reflected glory from the
     good works of his fellow believers, yet, when they perpetrate some
     outrage, denounce them as not 'real' Christians at all. It becomes
     impossible to conceive of Christianity other than as a force for good.
     Earnest Sunday discussions may struggle with the question of what

Christians can do about Northern Ireland, before going on to stress
the need for compulsory religious instruction in all schools. This
kind of complacency is not always avoided in current discussions of
science.

6   SCIENCE AND IDEOLOGY

1   The whole of the discussion should be treated as relevant only to
the beliefs of a highly differentiated society.

2   I am referring here only to evaluations which get, as it were,
concretely entangled in the culture of science, and not to values
which may be considered basic to the enterprise. Criticisms of these
will not be discussed here, since the arguments of the monograph
add little to the debate surrounding them. Consider Marcuse, who
impeaches science as ideological because the fact-value distinction is
central to it. Essentially he wants to say that the distinction is
unnecessary (which it is easy to accept), and legitimates a social
order antipathetic to the essentials of human nature and corrosive of
human dignity and freedom; therefore we need a new kind of science.
The claim is straightforward enough, and nothing said here need
affect its assessment.

3   In this connection one thinks particularly of the Robbins Report
where credibility is clearly treated as a function of weight of paper
times the amount of scientific gloss upon it. Perhaps credibility is
well treated as varying in this way; in any case Robbins provided a
model for most subsequent educational policy reports produced in
Britain.

4   What follows, is of course, my own assessment. Nothing is to be
gained by presenting long technical commentary here upon a paper
of over one hundred pages, especially as anyone who wishes to do so
may check it himself.

5   Bodmer's work will be considered in so far as it contrasts with
Jensen's. Much of the time it does not. Many of Bodmer's points
may be seen as attempts to inoculate the public against arguments
and evaluations claiming spurious legitimacy as 'following from' or
'implied by' Jensen's work.

6   Bodmer's kind of argument can of course be used against any
scientific hypothesis. How seriously it is taken will often depend
upon what standards of proof or plausibility the critic expects the
hypothesis to fulfil.

   In practice, criticisms of hypotheses based entirely upon this
negative kind of consideration have not fared well, in the long term,
in scientific controversy. The hypothesized causal connection

between smoking and lung cancer was opposed in a related way, and still could be if anyone was still of a mind to do so. One thinks also of the Müller-Helmholtz controversy.

7   The myth of Galileo, of course, no longer possesses the power and potency it once enjoyed, but for those in danger of reading too much into the parallel the following points may be relevant. First, according to the standards of current scientific orthodoxy, Galileo was wrong—and not trivially wrong. Second, whereas the myth celebrates the virtues of open, unhindered research and communication, scientists today readily maintain an effective self-censorship whenever they think it expedient, and, as an occupational group, they have tended to be indifferent to whether the right to free thought and communication is enjoyed by other groups or individuals. Consistently enough, the scientists referred to did not make a general moral stand, but sought to defend an occupational privilege (cf. Page *et al.* (1972)).

More recently, in a work to which he makes a curiously encapsulated contribution, Professor Jensen has been compared to Copernicus and Pasteur (Haskell (1972), p. 108). *Full Circle: the Moral Force of Unified Science* is indeed a remarkable volume. If anything might make a follower of Marcuse come to accept the importance of observing a fact-value distinction this would be it! And it has reminded the present writer of the need to add a proviso to his somewhat conservative analysis of social determinants of science. The discussion, it must be emphasized, concerns presently established science, not what may come to be accepted as science in the future; present conclusions are contingent on what science presently happens to be. Given an upward trend in enthusiasm for 'unified science', 'systems' of diverse kinds, 'general systems theory' and related materials, who knows what different conclusions may not be drawn at some future time!

8   It is interesting to note how it has become in the interests of industrial concerns to purchase formally certified *doubt*. Given the nature of scientific knowledge, such doubt is of course always available, but none the less high quality doubt can command high prices, and even a shoddy second-rate product is worth something, for temporary use, if the gains are large enough. The research on possible toxic effects of artificial sweeteners provides a good example here, as well as the smoking/cancer affair.

9   A diametrically opposed view to this may be found in the work of W. Stark (1958). Stark uses a distinction very close to the present division between thought which departs from normal practice and that which forms part of it. But he adopts a deterministic approach

to the former only, discussing the latter in terms of lyrical idealism.

10 One of the great virtues of this example is that brilliant scientists went as 'deeply' as they possibly could into the issues without resolving them. Those unimpressed by theoretical arguments against making external judgments may still have trepidations about making them in this case.

11 One would not for a moment wish to suggest that the implementation of their eugenic prescription would have produced a situation more to the liking of the members of that class than the one which actually transpired. The notion that ideologically motivated prescriptions would, if implemented, always serve their advocates' 'real' interests is not defended here!

12 I am greatly indebted to Donald MacKenzie of the Science Studies Unit at Edinburgh for suggesting this last point and convincing me of its plausibility as well as for greatly adding to my knowledge of the example generally.

13 It is interesting to note how Haller (1971), who sees this point clearly, is still content to comment on the 'prejudices' of the time with an implied superiority grounded in present taken for granted preconceptions and fashionable morality. It is always expedient, when noting how others have taken confident stances upon insecure ground, to avoid glancing at one's own feet.

14 Technically, the selection of a model with an eye to the social consequences of the choice need not be incompatible with good practice according to other standards. It may, for example, facilitate the choice of a working model which otherwise would have had to to be made randomly. Thus, secondary social considerations could play a part in bona fide science, and be openly acknowledged by scientists. For obvious reasons, however, a prohibition against taking *any* note of secondary considerations generally appertains in science. It does come under pressure from time to time; in the last decade particularly, strong attacks have been made upon it; none the less it persists.

15 It puts the case too strongly to say that we are 'trapped' by our culture and can never fundamentally criticize or restructure it. True, we can never set it aside entirely, or filter the whole of it and retain only that which conforms to certain formal requirements. Such a radical, Cartesian operation is a practical impossibility. But what can be done (and what Descartes actually did) is to operate within one differentiated sector of belief and action, and from that taken for granted base appraise the rest of our knowledge. This is a very considerable freedom.

16 Elias (1971) attaches great importance to this kind of effect. He equates smoothing out with the attainment of greater 'object adequacy' as knowledge is transmitted and modified over the ages.

EPILOGUE

1 It is left to the reader to decide whether to call the position taken here relativistic or not. I would urge him, however, to set aside the inane argument that relativism is equivalent to believing that 'might is right'. This would certainly save this essay from being criticized as relativistic, since I tend to believe that might is generally wrong, and find this consistent with my arguments. However, I have no wish to be rescued in such a trivial way.

2 Thus, in Popper's *Logic of Scientific Discovery* (1934), we find trenchant criticism of inductivism, characterization of the crucial basic statements in science as dogmas which can only be decided upon at any particular time by agreement, and explicit opposition to the idea that science ever arrives at final or absolute truth. Here are many arguments which may be used to support a sociological treatment of scientific knowledge, in a work which neither suggested nor stimulated such an enterprise. At the time, these points arose out of the task of justifying 'scientific method' as an ideal for all rational activity to aspire to.

3 John Ziman, a physicist, wrote recently: 'The public adoration of the scientist, as the sage and saviour, is a thing of the past: now we seem to hear nothing but scorn for his pretensions and hatred of his arrogance' (1971, p. 122).

4 A stronger case than this can, of course, be argued. Association with government, industry and the military is association with lies, corruption and brutality, and with science the association has involved particularly unfortunate concrete connections: the long series of American atrocities in South East Asia, the obscene symbol of the Space Programme, the routinized racketeering and 'scientific' exploitation of ignorance which passes for business in the pharmaceutical industry, the high farce of Concorde, the disaster with thalidomide. In the face of this it could be said, no image, however bright and shining, could hope to remain untarnished.

Yet, societies are perfectly capable of cleaving to obscene symbols, and brutality may call forth effusions of patriotism. So an analysis like the above can be, at best, superficial; more basic explanations must be sought. Perhaps a major factor is that contributions from the frontiers of research no longer clearly improve the quality of life in the developed countries, even when judged by materialistic criteria.

N

Alternatively, it could be that special causes are being sought for the wrong phenomenon. The perceived link of science with other institutions is not new; neither is vigorous criticism of science and intense opposition to it. It might be that the present range of attitudes to science is normal historically, and seems new only in comparison with the extraordinarily favourable perceptions characteristic of the postwar period. What might really be in need of explanation is how, in highly differentiated modern societies, an institution could exist for a considerable period without being subjected to serious criticism or engendering any significant hostility.

5   Relativism in the literature of the sociology of knowledge has generally taken the 'everything is invalid' form, and not the 'everything is equally valid' form. It has been opposed, traditionally, by demonstrations of its logical inconsistency : if it is true, then by its own tenets it is untrue. The debate has been most unsociological, with nobody talking of the ways in which different groups or societies deploy true/false predicates differently, and most protagonists tending to assume a correspondence theory of truth.

But then, despite Mannheim, relativism has never really been an *issue* in sociology. Rather, sociologists have seized gratefully upon some convenient conundrums with which to inoculate themselves and their successors against doubt about their enterprise.

Bibliography

ADVISORY COMMITTEE ON DRUG DEPENDENCE (1968), *Cannabis* (Wootton Report), HMSO, London.

AGASSI, J. (1963), *Towards an Historiography of Science*, North Holland Publishing Co., The Hague.

AYER, A. J. (1968), *The Origins of Pragmatism*, Macmillan, London.

BARBER, B. (1961), 'Resistance by scientists to scientific discovery', *Science*, vol. 134, no. 3479, pp. 596–602.

BARBER, B. and FOX, R. (1958), 'The case of the floppy-eared rabbits'. *A.J.S.*, no. 64, pp. 128–36.

BARNES, S. B. (1972), 'Sociological explanation and natural science', *Eur. J. Soc.*, vol. 13, pp. 373–91.

BARNES, S. B. (1973), 'The Comparison of Belief Systems: Anomaly versus Falsehood', in R. Horton and R. Finnegan (eds), *Modes of Thought*, London.

BEATTIE, J. H. M. (1966), 'Ritual and social change', *Man*, N.S., 1, pp. 60–74.

BEATTIE, J. H. M. (1970), 'On Understanding Ritual', in B. Wilson (ed.), *Rationality*, Blackwell, Oxford.

BEN-DAVID, J. (1960), 'Roles and innovations in medicine', *A.J.S.*, vol. 65, pp. 557–68.

BEN-DAVID, J. (1971), *The Scientist's Role in Society*, Prentice-Hall, Englewood Cliffs, N.J.

BERGER, P. (1961), *The Sacred Canopy*, Doubleday, New York.

BERNSTEIN, B. (1971), *Class, Codes and Control*, vol. 1, Routledge & Kegan Paul, London.

BLACK, M. (1962), *Models and Metaphors*, Cornell University Press, Ithaca, New York.

BLOOR, D. (1971), 'Two paradigms for scientific knowledge?', *Science Studies*, vol. 1, no. 1, pp. 101–15.

BLOOR, D. (1973a), 'Are Philosophers Averse to Science?', in D. O. Edge and J. N. Wolfe (eds), *Meaning and Control*, Tavistock Publications, London.

BLOOR, D. (1973b), 'Wittgenstein and Mannheim on the sociology of mathematics', *Stud. Hist. Phil. Sci.*, vol. 4, no. 2, pp. 173–91.

BODMER, W. F. and CAVALLI-SFORZA, L. L. (1970), 'Intelligence and race', *Scientific American*, vol. 223, no. 4, pp. 19–29.

BODMER, W. F. (1972), 'Race and IQ: the Genetic Background', in K. Richardson and D. Spears (eds), *Race, Culture and Intelligence*, Penguin, Harmondsworth.

BRUSH, S. G. (1970), 'The wave theory of heat', *Br. J. Hist. Sci.*, vol. 5, no. 18, pp. 145–67.

BULMER, R. (1967), 'Why is the Cassowary not a bird? A problem of zoological taxonomy among the Karam of the New Guinea Highlands', *Man*, vol. 2, no. 1, pp. 5–25.

BURTT, E. A. (1932), *The Metaphysical Foundations of Modern Physical Science*, Routledge & Kegan Paul, London.

CANTOR, G. (forthcoming), 'The reception of the wave theory of light in England'.

CARDWELL, D. S. L. (1971), *From Watt to Clausius*, Heinemann, London.

CARNOT, S. (1960), *Reflections on the Motive Powers of Fire* (English translation of his 1824, plus other works), Dover, New York.

CASSIRER, E. (1946), *Language and Myth* (English translation), Dover, New York.

CASSIRER, E. (1953), *Philosophy of Symbolic Forms* (3 vols English translation), Yale University Press, New Haven.

COWAN, R. S. (1968), 'Sir Francis Galton and the continuity of germ plasm: A biological idea with political roots', *C.I.H.S.*, vol. 12e, pp. 181–6.

COWAN, R. S. (1972), 'Francis Galton's statistical ideas: the influence of eugenics', *Isis*, vol. 63, pp. 509–28.

CRANE, D. (1972), *Invisible Colleges*, University of Chicago Press.

DOLBY, A. (forthcoming), 'Debates over the theory of solutions. A study of dissent in physical chemistry in the English Speaking World in the late nineteenth and early twentieth centuries'.

DOUGLAS, M. (1966), *Purity and Danger*, Routledge & Kegan Paul, London.

DOUGLAS, M. (1970a), *Natural Symbols*, Barrie & Jenkins, London.

DOUGLAS, M. (1970b), 'Environments at risk', *Times Lit. Supp.*, 30 October, pp. 1273–5.

DOUGLAS, M. (1972), 'Self-evidence', *Proc. Roy. Anthrop. Inst.*, pp. 27–43.

DOUGLAS, M. (1973), *Rules and Meanings*, Penguin, Harmondsworth.

DURKHEIM, E. (1912), *The Elementary Forms of the Religious Life*, Paris (English translation, Free Press, New York 1961).

EDGE, D. O. and MULKAY, M. (1974), *A study of the emergence of radio-astronomy in Great Britain* (available from Department of Engineering Science, Cambridge University).

ELIAS, N. (1971), 'Sociology of knowledge—new perspectives', *Sociology*, vol. 5, no. 2, pp. 149ff; vol. 5, no. 3, pp. 368ff.

ENGELS, F. (1893), Letter to Mehring of 14th July, cf. *Selected Works* (1962), vol. 2, p. 497, Moscow.

EVANS-PRITCHARD, E. E. (1937), *Witchcraft Oracles and Magic among the Azande*, Oxford University Press, London.

EVANS-PRITCHARD, E. E. (1956), *Nuer Religion*, Oxford University Press, London.

EZRAHI, Y. (1971), 'The political resources of American science', *Science Studies*, vol. 1, no. 2, pp. 117–34.

FELLOWS, E. W. (1961), 'Social and cultural influences in the development of science', *Synthese*, vol. 13, no. 2, pp. 154–72.

FEYERABEND, P. (1958), 'Attempt at a realistic interpretation of experience', *Proc. Arist. Soc.*, New Series, vol. 58, pp. 143–70.

FEYERABEND, P. (1970), 'Against Method', in M. Radner and S. Winokur (eds), *Analyses of Theories and Methods of Physics and Psychology*, University of Minnesota Press, Minneapolis.

FISHER, R. A. (1936), 'Has Mendel's work been rediscovered?', *Ann. Sci.*, vol. 1, pp. 115–37.

FORMAN, P. (1971), 'Weimar culture, causality and quantum theory, 1918–1927', *Historical Studies in the Physical Sciences*, vol. 3, pp. 1–115. University of Pennsylvania Press, Philadelphia.

GEERTZ, C. (1964), 'Ideology as a Cultural System', in D. E. Apter (ed.), *Ideology and Discontent*, Free Press, New York.

GELLNER, E. (1959), *Words and Things*, Gollancz, London.

GELLNER, E. (1962), 'Concepts and Society', as reprinted in B. R. Wilson (ed.), *Rationality*, 1970, Blackwell, Oxford.

GELLNER, E. (1968), 'The New Idealism', in I. Lakatos and A. Musgrave (eds), *Problems in the Philosophy of Science*, Wesleyan University Press, Middletown, Conn.

GOLDMANN, L. (1964), *The Hidden God* (English translation), Routledge & Kegan Paul, London.

GOODY, J. (1961), 'Religion and ritual: the definitional problem', *B.J.S.*, vol. 12, pp. 142–64.

GREGORY, R. L. (1966), *Eye and Brain*, Weidenfeld & Nicolson, London.

HAGSTROM, W. O. (1965), *The Scientific Community*, Basic Books, New York.

HAHN, R. (1971), *The Anatomy of a Scientific Institution: the Paris Academy of Sciences, 1666–1803*, University of California Press, Berkeley.

HALL, A. R. (1952), *Ballistics in the Seventeenth Century*, Cambridge University Press.

HALL, A. R. (1963), 'Merton revisited', *History of Science*, vol. 2, no. 1, pp. 1–16.

HALLER, J. B. (1971), *Outcasts from Evolution*, University of Illinois Press, Urbana.

HANSON, N. (1958), *Patterns of Discovery*, Cambridge University Press.

HASKELL, E. (ed.) (1972), *Full Circle: the Moral Force of Unified Science*, Gordon & Breach, New York.

HEILBRON, J. L. and KUHN, T. S. (1969), 'The genesis of the Bohr atom', *Hist. Stud. Phys. Sci.*, vol. 1, pp. 221–90.

HESSE, M. (1961), *Forces and Fields*, Nelson, London.

HESSE, M. (1963), *Models and Analogies in Science*, Sheed & Ward, London.

HESSE, M. (1964), 'The Explanatory Function of Metaphor', in *International*

Congress for Logic, Methodology and Philosophy of Science,
  Amsterdam.
HESSE, M. (1970a), 'Is There an Independent Observation Language?', in
  R. G. Colodney (ed.), The Nature and Function of Scientific Theories,
  University of Pittsburgh Press.
HESSE, M. (1970b), 'An Inductive Logic of Theories', in M. Radner and
  S. Winokur (eds), Analyses of Theories and Methods of Physics and
  Psychology, University of Minnesota Press, Minneapolis.
HESSE, M. (1970c), 'Hermeticism and Historiography : An Apology for
  the Internal History of Science', in R. H. Stuewer (ed.), Historical
  and Philosophical Perspectives of Science, University of Minnesota Press,
  Minneapolis.
HESSEN, B. (1931), 'The Social and Economic Roots of Newton's Principia',
  in N. Bukharin (ed.), Science at the Crossroads, reprinted (1971), Cass,
  London.
HILL, C. (1965), Intellectual Origins of the English Revolution, Oxford
  University Press, London.
HOFF, J. H. VAN'T (1967), Imagination in Science, Springer Verlag, New
  York.
HOLLIS, M. (1967), 'The limits of irrationality', Eur. J. Soc., vol. 8, pp.
  265–71.
HORTON, R. (1967), 'African traditional thought and Western science',
  Africa, vol. 37, pp. 50–71, 155–87.
JARVIE, I. C. and AGASSI, J. (1967), 'The problem of the rationality of
  magic', B.J.S., vol. 18, pp. 55–74.
JENSON, A. R. (1969), 'How Much Can We Boost I.Q. and Scholastic
  Achievement?', reprinted in A. R. Jensen (1972) below.
JENSEN, A. R. (1972), Genetics and Education, Methuen, London.
KALANT, O. J. (1968), An Interim Guide to the Cannabis Literature,
  Addiction Research Foundation Bibliographic Series No. 2, University
  of Toronto Press.
KARGON, R. H. (1966), Atomism in England from Hariot to Newton,
  Oxford University Press, London.
KING, M. D. (1971), 'Reason, tradition and the progressiveness of science',
  History and Theory, vol. 10, no. 1, pp. 3–32.
KNIGHT, D. M. (1967), Atoms and Elements, Hutchinson, London.
KNIGHT, D. M. (ed.) (1968), Classical Scientific Papers: Chemistry, 1st series,
  Mills & Boon, London.
KOYRÉ, A. (1968), Metaphysics and Measurement (English translation),
  Chapman & Hall, London.
KUHN, T. S. (1957), The Copernican Revolution, Harvard University Press,
  Cambridge, Mass.
KUHN, T. S. (1961), 'Sadi Carnot and the Cagnard engine', Isis, 52, pp.
  567–74.
KUHN, T. S. (1962), 'The function of measurement in modern physical
  science', Isis, vol. 52, pp. 161–93.
KUHN, T. S. (1968), 'The History of Science', International Encyclopedia
  of the Social Sciences, vol. 14, pp. 74–83.

KUHN, T. S. (1970), *The Structure of Scientific Revolutions*, 2nd edition, University of Chicago Press.

KUHN, T. S. (1972), 'Scientific growth: Reflections on Ben-David's "Scientific Role" ', *Minerva*, vol. 10, no. 1, pp. 166–78.

LAKATOS, I. (1963), 'Proofs and refutations', *Br. J. Phil. Sci.*, vol. 14, pp. 1–25, 120–39, 221–45, 296–342.

LAKATOS, I. (1971), 'History of Science and its Rational Reconstructions', in Buck and Cohen (eds), *Boston Studies*, vol. 8, Reidel, Dordrecht.

LANGMUIR, I. (1953), edited (1968) by R. N. Hall, *Pathological Science*, General Electric R. & D. Center Report No. 68-C-035, New York.

LEITENBERG, M. (1971), 'The classical scientific ethic and strategic-weapons development', *Impact of Science on Society*, vol. 21, no. 2, pp. 123–36.

LÉVI STRAUSS, C. (1966), *The Savage Mind* (English translation of *La Pensée sauvage*), Weidenfeld & Nicolson, London.

LUKES, S. (1967), 'Some problems about rationality', *Eur. J. Soc.*, vol. 8, pp. 247–64.

LUKES, S. (1973), 'On the Social Determination of Truth', in R. Horton and R. Finnegan (eds), *Modes of Thought*, London.

MACINTYRE, A. (1966), 'The Antecedents of Action', in B. Williams and A. Montefiore (eds), *British Analytical Philosophy*, Routledge & Kegan Paul, London.

MACINTYRE, A. (1967), *Secularisation and Moral Change*, Oxford University Press, London.

MCMULLEN, E. (1970), 'The History and Philosophy of Science: A Taxonomy', in R. H. Stuewer (ed.), *Historical & Philosophical Perspectives of Science*, University of Minnesota Press, Minneapolis.

MANNHEIM, K. (1936), *Ideology and Utopia* (translated and introduced by L. Wirth and E. Shils), Routledge & Kegan Paul, London.

MANUEL, F. (1968), *A Portrait of Isaac Newton*, Harvard University Press, Cambridge, Mass.

MENDELSOHN, E. (1964), 'The Emergence of Science as a Profession in Nineteenth-Century Europe', in K. Hill (ed.), *The Management of Scientists*, Beacon Press, Boston.

MERTON, R. K. (1938), *Science, Technology and Society in Seventeenth-Century England*, reprinted (1970), Harper & Row, New York.

MERTON, R. K. (1957), 'Priorities in scientific discovery', *A.J.S.*, vol. 22, pp. 635–59.

MERTON, R. K. (1961), 'Singletons and multiples in scientific discovery', *Proc. Amer. Phil. Soc.*, vol. 105, no. 5, pp. 470–86.

MERTON, R. K. (1963), 'Resistance to the systematic study of multiple discoveries in science', *Eur. J. Soc.*, vol. 4, pp. 237–82.

MILLER, J. (1972), 'The dog beneath the skin', *Listener*, 20 July, pp. 74–6.

MULKAY, M. (1972), *The Social Process of Innovation*, Macmillan, London.

NASH, L. K. (1948), 'The Atomic-Molecular Theory', in J. B. Conant *et al.* (eds), *Harvard Case Histories in Experimental Science*, Harvard University Press, Cambridge, Mass.

NASH, L. K. (1956), 'The origin of Dalton's chemical atomic theory', *Isis*, vol. 47, pp. 101–16.

NEEDHAM, J. (1969), *The Grand Titration*, Allen & Unwin, London.

OGBURN, W. F. and THOMAS, D. (1922), 'Are inventions inevitable?', *Pol. Sci. Quart.*, vol. 37, no. 1, pp. 83–98.

PAGE, E. B. *et al.* (1972), Letter to *Am. Psychologist*, vol. 27, July, pp. 660–1.

PALMER, A. (1972), 'The Development of Scientific Interest in Cannabis', Department of Liberal Studies in Science, Manchester University (unpublished).

PANNEKOEK, A. (1961), *A History of Astronomy*, Allen & Unwin, London.

PARSONS, T. (1959), 'An Approach to the Sociology of Knowledge', reprinted in Curtis and Petras (eds) (1970), *The Sociology of Knowledge*, Duckworth, London.

POLANYI, M. (1958), *Personal Knowledge*, Routledge & Kegan Paul, London.

POPPER, K. R. (1934), *Logik der Forschung*, Vienna (English translation, *The Logic of Scientific Discovery*, 1959, Hutchinson, London).

RATTANSI, P. M. (1963), 'Paracelsus and the puritan revolution', *Ambix*, vol. 11, pp. 24–32.

RATTANSI, P. M. (1964), 'The Helmontian-Galenist controversy in Restoration England', *Ambix*, vol. 12, pp. 1–23.

RAVETZ, J. R. (1971), *Scientific Knowledge and its Social Problems*, Oxford University Press, London.

REISER, S. J. (1966), 'Smoking and Health : the Congress and Causality', in S. A. Lakoff (ed.), *Knowledge and Power*, Free Press, New York.

ROSENBERG, C. E. (1966), 'Science and American Social Thought', in D. Van Tassel and M. G. Hall (eds), *Science and Society in the United States*, Dorsey, New York.

SALMON, W. (1966), 'The Foundations of Scientific Inference', in R. G. Colodney, (ed.), *Mind and Cosmos*, University of Pittsburgh Press.

SALMON, W. (1970), 'Bayes's Theorem and the History of Science', in R. H. Stuewer (ed.), *Historical and Philosophical Perspectives on Science*, University of Minnesota Press, Minneapolis.

SCHEFFLER, I. (1967), *Science and Subjectivity*, Bobbs-Merrill, New York.

SCHON, D. (1963), *Displacement of Concepts*, Tavistock Publications, London.

SCHON, D. (1966), 'The Fear of Innovation', reprinted (1967) in R. N. Hainer, S. Kingsbury, and D. B. Gleicher (eds), *Uncertainty in Research Management*, Reinhold, Cambridge, Mass., pp. 11–25.

SHIBLES, W. A. (1971), *Metaphor*, Language Press, Whitewater, Wisconsin.

SLACK, J. (1972), 'Class Struggle Among the Molecules', in Pateman (ed.), *Counter Course*, pp. 202–17, Penguin, Harmondsworth.

STANTON, W. (1960), *The Leopard's Spots*, University of Chicago Press.

STARK, W. (1958), *The Sociology of Knowledge*, Routledge & Kegan Paul, London.

STRAWSON, P. E. (1952), *Introduction to Logical Theory*, Methuen, London.

STRONG, E. W. (1936) (republished 1966), *Procedures and Metaphysics*, Georg Olms, Hildesheim.

THACKRAY, A. W. (1966), 'The origins of Dalton's chemical atomic theory : Daltonian doubts resolved', *Isis*, vol. 57, no. 1, pp. 35–55.

THACKRAY, A. W. (1970), 'Science and technology in the industrial revolution', *History of Science*, vol. 9, pp. 76–89.

TOULMIN, S. (1953), *The Philosophy of Science*, Hutchinson, London.

TURVEY, P. M. and GIBBONS, M., 'Continental Drift: A Case Study in Kuhn's Theory of Scientific Revolutions' (available from the authors, Department of Liberal Studies in Science, Manchester University).

VEBLEN, T. (1908), 'The Place of Science in Modern Civilisation', and 'The Evolution of the Scientific Point of View', reprinted (1961) in T. Veblen, *The Place of Science in Modern Civilization and Other Essays*, Russell, New York.

WALLER, C. W. and DENNY, J. J. (1971), *Bibliography of Marijuana*, University of Mississippi Press.

WINCH, P. (1958), *The Idea of a Social Science*, Routledge & Kegan Paul, London.

WINCH, P. (1964), 'Understanding a primitive society', *American Phil. Quart.*, vol. 1, pp. 307–24.

WITTGENSTEIN, L. (1953), *Philosophical Investigations*, Blackwell, Oxford.

WITTGENSTEIN, L. (1964), *Remarks on the Foundations of Mathematics*, Blackwell, Oxford.

YATES, F. A. (1964), *Giordano Bruno and the Hermetic Tradition*, Routledge & Kegan Paul, London.

YOUNG, M. (ed.) (1971), *Knowledge and Control*, Collier-Macmillan, London.

YOUNG, R. M. (1969), 'Malthus and the evolutionists', *Past and Present*, vol. 43, pp. 109–45.

YOUNG, R. M. (1971), 'Darwin's metaphor: Does Nature select?', *Monist*, vol. 55, pp. 442–503.

YOUNG, R. M. (1972), 'The Historiographic and Ideological Contexts of the Nineteenth-Century Debate on Man's Place in Nature', in M. Teich and R. M. Young (eds), *Changing Perspectives in the History of Science*, Heinemann, London.

ZILSEL, E. (1941), 'The sociological roots of science', *Am. Sociol.*, vol. 2, pp. 544–60.

ZIMAN, J. (1971), 'The impact of social responsibility on science', *Impact of Science on Society*, vol. 21, no. 2, pp. 113–22.

Author Index

Agassi, J., 6
Ayer, A.J., 153

Barber, B., 172
Barnes, S. B., 30, 117, 165, 172
Beattie, J. H. M., 6
Ben-David, J., 104, 174
Berger, P., 1
Bernstein, B., 102
Black, M., 165
Bloor, D., 148, 162, 164, 166, 175
Bodmer, W. F., 134–5, 176
Brush, S. G., 167
Bulmer, R., 35
Burtt, E. A., 118

Cantor, G., 95, 166
Cardwell, D. S. L., 120
Carnot, S., 120
Cassirer, E., 57
Cavalli-Sforza, L. L., 134
Collingwood, R. G., 109
Cowan, R. S., 118–19
Crane, D., 48

Denny, J. J., 138
Dolby, R. G. A., 63, 166, 173
Douglas, M., 117, 150, 165, 167
Durkheim, E., 165, 167

Edge, D. O., 172
Elias, N., 179
Engels, F., 143
Evans-Pritchard, E. E., 27, 31–2, 164
Ezrahi, Y., 102

Fellows, E. W., 104
Feyerabend, P., 160–1, 165
Fisher, R. A., 165
Forman, P., 109–11, 116, 141, 175
Fox, R., 172

Geertz, C., 3–4
Gellner, E., 27, 31, 76, 159, 169, 175
Gibbons, M., 95
Goldmann, L., 175
Goody, J., 6
Gregory, R. L., 20–1, 160

Hagstrom, W. O., 48, 86
Hahn, R., 104
Hall, A. R., 105–7, 109
Haller, J. S., 144, 178
Hanson, N., 21
Haskell, E., 177
Heilbron, J. L., 173
Hesse, M., 16–18, 160–1, 163, 165, 167
Hessen, B., 104, 106
Hill, C., 104
Hollis, M., 163
Horton, R., 2, 27, 30, 117, 165, 167

Jarvie, I. C., 6
Jensen, A. R., 132–5

Kalant, O. J., 138
Kargon, R. H., 104
King, M. D., 5
Knight, D. M., 166
Koyré, A., 108–9, 114, 165

Kuhn, T. S., 21, 30, 48, 50, 52, 56,
   60–1, 63–4, 67, 84, 87, 93–6, 107,
   120, 123, 160, 165, 173–4

Lakatos, I., 172, 174
Langmuir, I., 21
Leitenberg, M., 174
Lévi-Strauss, C., 57–9, 165
Lilley, S., 106
Lukes, S., 33–41, 163

MacIntyre, A., 70–4, 76, 170
McMullen, E., 162
Mannheim, K., 131, 145, 147–8
Manuel, F., 173
Marcuse, H., 176
Mendelsohn, E., 104
Merton, R. K., 4–5, 48, 99, 104, 106
Miller, J., 175
Mulkay, M., 86, 172

Nash, L. K., 166
Needham, J., 104, 106–7

Ogburn, W. F., 48

Page, E. B., 177
Palmer, A., 138
Pannekoek, A., 104
Parsons, T., 3
Polanyi, M., 27, 67, 166

Popper, K. R., 23–4, 32, 45, 160,
   162, 179
Price, D. J. de S., 48

Rattansi, P. M., 174
Ravetz, J. R., 166
Rosenberg, C. E., 175

Salmon, W., 161
Scheffler, I., 20, 160
Schon, D., 57, 165, 167
Shibles, W. A., 57
Slack, J., 103
Stanton, W., 144
Stark, W., 177
Strawson, P. F., 161
Strong, E. W., 118, 175

Thackray, A. W., 104, 166
Thomas, D., 48
Toulmin, S., 10
Turvey, P. M., 95

Veblen, T., 13–15

Waller, C. W., 138
Winch, P., 27, 69, 76–8, 168–9
Wittgenstein, L., 163, 168, 170–1

Yates, F., 174
Young, R. M., 110–13, 174

Zilsel, E., 104
Ziman, J., 179

Subject Index

Acausality, 109–10, 141–2
Anomaly, 61, 94–5
Anthropology, 6
Anthropomorphism, 14, 45
  decline of, 117, 164–5
Azande poison oracles, 27–31, 164

Bricolage, 58, 146

Cancer and smoking, 138–9
Cannabis, 137–8
Carnot's cycle, 119–20
Contradiction, 37–41

Daltonian atomism, 50–7, 167
Definition in science, 65–6 .
Determinism, 71–84
Doubt as commodity, 177

Epistemology, 148, 153–7, 159
Evaluative elements in science,
  125–7
External factors in scientific change,
  99–124

Falsifiability, 23–5, 30–1, 46–7
Functional explanation, 128, 159

Galton's mathematical innovations,
  118–19

Habituation, 14
History of science, 6, 99–124
  teleological conception of, 7, 119,
  122–3

Ideological determination, 131, 138,
  142–3
Ideology, 125–51
  total, 145, 147–8
Induction, 9
Inductive processing, 22–3, 161
Inductivism, 8–9, 36

Jensen controversy, 131–6

Legitimation, 146, 149–51
Linguistic philosophy, 161, 163,
  166, 169–70

Magic, 6, 101
Marcuse's indictment of science,
  176
Metaphor, 57–9, 165
  extension of, 86–92
  in science, 49, 53–7, 146–7
  replacement of, 93–6
Methodological anarchy, 165

Normal science, 60

Observation languages, 16–18

Perception,
  theory dependence of, 19–21
Popper's (1934) epistemology, 23–4
Positivism, 55–6, 166
Psychology of perception, 11, 20–1,
  160

Quantum physics, 109, 141–2

Rationality, 22–44
  conventional as opposed to
    natural, 26
  universal criteria of, 33–41
Reasons as opposed to causes in the
  explanation of action, 70–84
Relativism, 154, 156, 179, 180

Science as an accredited knowledge
  source, 64
Science as an actors' category,
  99–101
Scientific exemplars, 52, 87–92
Scientific method, 45–8
Scientific progress, 122–4
Scientific revolution, 104–9

Scientific routines, 84–6
Scientific sub-cultures (specialties),
  48, 60–1
Scientific training, 21, 64–8, 84
Serendipity, 172
Social differentiation, 117, 165
Social functions of beliefs, 128–30
Sociological idealism, 69–71

Technique, 92
Tobacco addiction and lung cancer,
  138–9

Veblen's sociology of knowledge,
  13–15

International Library of Sociology

Edited by
John Rex
University of Warwick

Founded by
Karl Mannheim

as The International Library of Sociology
and Social Reconstruction

*This Catalogue also contains other Social Science
series published by Routledge*

Routledge & Kegan Paul   London and Boston

68-74 Carter Lane   London EC4V 5EL
9 Park Street Boston Mass 02108

Contents

General Sociology 3
Foreign Classics of Sociology 3
Social Structure 3
Sociology and Politics 4
Foreign Affairs 5
Criminology 5
Social Psychology 5
Sociology of the Family 6
Social Services 6
Sociology of Education 7
Sociology of Culture 8
Sociology of Religion 8
Sociology of Art and Literature 9
Sociology of Knowledge 9
Urban Sociology 9
Rural Sociology 10
Sociology of Industry and Distribution 10
Anthropology 11
Documentary 11
Sociology and Philosophy 11

Other Routledge Social Science Series
International Library of Anthropology 12
International Library of Social Policy 12
Primary Socialization, Language and Education 12
Reports of the Institute of Community Studies 13
Reports of the Institute for Social Studies in Medical Care 14
Medicine, Illness and Society 14
Monographs in Social Theory 14
Routledge Social Science Journals 14

● *Books so marked are available in paperback*
All books are in Metric Demy 8vo format (216 × 138mm approx.)

GENERAL SOCIOLOGY

Belshaw, Cyril. The Conditions of Social Performance. *An Exploratory Theory. 144 pp.*

Brown, Robert. Explanation in Social Science. *208 pp.*
● Rules and Laws in Sociology.

Cain, Maureen E. Society and the Policeman's Role. *About 300 pp.*

Gibson, Quentin. The Logic of Social Enquiry. *240 pp.*

Gurvitch, Georges. Sociology of Law. *Preface by Roscoe Pound. 264 pp.*

Homans, George C. Sentiments and Activities: *Essays in Social Science. 336 pp.*

Johnson, Harry M. Sociology: *a Systematic Introduction. Foreword by Robert K. Merton. 710 pp.*

Mannheim, Karl. Essays on Sociology and Social Psychology. *Edited by Paul Keckskemeti. With Editorial Note by Adolph Lowe. 344 pp.*
Systematic Sociology: *An Introduction to the Study of Society. Edited by J. S. Erös and Professor W. A. C. Stewart. 220 pp.*

Martindale, Don. The Nature and Types of Sociological Theory. *292 pp.*

● **Maus, Heinz.** A Short History of Sociology. *234 pp.*

Mey, Harald. Field-Theory. *A Study of its Application in the Social Sciences. 352 pp.*

Myrdal, Gunnar. Value in Social Theory: *A Collection of Essays on Methodology. Edited by Paul Streeten. 332 pp.*

Ogburn, William F., and **Nimkoff, Meyer F.** A Handbook of Sociology. *Preface by Karl Mannheim. 656 pp. 46 figures. 35 tables.*

Parsons, Talcott, and **Smelser, Neil J.** Economy and Society: *A Study in the Integration of Economic and Social Theory. 362 pp.*

● **Rex, John.** Key Problems of Sociological Theory. *220 pp.*

Urry, John. Reference Groups and the Theory of Revolution.

FOREIGN CLASSICS OF SOCIOLOGY

● **Durkheim, Emile.** Suicide. *A Study in Sociology. Edited and with an Introduction by George Simpson. 404 pp.*
Professional Ethics and Civic Morals. *Translated by Cornelia Brookfield. 288 pp.*

● **Gerth, H. H.,** and **Mills, C. Wright.** From Max Weber: *Essays in Sociology. 502 pp.*

Tönnies, Ferdinand. Community and Association. *(Gemeinschaft und Gesellschaft.) Translated and Supplemented by Charles P. Loomis. Foreword by Pitirim A. Sorokin. 334 pp.*

SOCIAL STRUCTURE

Andreski, Stanislav. Military Organization and Society. *Foreword by Professor A. R. Radcliffe-Brown. 226 pp. 1 folder.*

Coontz, Sydney H. Population Theories and the Economic Interpretation. *202 pp.*

Coser, Lewis. The Functions of Social Conflict. *204 pp.*

Dickie-Clark, H. F. Marginal Situation: *A Sociological Study of a Coloured Group. 240 pp. 11 tables.*

Glass, D. V. (Ed.). Social Mobility in Britain. *Contributions by J. Berent, T. Bottomore, R. C. Chambers, J. Floud, D. V. Glass, J. R. Hall, H. T. Himmelweit, R. K. Kelsall, F. M. Martin, C. A. Moser, R. Mukherjee, and W. Ziegel. 420 pp.*

Glaser, Barney, and **Strauss, Anselm L.** Status Passage. *A Formal Theory. 208 pp.*

Jones, Garth N. Planned Organizational Change: *An Exploratory Study Using an Empirical Approach. 268 pp.*

Kelsall, R. K. Higher Civil Servants in Britain: *From 1870 to the Present Day. 268 pp. 31 tables.*

König, René. The Community. *232 pp. Illustrated.*

● **Lawton, Denis.** Social Class, Language and Education. *192 pp.*

McLeish, John. The Theory of Social Change: *Four Views Considered. 128 pp.*

Marsh, David C. The Changing Social Structure of England and Wales, 1871-1961. *288 pp.*

Mouzelis, Nicos. Organization and Bureaucracy. *An Analysis of Modern Theories. 240 pp.*

Mulkay, M. J. Functionalism, Exchange and Theoretical Strategy. *272 pp.*

Ossowski, Stanislaw. Class Structure in the Social Consciousness. *210 pp.*

SOCIOLOGY AND POLITICS

Hertz, Frederick. Nationality in History and Politics: *A Psychology and Sociology of National Sentiment and Nationalism. 432 pp.*

Kornhauser, William. The Politics of Mass Society. *272 pp. 20 tables.*

Laidler, Harry W. History of Socialism. *Social-Economic Movements: An Historical and Comparative Survey of Socialism, Communism, Co-operation, Utopianism; and other Systems of Reform and Reconstruction. 992 pp.*

Mannheim, Karl. Freedom, Power and Democratic Planning. *Edited by Hans Gerth and Ernest K. Bramstedt. 424 pp.*

Mansur, Fatma. Process of Independence. *Foreword by A. H. Hanson. 208 pp.*

Martin, David A. Pacificism: *an Historical and Sociological Study. 262 pp.*

Myrdal, Gunnar. The Political Element in the Development of Economic Theory. *Translated from the German by Paul Streeten. 282 pp.*

Wootton, Graham. Workers, Unions and the State. *188 pp.*

FOREIGN AFFAIRS: THEIR SOCIAL, POLITICAL AND ECONOMIC FOUNDATIONS

Mayer, J. P. Political Thought in France from the Revolution to the Fifth Republic. *164 pp.*

CRIMINOLOGY

Ancel, Marc. Social Defence: *A Modern Approach to Criminal Problems.* *Foreword by Leon Radzinowicz. 240 pp.*

Cloward, Richard A., and **Ohlin, Lloyd E.** Delinquency and Opportunity: *A Theory of Delinquent Gangs. 248 pp.*

Downes, David M. The Delinquent Solution. *A Study in Subcultural Theory. 296 pp.*

Dunlop, A. B., and **McCabe, S.** Young Men in Detention Centres. *192 pp.*

Friedlander, Kate. The Psycho-Analytical Approach to Juvenile Delinquency: *Theory, Case Studies, Treatment. 320 pp.*

Glueck, Sheldon, and **Eleanor.** Family Environment and Delinquency. *With the statistical assistance of Rose W. Kneznek. 340 pp.*

Lopez-Rey, Manuel. Crime. *An Analytical Appraisal. 288 pp.*

Mannheim, Hermann. Comparative Criminology: *a Text Book. Two volumes. 442 pp. and 380 pp.*

Morris, Terence. The Criminal Area: *A Study in Social Ecology. Foreword by Hermann Mannheim. 232 pp. 25 tables. 4 maps.*

● **Taylor, Ian, Walton, Paul,** and **Young, Jock.** The New Criminology. *For a Social Theory of Deviance.*

SOCIAL PSYCHOLOGY

Bagley, Christopher. The Social Psychology of the Epileptic Child. *320 pp.*

Barbu, Zevedei. Problems of Historical Psychology. *248 pp.*

Blackburn, Julian. Psychology and the Social Pattern. *184 pp.*

● **Brittan, Arthur.** Meanings and Situations. *224 pp.*

● **Fleming, C. M.** Adolescence: Its Social Psychology. *With an Introduction to recent findings from the fields of Anthropology, Physiology, Medicine, Psychometrics and Sociometry. 288 pp.*

● The Social Psychology of Education: *An Introduction and Guide to Its Study. 136 pp.*

Homans, George C. The Human Group. *Foreword by Bernard DeVoto. Introduction by Robert K. Merton. 526 pp.*

Social Behaviour: *its Elementary Forms. 416 pp.*

Klein, Josephine. The Study of Groups. *226 pp. 31 figures. 5 tables.*

Linton, Ralph. The Cultural Background of Personality. *132 pp.*

Mayo, Elton. The Social Problems of an Industrial Civilization. *With an appendix on the Political Problem. 180 pp.*

Ottaway, A. K. C. Learning Through Group Experience. *176 pp.*

Ridder, J. C. de. The Personality of the Urban African in South Africa. *A Thematic Apperception Test Study. 196 pp. 12 plates.*

● **Rose, Arnold M.** (Ed.). Human Behaviour and Social Processes: *an Interactionist Approach. Contributions by Arnold M. Rose, Ralph H. Turner, Anselm Strauss, Everett C. Hughes, E. Franklin Frazier, Howard S. Becker, et al. 696 pp.*

Smelser, Neil J. Theory of Collective Behaviour. *448 pp.*
Stephenson, Geoffrey M. The Development of Conscience. *128 pp.*
Young, Kimball. Handbook of Social Psychology. *658 pp. 16 figures. 10 tables.*

SOCIOLOGY OF THE FAMILY

Banks, J. A. Prosperity and Parenthood: *A Study of Family Planning among The Victorian Middle Classes. 262 pp.*
Bell, Colin R. Middle Class Families: *Social and Geographical Mobility. 224 pp.*
Burton, Lindy. Vulnerable Children. *272 pp.*
Gavron, Hannah. The Captive Wife: *Conflicts of Household Mothers. 190 pp.*
George, Victor, and **Wilding, Paul.** Motherless Families. *220 pp.*
Klein, Josephine. Samples from English Cultures.
  1. Three Preliminary Studies and Aspects of Adult Life in England. *447 pp.*
  2. Child-Rearing Practices and Index. *247 pp.*
Klein, Viola. Britain's Married Women Workers. *180 pp.*
  The Feminine Character. *History of an Ideology. 244 pp.*
McWhinnie, Alexina M. Adopted Children. *How They Grow Up. 304 pp.*
Myrdal, Alva, and **Klein, Viola.** Women's Two Roles: *Home and Work. 238 pp. 27 tables.*
Parsons, Talcott, and **Bales, Robert F.** Family: Socialization and Interaction Process. *In collaboration with James Olds, Morris Zelditch and Philip E. Slater. 456 pp. 50 figures and tables.*

SOCIAL SERVICES

Bastide, Roger. The Sociology of Mental Disorder. *Translated from the French by Jean McNeil. 260 pp.*
Carlebach, Julius. Caring For Children in Trouble. *266 pp.*
Forder, R. A. (Ed.). Penelope Hall's Social Services of England and Wales. *352 pp.*
George, Victor. Foster Care. *Theory and Practice. 234 pp.*
  Social Security: *Beveridge and After. 258 pp.*
● **Goetschius, George W.** Working with Community Groups. *256 pp.*
Goetschius, George W., and **Tash, Joan.** Working with Unattached Youth. *416 pp.*
Hall, M. P., and **Howes, I. V.** The Church in Social Work. *A Study of Moral Welfare Work undertaken by the Church of England. 320 pp.*
Heywood, Jean S. Children in Care: *the Development of the Service for the Deprived Child. 264 pp.*
Hoenig, J., and **Hamilton, Marian W.** The De-Segration of the Mentally Ill. *284 pp.*
Jones, Kathleen. Mental Health and Social Policy, 1845-1959. *264 pp.*

King, Roy D., Raynes, Norma V., and **Tizard, Jack.** Patterns of Residential Care. *356 pp.*

Leigh, John. Young People and Leisure. *256 pp.*

Morris, Mary. Voluntary Work and the Welfare State. *300 pp.*

Morris, Pauline. Put Away: *A Sociological Study of Institutions for the Mentally Retarded. 364 pp.*

Nokes, P. L. The Professional Task in Welfare Practice. *152 pp.*

Timms, Noel. Psychiatric Social Work in Great Britain (1939-1962). *280 pp.*

● Social Casework: *Principles and Practice. 256 pp.*

Young, A. F., and **Ashton, E. T.** British Social Work in the Nineteenth Century. *288 pp.*

Young, A. F. Social Services in British Industry. *272 pp.*

SOCIOLOGY OF EDUCATION

Banks, Olive. Parity and Prestige in English Secondary Education: a Study in Educational Sociology. *272 pp.*

Bentwich, Joseph. Education in Israel. *224 pp. 8 pp. plates.*

● **Blyth, W. A. L.** English Primary Education. *A Sociological Description.*
1. Schools. *232 pp.*
2. Background. *168 pp.*

Collier, K. G. The Social Purposes of Education: *Personal and Social Values in Education. 268 pp.*

Dale, R. R., and **Griffith, S.** Down Stream: *Failure in the Grammar School. 108 pp.*

Dore, R. P. Education in Tokugawa Japan. *356 pp. 9 pp. plates*

Evans, K. M. Sociometry and Education. *158 pp.*

Foster, P. J. Education and Social Change in Ghana. *336 pp. 3 maps.*

Fraser, W. R. Education and Society in Modern France. *150 pp.*

Grace, Gerald R. Role Conflict and the Teacher. *About 200 pp.*

Hans, Nicholas. New Trends in Education in the Eighteenth Century. *278 pp. 19 tables.*

● Comparative Education: *A Study of Educational Factors and Traditions. 360 pp.*

Hargreaves, David. Interpersonal Relations and Education. *432 pp.*

● Social Relations in a Secondary School. *240 pp.*

Holmes, Brian. Problems in Education. *A Comparative Approach. 336 pp.*

King, Ronald. Values and Involvement in a Grammar School. *164 pp.*
School Organization and Pupil Involvement. *A Study of Secondary Schools.*

● **Mannheim, Karl,** and **Stewart, W. A. C.** An Introduction to the Sociology of Education. *206 pp.*

Morris, Raymond N. The Sixth Form and College Entrance. *231 pp.*

● **Musgrove, F.** Youth and the Social Order. *176 pp.*

● **Ottaway, A. K. C.** Education and Society: An Introduction to the Sociology of Education. *With an Introduction by W. O. Lester Smith. 212 pp.*

Peers, Robert. Adult Education: *A Comparative Study. 398 pp.*

7

Pritchard, D. G. Education and the Handicapped: *1760 to 1960. 258 pp.*
Richardson, Helen. Adolescent Girls in Approved Schools. *308 pp.*
Stratta, Erica. The Education of Borstal Boys. *A Study of their Educational Experiences prior to, and during Borstal Training. 256 pp.*

SOCIOLOGY OF CULTURE

Eppel, E. M., and M. Adolescents and Morality: *A Study of some Moral Values and Dilemmas of Working Adolescents in the Context of a changing Climate of Opinion. Foreword by W. J. H. Sprott. 268 pp. 39 tables.*
● **Fromm, Erich.** The Fear of Freedom. *286 pp.*
The Sane Society. *400 pp.*
Mannheim, Karl. Essays on the Sociology of Culture. *Edited by Ernst Mannheim in co-operation with Paul Kecskemeti. Editorial Note by Adolph Lowe. 280 pp.*
Weber, Alfred. Farewell to European History: *or The Conquest of Nihilism Translated from the German by R. F. C. Hull. 224 pp.*

SOCIOLOGY OF RELIGION

Argyle, Michael. Religious Behaviour. *224 pp. 8 figures. 41 tables.*
Nelson, G. K. Spiritualism and Society. *313 pp.*
Stark, Werner. The Sociology of Religion. *A Study of Christendom.*
Volume I. *Established Religion. 248 pp.*
Volume II. *Sectarian Religion. 368 pp.*
Volume III. *The Universal Church. 464 pp.*
Volume IV. *Types of Religious Man. 352 pp.*
Volume V. *Types of Religious Culture. 464 pp.*
Watt, W. Montgomery. Islam and the Integration of Society. *320 pp.*

SOCIOLOGY OF ART AND LITERATURE

Jarvie, Ian C. Towards a Sociology of the Cinema. *A Comparative Essay on the Structure and Functioning of a Major Entertainment Industry. 405 pp.*
Rust, Frances S. Dance in Society. *An Analysis of the Relationships between the Social Dance and Society in England from the Middle Ages to the Present Day. 256 pp. 8 pp. of plates.*
Schücking, L. L. The Sociology of Literary Taste. *112 pp.*

SOCIOLOGY OF KNOWLEDGE

Mannheim, Karl. Essays on the Sociology of Knowledge. *Edited by Paul Kecskemeti. Editorial Note by Adolph Lowe. 353 pp.*

Remmling, Gunter W. (Ed.). Towards the Sociology of Knowledge. *Origins and Development of a Sociological Thought Style.*

Stark, Werner. The Sociology of Knowledge: *An Essay in Aid of a Deeper Understanding of the History of Ideas. 384 pp.*

URBAN SOCIOLOGY

Ashworth, William. The Genesis of Modern British Town Planning: *A Study in Economic and Social History of the Nineteenth and Twentieth Centuries. 288 pp.*

Cullingworth, J. B. Housing Needs and Planning Policy: *A Restatement of the Problems of Housing Need and 'Overspill' in England and Wales. 232 pp. 44 tables. 8 maps.*

Dickinson, Robert E. City and Region: *A Geographical Interpretation. 608 pp. 125 figures.*

The West European City: *A Geographical Interpretation. 600 pp. 129 maps. 29 plates.*

● The City Region in Western Europe. *320 pp. Maps.*

Humphreys, Alexander J. New Dubliners: *Urbanization and the Irish Family. Foreword by George C. Homans. 304 pp.*

Jackson, Brian. Working Class Community: *Some General Notions raised by a Series of Studies in Northern England. 192 pp.*

Jennings, Hilda. Societies in the Making: *a Study of Development and Redevelopment within a County Borough. Foreword by D. A. Clark. 286 pp.*

● **Mann, P. H.** An Approach to Urban Sociology. *240 pp.*

Morris, R. N., and **Mogey, J.** The Sociology of Housing. *Studies at Berinsfield. 232 pp. 4 pp. plates.*

Rosser, C., and **Harris, C.** The Family and Social Change. *A Study of Family and Kinship in a South Wales Town. 352 pp. 8 maps.*

RURAL SOCIOLOGY

Chambers, R. J. H. Settlement Schemes in Tropical Africa: *A Selective Study. 268 pp.*

Haswell, M. R. The Economics of Development in Village India. *120 pp.*

Littlejohn, James. Westrigg: *the Sociology of a Cheviot Parish. 172 pp. 5 figures.*

Mayer, Adrian C. Peasants in the Pacific. *A Study of Fiji Indian Rural Society. 248 pp. 20 plates.*

Williams, W. M. The Sociology of an English Village: *Gosforth. 272 pp. 12 figures. 13 tables.*

SOCIOLOGY OF INDUSTRY AND DISTRIBUTION

Anderson, Nels. Work and Leisure. *280 pp.*

● **Blau, Peter M.,** and **Scott, W. Richard.** Formal Organizations: *a Comparative approach. Introduction and Additional Bibliography by J. H. Smith. 326 pp.*

Eldridge, J. E. T. Industrial Disputes. *Essays in the Sociology of Industrial Relations. 288 pp.*

Hetzler, Stanley. Applied Measures for Promoting Technological Growth. *352 pp.*

Technological Growth and Social Change. *Achieving Modernization. 269 pp.*

Hollowell, Peter G. The Lorry Driver. *272 pp.*

Jefferys, Margot, *with the assistance of Winifred Moss.* Mobility in the Labour Market: *Employment Changes in Battersea and Dagenham. Preface by Barbara Wootton. 186 pp. 51 tables.*

Millerson, Geoffrey. The Qualifying Associations: *a Study in Professionalization. 320 pp.*

Smelser, Neil J. Social Change in the Industrial Revolution: *An Application of Theory to the Lancashire Cotton Industry, 1770-1840. 468 pp. 12 figures. 14 tables.*

Williams, Gertrude. Recruitment to Skilled Trades. *240 pp.*

Young, A. F. Industrial Injuries Insurance: *an Examination of British Policy. 192 pp.*

DOCUMENTARY

Schlesinger, Rudolf (Ed.). Changing Attitudes in Soviet Russia.

2. The Nationalities Problem and Soviet Administration. *Selected Readings on the Development of Soviet Nationalities Policies. Introduced by the editor. Translated by W. W. Gottlieb. 324 pp.*

ANTHROPOLOGY

Ammar, Hamed. Growing up in an Egyptian Village: *Silwa, Province of Aswan. 336 pp.*

Brandel-Syrier, Mia. Reeftown Elite. *A Study of Social Mobility in a Modern African Community on the Reef. 376 pp.*

Crook, David, and **Isabel.** Revolution in a Chinese Village: *Ten Mile Inn. 230 pp. 8 plates. 1 map.*

Dickie-Clark, H. F. The Marginal Situation. *A Sociological Study of a Coloured Group. 236 pp.*

Dube, S. C. Indian Village. *Foreword by Morris Edward Opler. 276 pp. 4 plates.*

India's Changing Villages: *Human Factors in Community Development. 260 pp. 8 plates. 1 map.*

Firth, Raymond. Malay Fishermen. *Their Peasant Economy. 420 pp. 17 pp. plates.*

Gulliver, P. H. Social Control in an African Society: a Study of the Arusha, Agricultural Masai of Northern Tanganyika. *320 pp. 8 plates. 10 figures.*

Ishwaran, K. Shivapur. *A South Indian Village. 216 pp.*
Tradition and Economy in Village India: *An Interactionist Approach. Foreword by Conrad Arensburg. 176 pp.*

Jarvie, Ian C. The Revolution in Anthropology. *268 pp.*

Jarvie, Ian C., and **Agassi, Joseph.** Hong Kong. *A Society in Transition. 396 pp. Illustrated with plates and maps.*

Little, Kenneth L. Mende of Sierra Leone. *308 pp. and folder.*
Negroes in Britain. *With a New Introduction and Contemporary Study by Leonard Bloom. 320 pp.*

Lowie, Robert H. Social Organization. *494 pp.*

Mayer, Adrian C. Caste and Kinship in Central India: *A Village and its Region. 328 pp. 16 plates. 15 figures. 16 tables.*

Smith, Raymond T. The Negro Family in British Guiana: *Family Structure and Social Status in the Villages. With a Foreword by Meyer Fortes. 314 pp. 8 plates. 1 figure. 4 maps.*

SOCIOLOGY AND PHILOSOPHY

Barnsley, John H. The Social Reality of Ethics. *A Comparative Analysis of Moral Codes. 448 pp.*

Diesing, Paul. Patterns of Discovery in the Social Sciences. *362 pp.*

Douglas, Jack D. (Ed.). Understanding Everyday Life. *Toward the Reconstruction of Sociological Knowledge. Contributions by Alan F. Blum. Aaron W. Cicourel, Norman K. Denzin, Jack D. Douglas, John Heeren, Peter McHugh, Peter K. Manning, Melvin Power, Matthew Speier, Roy Turner, D. Lawrence Wieder, Thomas P. Wilson and Don H. Zimmerman. 370 pp.*

Jarvie, Ian C. Concepts and Society. *216 pp.*

Roche, Maurice. Phenomenology, Language and the Social Sciences. *About 400 pp.*

Sahay, Arun. Sociological Analysis.

Sklair, Leslie. The Sociology of Progress. *320 pp.*

International Library of Anthropology
General Editor Adam Kuper

Brown, Raula. The Chimbu. *A Study of Change in the New Guinea Highlands.*
Van Den Berghe, Pierre L. Power and Privilege at an African University.

International Library of Social Policy

General Editor Kathleen Jones

Holman, Robert. Trading in Children. *A Study of Private Fostering.*
Jones, Kathleen. History of the Mental Health Services. *428 pp.*
Thomas, J. E. The English Prison Officer since 1850: *A Study in Conflict. 258 pp.*

Primary Socialization, Language and Education

General Editor Basil Bernstein

Bernstein, Basil. Class, Codes and Control. *2 volumes.*
　1. *Theoretical Studies Towards a Sociology of Language. 254 pp.*
　2. *Applied Studies Towards a Sociology of Language. About 400 pp.*
Brandis, Walter, and **Henderson, Dorothy.** Social Class, Language and Communication. *288 pp.*
Cook-Gumperz, Jenny. Social Control and Socialization. *A Study of Class Differences in the Language of Maternal Control.*
Gahagan, D. M., and **G. A.** Talk Reform. *Exploration in Language for Infant School Children. 160 pp.*
Robinson, W. P., and **Rackstraw, Susan, D. A.** A Question of Answers. *2 volumes. 192 pp. and 180 pp.*
Turner, Geoffrey, J., and **Mohan, Bernard, A.** A Linguistic Description and Computer Programme for Children's Speech. *208 pp.*

Reports of the Institute of Community Studies

Cartwright, Ann. Human Relations and Hospital Care. *272 pp.*
　Parents and Family Planning Services. *306 pp.*
　Patients and their Doctors. *A Study of General Practice. 304 pp.*
● **Jackson, Brian.** Streaming: *an Education System in Miniature. 168 pp.*
Jackson, Brian, and **Marsden, Dennis.** Education and the Working Class: *Some General Themes raised by a Study of 88 Working-class Children in a Northern Industrial City. 268 pp. 2 folders.*
Marris, Peter. The Experience of Higher Education. *232 pp. 27 tables.*
Marris, Peter, and **Rein, Martin.** Dilemmas of Social Reform. *Poverty and Community Action in the United States. 256 pp.*
Marris, Peter, and **Somerset, Anthony.** African Businessmen. *A Study of Entrepreneurship and Development in Kenya. 256 pp.*
Mills, Richard. Young Outsiders: *a Study in Alternative Communities.*

Runciman, W. G. Relative Deprivation and Social Justice. *A Study of Attitudes to Social Inequality in Twentieth Century England. 352 pp.*

Townsend, Peter. The Family Life of Old People: *An Inquiry in East London. Foreword by J. H. Sheldon. 300 pp. 3 figures. 63 tables.*

Willmott, Peter. Adolescent Boys in East London. *230 pp.*

The Evolution of a Community: *a study of Dagenham after forty years. 168 pp. 2 maps.*

Willmott, Peter, and **Young, Michael.** Family and Class in a London Suburb. *202 pp. 47 tables.*

Young, Michael. Innovation and Research in Education. *192 pp.*

● **Young, Michael,** and **McGeeney, Patrick.** Learning Begins at Home. *A Study of a Junior School and its Parents. 128 pp.*

Young, Michael, and **Willmott, Peter.** Family and Kinship in East London. *Foreword by Richard M. Titmuss. 252 pp. 39 tables.*

The Symmetrical Family.

Reports of the Institute for Social Studies in Medical Care

Cartwright, Ann, Hockey, Lisbeth, and **Anderson, John L.** Life Before Death.

Dunnell, Karen, and **Cartwright, Ann.** Medicine Takers, Prescribers and Hoarders. *190 pp.*

Medicine, Illness and Society
General Editor W. M. Williams

Robinson, David. The Process of Becoming Ill.

Stacey, Margaret. *et al.* Hospitals, Children and Their Families. *The Report of a Pilot Study. 202 pp.*

Monographs in Social Theory
General Editor Arthur Brittan

Bauman, Zygmunt. Culture as Praxis.

Dixon, Keith. Sociological Theory. *Pretence and Possibility.*

Smith, Anthony D. The Concept of Social Change. *A Critique of the Functionalist Theory of Social Change.*

Routledge Social Science Journals

The British Journal of Sociology. *Edited by Terence P. Morris. Vol. 1, No. 1, March 1950 and Quarterly. Roy. 8vo. Back numbers available. An international journal with articles on all aspects of sociology.*

Economy and Society. *Vol. 1, No. 1. February 1972 and Quarterly. Metric Roy. 8vo. A journal for all social scientists covering sociology, philosophy, anthropology, economics and history. Back numbers available.*

Year Book of Social Policy in Britain, The. *Edited by Kathleen Jones. 1971. Published Annually.*